G. K. Chesterton & Hilaire Belloc

The Battle Against Modernity

G. K. Chesterton
& Hilaire Belloc

The Battle Against Modernity

by
JAY P. CORRIN

OHIO UNIVERSITY PRESS,

Athens/London

Library of Congress Cataloging in Publication Data

Corrin, Jay P., 1943-
  G. K. Chesterton and Hilaire Belloc: the battle against modernity.

  Bibliography: p.
  Includes index.
  1. Authors—English—20th century—Political and social views. 2.
Chesterton, G. K. (Gilbert Keith), 1874-1936—Political and social views.
3. Belloc, Hilaire, 1870-1953—Political and social views. 4. Distributist League. 5. Great Britain—Politics and government—1910-
1936. 6. Politics and literature—Great Britain. I. Title.
PR478.P64C6   820'.9'358   81-4756
ISBN 0-8214-0604-3   AACR2

To Nancy

Contents

Acknowledgements

It gives me pleasure to express my gratitude to those who made this book possible. First, I wish to thank my teachers and colleagues at Boston University's Department of History who made my years as a fledgling graduate student an intellectually exciting and challenging experience. In particular, I am indebted to Professor F. M. Leventhal who suggested the Chesterbelloc as a dissertation topic and provided the steady guidance and criticism that were necessary to complete this book. Special thanks also go to Professor Sidney Burrell, not only for his kindness and sagacious academic counseling but, more importantly, for creating the very special learning environment that has made graduate study for many students such a rewarding endeavor at Boston University. I want to thank Professors Fritz Ringer and William Keylor, who read my manuscript in its early stages and offered a number of helpful criticisms and suggestions.

My appreciation also goes to Mr. Geoffrey Curran for his unflagging efforts at tracking down obscure books and journals, and to the many other staff members of the interlibrary loans department at Boston University's Mugar Library. The staffs of Bapst Library, Boston College; St. John's Seminary, Brighton, Massachusetts; the New York Public Library; and the Benedictine College Library, Atchison, Kansas, were extremely helpful in allowing me access to the many journals and manuscripts that concerned Chesterton and Belloc. Parts of this book (sections from Chapters V and VI) have appeared in articles published in *The Chesterton Review* (Spring/Summer, 1975 and Spring/Summer, 1976). I wish to thank its editor, Mr. Ian Boyd, for permission to reprint parts of these in the present revised form.

Throughout my research and writing, I was fortunate to have had the good counsel, criticism, and inspiration of Professor John G. Gagliardo. No teacher has given more to me. Professor Gagliardo has been my model in both pedagogy and scholarship, and I owe to him immeasurable gratitude. Finally, I extend my deepest appreciation to Nancy Corrin for the years of patience and understanding that she has provided as wife and friend, and to my parents who bequeathed to me an appreciation for learning.

Boston University   Jay P. Corrin

Introduction

Among the half-forgotten curiosities of the inter-war years in Britain was a composite of social and moral theories known as Distributism. The driving forces behind the Distributist movement were Gilbert Keith Chesterton (1874-1936) and Hilaire Belloc (1870-1953), two of the most masterful and popular writers of their generation. Few practitioners of the English language have ever equaled their extraordinary literary output. In a career that spanned almost forty years, Chesterton published approximately one hundred books, wrote introductions and contributions to about two hundred more, contributed to practically every major British periodical, and, for more than ten years, edited his own weekly journal. Belloc, nearly as prolific, produced more than a hundred books dealing with an astounding variety of subjects, and maintained high public visibility as a polemical journalist.

G. K. Chesterton was a man of brilliant personality and charm. As a writer, he collaborated intellectually with some of the seminal minds of his generation, men like George Bernard Shaw, H. G. Wells, and Belloc himself. But it was Belloc's Catholicism and singular political and historical ideas that shaped the development of Chesterton's world view. Neither man was influenced significantly by contemporary continental philosophical trends. Indeed, Chesterton's attempts to work out a Christian moral and political scheme for modern society preceded the efforts of the French neo-Thomist, Jacques Maritain, who only started to concentrate on this broad problem after the papal condemnation of *Action Française*, the French monarchist movement, in 1926. Maritain's major social writings did not appear until after 1934 (*True Humanism* published in that year set out his view for the application of Thomism to the contemporary world), whereas Chesterton's statements on the subject had been formulated and placed before the public by 1927.

If Chesterton sparked the neo-Thomist revival in England, his Thomism differed from that of most Catholic theologians: his thoughts were directed more to the social and political problems of his times than towards the lofty metaphysics of the schoolmen. Publicly engaging in battle with self-styled rationalists and positivists, in the tradition of St. Thomas, he never rested his arguments on appeals to an Augustinian fideism. Chesterton's adoption of Aquinas' common sense approach to secular problems meant that he was perfectly willing to use reason in dealing with the affairs of ordinary life. He chose to pursue a journalistic career because it kept him constantly in touch with the practical concerns of this world.

Popularly known as the "Chesterbelloc" (a portmanteau coined by George Bernard Shaw), Gilbert Chesterton and Hilaire Belloc deemed it their mission to warn the British public of the psychological and moral dangers implicit in the encroachment of big government, technology and science. Chesterton, in particular, sought to help the common man salvage his dignity in the depersonalized world of the twentieth century by calling for a rebirth of the Christian social conscience. Politically, Chesterton and Belloc proposed to restrain Liberal legislative proposals that were leading England further from the corporate ideals of medieval times towards the brave new world of state social control. Their religious beliefs dictated the view that it was better for individuals to starve in slums of their own making than to become part of a complacent herd of automatons who owed their opinions, jobs, and homes to the state. Vigorously opposed to the materialistic ethos of the industrial state, Chesterton and Belloc summoned modern man to return to the discipline of the Catholic tradition.

Many writers, concerning themselves strictly with the belletristic contributions of Chesterton and Belloc, have dismissed their social and political interests as intellectual folly, unworthy of the scholar's pen. Yet such mundane concerns always remained at the heart of the Chesterbelloc's writing, and all their works are imbued with the philosophy called Distributism. A complex of socio-political theories with anarchic affinities, Distributism essentially called for an equitable distribution of property and a restoration of worker control in commerce, agriculture, and industry through a return to the medieval guilds. The Distributists were rural-oriented, championing what Belloc called the "peasant state." Their ideal was a balanced or mixed economy of independent farmers and small industries owned and operated by the workers themselves. This would constitute a peasant state, in that small independent farming would be the mainstay of the nation's economy. By insisting on the efficacy of local power, decentralized control, self-sufficiency, and rural reconstruction, and in their distaste for the machinations of state bureaucracy and industrialism, the authors of Distributism came close to that ideal community of anarchism described in the writings of Kropotkin.

One might argue that Chesterton's and Belloc's belief in the necessity of private property disqualified them from being labeled true anarchists. Yet anarchists have not always rejected the notion of private property. Adam Smith's idea of free enterprise, which in its pure form consisted of owner-managers competing in a monopoly-free environment, has been warmly received by anarchists. Smith was even considered an anarchist in his own time.[1] A close examination of Belloc's economic views reveals that he was closely akin to Smith. Belloc waged a war against capitalists essentially because they erected monopolies, which disrupted the mechanisms of a free market system and victimized the small man. In their love of the small, their rejection of utopias, and in their concern for the ordinary man being swallowed by the machinery of the state, the Chesterbelloc belong to that tradition of anarchism which encompasses a collection of disparate writers from Bakunin through Herbert Read, Alex Comfort, and Paul Goodman. For example, Goodman's recommendation for reviving both peasant self-reliance and the democratic power of professional guilds[2] might well have qualified him for membership in Chesterton's Distributist League. Underlying all anarchist thought, wrote Goodman, is "a hankering for peasant independence, craft-guild self-management, and the democracy of the village meeting, or the medieval Free Cities."[3] Finally, like anarchism, which is a philosophy of life rather than an ideology, Distributism claimed to be more than simply an economic or social theory; it purported to be a dynamic approach to life firmly founded on religious principles (Thomism), which sought to retrieve the sanctity of human relationships in an impersonal and atomistic society by reintegrating the individual into a corporative state.

After many years of neglect, G. K. Chesterton's popularity is reviving. But even those who recognized his importance as a novelist, poet, and essayist in his centenary celebration largely ignored the social side of Chesterton's writing. Most of the books and articles that have appeared on Chesterton have been written by close admirers, usually Catholics. This literature has been laudatory; indeed, much of it has bordered on hagiolatry. The philosophical temperament of Chesterton's Catholic followers may have had much to do with the current dearth of literature dealing with his social and political ideas, for Chesterton, under the influence of Belloc, became associated with anti-Semitism and the political right. Historical events have caused his reputation to suffer for this; but they should not be allowed to efface Chesterton's insights, nor his influence. Misunderstood and maligned, the Distributist ideas of the Chesterbelloc have fallen under the cloud of a "black legend" which suggests that they should not be taken seriously and that Distributism itself was nothing more than a collection of medieval fantasies.[4] This study, among other things, will attempt to examine the black legend and recast it in a different light.

Chesterton and Belloc always operated on the fringe of British politics. Before 1914 their attitude toward labor unrest and imperialism brought them into leftist circles. After the war Chesterton's and Belloc's views shifted more towards the right. Their estrangement from mainstream politics was caused by a variety of factors, notably Belloc's disappointment with the Liberal Party, the Marconi scandal, and the Versailles Peace Treaty. Chesterton and Belloc eventually turned their backs on parliamentary government and called for a return to monarchical rule. Throughout the domestic and international turmoil of the inter-war years Chesterbelloc and their journals, *G. K.'s Weekly* and the *Weekly Review* (which were meant to function as mouthpieces for Distributist theory), steadily drifted toward the extreme right. At times these journals were anti-Semitic, sympathetic to the philosophy of *Action Française* and highly supportive of the rightist views of Francisco Franco, Antonio Salazar, and Benito Mussolini. Yet the Distributist movement had little connection with either contemporary continental ideas or English political thought. The Chesterbelloc alliance kept its distance from the British fascists (at least before Chesterton's death), and never approved of the philosophy and political practice of the Tory Right.

The purpose of this study is to analyze the social and political side of the Chesterbelloc, the circle of writers who fought for their cause, and the overall impact they had on British society. It draws upon the vast collection of materials published by Chesterton, Belloc, and their associates (including memoirs, essays, books and periodicals), but concentrates chiefly on the development of the Distributist world view as it emerged out of the Chesterbelloc's weekly journals: the *Eye* and *New Witness, G. K.'s Weekly*, and the *Weekly Review*. The reader will notice that in many instances Chesterton and Belloc have been allowed to speak for themselves. Chesterton, in particular, had such a genius for words (with Shakespeare, he remains the most quoted writer in the English language) that the full impact of his ideas are best revealed through the medium of his own pen. Finally, this work seeks to illuminate rightist political thought in Britain by focusing on a neglected group of ethically oriented traditionalists responding to the challenges and dislocations of the twentieth century. We will begin by examining the early ideas of the Chesterbelloc and the milieu out of which they emerged.

G. K. CHESTERTON AND HIS MILIEU

Gilbert Chesterton first attracted public recognition for his polemics on the issues of nationalism and imperialism. In 1899 he joined *The Speaker*, a radical Liberal weekly which had been taken over by Hilaire Belloc's Oxford colleagues. The so-called "*Speaker* group" (J. L. Hammond, Francis Hirst, Lucian Oldershaw, E. C. Bentley, John Simon, and F. Y. Eccles) were determined to make this journal the primary left-wing organ of the Liberal Party. As the brother-in-law of Oldershaw and a close friend of Bentley, Chesterton easily identified with the other members of the entourage by his opposition to the Boer War. *The Speaker* had gained a respectable niche within radical circles because of its persistent criticism of British imperialism. Those who wrote for the journal regarded the war as the result of dishonest business deals, and in particular of big-time capitalists seeking new markets for their investments. Chesterton became a well-known figure in this group because of his distinctive animus against the war and the magnificent style in which he expressed his views.

Chesterton's critique of Britain's South African entanglement and his subsequent condemnation of imperialism in general differed sharply from rank and file Liberal dissident opinion. Whereas Liberal nonconformists and Quakers were pro-Boer because of a cosmopolitan spirit of brotherhood and a hatred of wars in general,

Chesterton supported the Boers out of what he called a "love of nationalism." Unlike the particularistic nationalism of a Rudyard Kipling, which ignored the patriotism of others, Chesterton, in the tradition of earlier cosmopolitan nationalists such as Mazzini and Herder, possessed a deep sympathy for the rights and customs of all ethnic groups. Thus he supported the Boers chiefly because they were willing to take to horse and ride in defense of their farms against intruders. Chesterton's concept of nationalism was simply incompatible with imperialism. True British patriots, said he, could never be imperialists, "for if they believed in nationality they could not really believe in empire, because the cosmopolitan idea tends to destroy the nationality of others."[1] Yet Chesterton was not necessarily pro-Boer; he opposed the war mainly because it was unjust and degraded the honor of England. The point was artfully made in a *Speaker* essay on patriotism:

My country right or wrong [would be like saying] . . . my mother drunk or sober. What we really need for the frustration and overthrow of a deaf and raucous Jingoism is a renaissance of the love of the native land . . . . The extraordinary thing is that eating up provinces and pulling down princes is the chief boast of people who have Shakespeare, Newton, Darwin and Burke to boast of. . . . We that have produced sages who could have spoken with Socrates and poets who could talk with Dante, talk as if we have never done anything more intelligent than found colonies and kick niggers.[2]

Chesterton soon developed a reputation as the *bête noire* of the imperialist Fabians who rallied around George Bernard Shaw. Shaw defended the Boer War on the grounds that it would serve to bring benighted creatures into the mainstream of civilization via the British Empire. Chesterton considered this defense of imperialism the mortal enemy of patriotism and an affront to human dignity. He defined imperialism as an attempt by a European country to create a sham Europe which it could dominate, instead of the real Europe, which it could only share: "It is a love of living with one's inferiors."[3] Imperialism was seen as the enemy of liberty, for it negated the deepest of democratic principles—it denied the equality of man by imposing "our standards" on another nation, yet learning nothing from them.[4] And of course it also denied true liberty, which,

Chesterton believed, was obtainable only within a defined sphere of activity and by wielding power over "small things."

Chesterton's lifelong fear of bigness, plutocracy, and centralized government of any kind led him to the anarchistic position of believing that man could reach his full potential only under conditions of direct democracy practiced on the most basic level of politics, completely free of any outside supervision. It was this inclination towards anarchism, a belief in applying principles on a human scale, that aroused him against H. G. Wells' concept of the "World State." First articulated in Wells' *The Outline of History* (1920), this was a proposal to set up a highly structured global government based on the American model. How could Wells propose a truly representative government for the world, asked Chesterton, when the problem had not been solved even in the nearest parish council or with the smallest of nationalities? How would the world leader be controlled? For Chesterton the only purely popular government was local and founded on local knowledge:

The citizens can rule the city because they know the city; but it will always be an exceptional sort of citizen who has or claims the right to rule over ten cities, and these remote and altogether alien cities.[5]

Chesterton's answer to Wells' utopias, which always seemed indefinite yet simplistic to him, was an appeal to the practice of politics on a human scale so that men might better understand what they were doing. The Wellsian world government, just like Britain's South African escapade, ignored the historic pride of men that grew out of patriotism:

All normal men have received their civilization through their citizenship; and to lose their past would be to lose their link with mankind. . . . Nations have not always been seals or stoppers closing up the ancient wine of the world; they have been the vessels that received it. And, as with many ancient vessels, each of them is a work of art.[6]

Chesterton's feelings about freedom and imperialism were best revealed in a bizarre novel entitled *The Napoleon of Notting Hill*, which appeared just after World War I. The setting of this story was the London of 1984. Contrary to the prognostications of Chesterton's contemporaries, life in futuristic London had not improved but deteriorated. Yet, this deterioration was not necessarily inevitable. The story's hero, Adam Wayne, sallies forth willing to spill blood for the sake of private property; in so doing he prevents the stagnation of conformity in modern life. The drama begins when a small section of London attempts to hold out against big-time capitalists. Wayne's borough of Notting Hill is threatened by real-estate developers hoping to demolish a small row of shops on Pump Street for the construction of a new state highway. Rallying the local grocer, chemist, and other concerned citizens, the hero, dressed as a knight in full feudal colors and brandishing sword and halberd, destroys the enemy in a sea of blood.

On one level Chesterton's story can be seen as a satire on the futuristic fantasies of H. G. Wells, in which individuals are overshadowed by the technological achievements of science and big government. Adam Wayne is not dwarfed by the onslaught of modernizing developers, but rather takes up his sword and defends the dignity of Notting Hill. The citizens of Wayne's neighborhood defeated the leviathans of progress because they possessed the materials of creation—the freedom connected with owning one's own property.

On another level the story is a criticism of imperialism. The London developers had denied the citizens of Pump Street their fundamental democratic rights; in a sense, they denied the equality of men by imposing their "progressive" and "collectivist" standards on another nation. Eventually Wayne and the men of Notting Hill fell victim to their own success. Victory engendered pride, and Notting Hill made the dreadful mistake of imposing its powers and way of life on all of London itself. In the final pages Battersea, Hammersmith, and other boroughs revolted, defeating the armies of Notting Hill in a great battle in Kensington Gardens. Wayne admits that they have deserved defeat as a punishment for their materialism. Notting Hill, having made itself a nation, succumbed to vanity by becoming an empire.

These attacks on imperialism earned G. K. C. (he became known to the public by his initials) the affectionate respect of enemy and friend alike. His unusual appearance and flamboyant life-style brought him fame as a sort of white knight of Fleet Street. The Boer

War and its associated issue of imperialism were the occasions for Chesterton's initial appearance on the journalistic stage; but behind his distaste for imperialism lurked a myriad of personal sentiments which ran directly counter to the cultural trends of his day. Soon after establishing his niche as an anti-imperialist, this huge and eccentric man with cape and sword (Chesterton went about in public in a black flowing cape and wore a revolver and sword-stick) was charming the readers of *The Speaker* and the *Daily News* with a full-fledged assault on modern decadence and the general malaise of the *fin de siècle*.

"*Fin de siècle*" was a phrase popular in the nineties (meaning many things to many people), used to depict a confusing era of intellectual movements. Most people tended to see the last decade of the century as a transitional period in which England was moving into some new social, moral, or political system. In his book *The Eighteen-Nineties* (1925), Holbrook Jackson wrote that there was a new sense of freedom and enthusiasm and a desire to taste life during these years, yet there was no concerted action of any kind, and everybody, mentally and emotionally, was running about in a hundred different directions. London by the eighteen-nineties was not only the center of forward-looking movements (the accent was always on "progress" and that meant attacking religion, tradition and any other such thing considered sacred by the old Victorian establishment), but it was also afflicted with pessimism and cultured aberration, the latter reflected in the *Yellow Book* group—Oscar Wilde, Aubrey Beardsley, Henry Harland, and others. After being asked about the aims of the *Yellow Book* magazine, its editors, Harland and Beardsley, replied that it would contain "clever stuff" and be distinctly modern—though neither, it seems, knew what "modern" meant.[7]

The cultural ennui of the *fin de siècle* was abetted by disquieting changes in the real world. By the end of the nineteenth century, Britain's expansive economy had begun to atrophy, and the public was suddenly made aware of the seriousness of mass poverty. In conjunction with new doctrines of biological evolution, this occasioned profound feelings of anxiety in English intellectual circles. Charles Darwin's biological theories evoked popular religious controversy and generated considerable philosophical despair. *On The*

Origin of Species, in particular, had the effect of removing teleology from nature and the universe. Darwin brought man from his former special position in the cosmos down to the animal level. Man was now to struggle with a blind and purposeless nature without having the advantage of a special creation or free will. Bertrand Russell wrote that Darwin had made everything a "matter of degree" and so with his triumph "all splendid things vanished."[8] Even the irrepressible Shaw had difficulty mustering great faith for the morrow: by 1889 he announced that it was statistically proven that England's civilization was "in an advanced state of rottenness."[9]

This pessimistic aspect of the *fin de siècle* had a certain blend of cold air and emptiness about it. Chesterton called it "the Evil Day." This constituted a dark interlude, said he, starting about 1870, the year Paris fell and Dickens died, and continuing roughly up to the retirement of Gladstone and the abandonment of Home Rule. G. K.'s impression was that devious hands had closed the doors on man's two great outlets—liberty and faith: The one was blocked by Bismarck with his "blood and iron," and the other by Darwin with his "blood and bones." The evil Prussian had brought political materialism to Europe, destroying idealism forever, while Darwin destroyed the uniqueness of man. The significance of *The Descent of Man* "was that it really was a descent of man—that man had been kicked off his pedestal onto the floor." And the ensuing despair led to boredom, for these were the years of yawning—"They were like the hours of an afternoon 'at Home' in a rich house on a rainy day when nobody comes to call."[10] Chesterton's first impulse was to revolt against this despair and boredom. The *fin de siècle* seemed so final that he envisioned it as the end of the world rather than the end of the century. The urge to retrieve some dignity and hope for man was so intense in Chesterton that a deep-seated rebellion against the *fin de siècle* permanently marked all of his writings.

Chesterton's fears about the moral confusions of his generation ultimately forced him back to some fundamental questions about society and the nature of man. He concluded that Bertrand Russell's view of everything as simply a "matter of degree" and Shaw's sniping at idealism represented a certain philosophical nihilism which, if carried to its logical dimensions, would result in a completely valueless society. The art for art's sake theme of the *Yellow*

Book circle was the aesthetic face of this intellectual anomie. At the time, Chesterton remarked, he was more inclined to substitute no art, for God's sake:

I would rather have no art at all than one which occupies itself in matching shades of peacock and turquoise for a decorative scheme of blue devils.[11]

In two of his major polemics, *Heretics* (1905) and *Orthodoxy* (1908), Chesterton defined the errors of the "moderns" (a term he used, it seems, to depict anybody with whom he disagreed) and offered some well-thought-out remedies for the contemporary intellectual malaise. The central criticism of *Heretics*, in which the leading publicists of the day were unmercifully rebuked, was that men were mistakenly trying to broaden themselves by attacking the fundamental institutions (e.g., family, church, Christmas, and pubs) in the name of science. Lasting values were seen to have been sacrificed for the immediate gains of "progress" and efficiency, and doubts concerning the basic fundamentals of life were leaving men's minds derelict on a sea of uncertainty. Thus, *Heretics* made an appeal for returning to fundamentals in order to reform modern ethics, which G. K. considered void of purity and spiritual triumph. As Chesterton saw it, "the ordinary honest man" was disgusted with modern realistic literature, not because of realism, but because it lacked a clear idealism. He resented this type of modern literature, typified by Shaw and Ibsen, because it developed an eye for criticism but became blind to what was right: "If we compare . . . the morality of the *Divine Comedy* with the morality of Ibsen's *Ghosts*, we shall see all that modern ethics have really done."[12] The moderns lacked a sense of proportion and standards. Shaw's *Quintessence of Ibsenism* acknowledged as much; the essay summed up Ibsen's teaching in the phrase, "the golden rule is that there is no golden rule." Chesterton pointed out that this omission had the effect of leaving human consciousness with very definite images of evil but with no clear image of good: "The human race, according to religion, fell once, and in falling gained the knowledge of good and evil. Now we have fallen a second time, and only the knowledge of evil remains to us."[13]

There was also a certain underlying determinism to modernist thought that upset Chesterton. The fact that Shaw doubted the existence of any permanent element in morality and that H. G. Wells doubted the permanence of anything, seemed to Chesterton to preclude the necessity of human effort. Yet some of these heretics blindly believed in a socialist utopia of mechanical orderliness and materialistic plenitude, all insured by inevitable biological "progress." Chesterton believed that evolutionary doctrine was the source of this false pride which led the heretics to criticize the universe because it was not constructed to their liking. This he considered to be the great spiritual sin of the age, since it led to limitless pessimism and prevented man from doing anything constructive about improving the condition of his worldly estate.

This modernist disease also had affected religion, in particular the preachers of the "New Theology," which was an attempt to present Christianity in terms intelligible to the "modern man" by taking into account revolutionary changes in biology and Biblical Higher Criticism. One of the originators of this effort to modernize Christianity, the Protestant theologian R. J. Campbell, felt that man, thanks to a gradual moral evolution, was becoming more and more Christlike. Chesterton vehemently castigated Campbell's position because it attempted to explain away evil by rejecting the doctrines of original sin. But his real objection to the New Theology was that it aimed to reconcile Christianity with the modern world, whereas it was a violent reaction against modernity which was rapidly driving Chesterton into a reconciliation with Christianity.

In Chesterton's mind, the modern heretics had forsaken the older, established standards for something as yet untried. Such an approach to life was false on two grounds. Not only was it unproven historically; it also lacked proportion and balance: "Heresy is the subtraction of one particular idea from a necessary complex balance of ideas, and the exaltation of it at the expense of others which must also be maintained."[14] After lashing out at these fundamental philosophical errors, Chesterton offered his own system which in contrast he labeled "orthodoxy." He felt that English philosophers and reformers could not work towards a social ideal until it was determined what that ideal should be. In other words, one had to begin with first principles—the nature of man and his primary spiritual needs. For Chesterton the spiritual need was a dual one: "The need for that mixture of the familiar and the unfamiliar which Christen-

dom has rightly named romance."[15] Most men, he felt, needed a
practical romance, the combination of something strange with
something secure; the mystery of the cosmos had to be balanced with
man's certainty about his place within it. Hence, in *Orthodoxy*
(1908), Chesterton developed an argument for utilizing tradition as
the only reasonable basis for reform and securing man's freedom.
Moving away from an earlier position of agnosticism, he embraced
the dogma of Christian theology as the sole foundation for sound
ethics. At the root of this acceptance of Christianity is what J. M.
Ryan has called G. K.'s "sense of limits":

When Chesterton said: 'All my life I have loved edges, and the boundary
line that brings one thing sharply against another,' he was voicing that
opposition to vagueness and drift which finds one expression in dogma.[16]

Chesterton's sense of limits, which was at the core of his distaste
for imperialism ("I think the first thing that made me dislike
imperialism was the statement that the sun never sets on the British
Empire. What good is a country with no sunset?"), and the yearning
for the firmness of dogma inevitably brought him to Catholicism.[17,18]

Before Gilbert Chesterton, the proponents of Christian orthodoxy
against modernism, i.e., the whole complex of ideas associated with
Darwin and scientism, defended their creed with appropriate solem-
nity. However, Chesterton's belief in divine grace made him a
philosophic optimist: man was a fallen creature, but he was re-
deemed by Christ. Gaiety and optimism set Chesterton apart from
many Catholic writers and especially from his conservative colleagues. Both T.E. Hulme and Ramon de Maetzu, who wrote with
G.K.in A.R. Orage's *The New Age*, shared his feelings about original sin and the need for dogma and discipline.[19] Yet Orage persistently asked the sardonic Hulme and de Maetzu to qualify their
doctrines of Christianity, since an excessive concern with original
sin had led them to neglect its counterpart—the doctrine of redemp-
tion.[20]

Orthodoxy was Chesterton's answer to the moral skepticism of
Edwardian England. Darwin and the "evolutionary thing" had led
to a natural confusion of priorities and an unnatural boom in man's
pride; the modern heretics had torn fragments of truth from Darwin

and stretched them completely out of proportion. *On the Origin of Species* and *The Descent of Man* had become erroneously identified with progress and hence used to establish the doctrine of human perfectibility. Chesterton felt that if men were perpetually evolving into something higher, morality, lacking a permanent base, must fail. What was immoral today might be moral tomorrow, and eventually everything would become relative:

All had grown dizzy with degree and relativity . . . so that there would be very little difference between eating dog and eating darkee, or between eating darkee and eating dago.[21]

Chesterton's social philosophy also began to take shape during these years, a dimension of his work which brought him considerable attention within radical circles. While he was writing for the *Daily News* he challenged the inequalities of English social life, as defended by conservatives, no less than leftist pleas for social planning through the mechanistic regulation of men's lives. His articles also poked fun at the ideals of vegetarianism, teetotaling, and pacifism, thus greatly annoying the publisher, the teetotaling Quaker gentleman, George Cadbury. In fact, Chesterton's bombasts assailed so many basic axioms of nonconformity that they often had to be qualified by a leader on the same page. Yet these vitriolic words, garnished with just the right spice of wit, went over extremely well with the reading public. It was alleged that Chesterton's weekly article proved so popular that the circulation of the *Daily News* on Saturdays doubled that of any other day of the week.[22]

Chesterton's special hatred for socialism and big government can best be understood by appreciating his strong feelings on the subjects of democracy and the common man. G.K.C. had a profound love of mankind which might properly be called humanism. He felt that the fundamental assumption of humanism, that man is by nature noble and unique, was first articulated in the teachings of Christianity. Christ had taught that man was made in the image of God, hence he must have been unique and, at the same time, created equal. This quickly explained, in G. K.'s mind, why Christianity was the first religion to oppose slavery; slavery was a denial of liberty, "the god in Man." Since Chesterton believed that liberty and one's freedom could best be exercised in small units, he concluded that democracy—the system in which men could truly use their liberty—could only function in very small places.

Most of Chesterton's polemical essays and literary criticisms were aimed at writers who either ignored or deprecated ordinary man. One of his main objections to the aesthetes, among whom he considered Oscar Wilde and Shaw, was their fundamental detachment "from the vulgar mob."[23] He considered these writers elitists who had lost touch with the people. Shaw's basic contempt for man, "the old beer-drinking, creed-making, fighting, failing, sensual, respectable man," was just the sort of thing Chesterton found objectionable in modern writers.[24] It was because Shaw did not understand this quality of man that he came to preach the doctrine of Superman, which G.K. considered not only false, since it ignored the nature of man, but evil because it denied the principles of democracy.

Chesterton found his literary heroes in Johnson, Swift, Browning, and Dickens. Like Chesterton, these writers demonstrated a true love of humanity, were intoxicatingly good-humored and boldly attacked many of the same evils against which G.K. was fighting in twentieth-century England. Dickens, in particular, was singled out and honored because he had contact with the people, something modern poets and intellectuals had lost. Chesterton objected to much of modern poetry, because it required an interpreter to be understood easily: "The ideal condition is that the poet should put his meaning more and more into the language of the people, that the people would enjoy more and more of the meaning of the poet."[25] Instead modern writers and artists were "mystagogues," specializing in obfuscation:

The cloud is their banner; they cry to chaos and old night. They circulate a piece of paper on which Mr. Picasso has had the misfortune to upset the ink and tried to dry it with his boots, and they seek to terrify democracy by the good old anti-democratic muddlements: that 'the public' does not understand these things; that 'the likes of us' cannot dare to question the dark decisions of our lords.[26]

In a sense, this split between people and artist points up what G.K.C. considered to be the fundamental problem of modern society: the common man had become alienated from his government and its leaders. The rootlessness of Shaw and the heretics was simply a literary manifestation of this malaise.

In *The Everlasting Man* (1925), Chesterton explained that the dichotomy between common man and poet-intellectual was an ancient problem. In pagan times the search for truth proceeded through both mythology and philosophy, the former being of popular origin (the spontaneous expression of a nameless multitude), the latter an effort by the erudite. Chesterton considered the great virtue of Christianity to be its remarkable success in bridging the gap between these two roads to truth. *The Everlasting Man* is, in particular, an explanation of how Christianity condemned the dichotomy and eventually succeeded in satisfying both the intellect of the philosophers and the more mundane needs of the multitude, the latter having been fulfilled previously only through mythology. Christianity did away with mythology and brought intellectual poet and everyman together through Biblical literature.

G.K.C., the jolly white knight of Fleet Street, ultimately linked his Christian democratic ideals to a man of far different temperament. Chesterton's orthodox critique of modern social philosophy found its natural counterpart in the world view of Hilaire Belloc. A man of uncompromising opinions, Belloc became Chesterton's mentor; his influence, not entirely positive, forced Chesterton to focus more closely on practical social and political issues.

CHAPTER
II

Hilaire Belloc

As a writer, Hilaire Belloc was known chiefly as an historian and political commentator. At the base of his world view was a militant Catholicism and a loyalty to French culture. The latter made him obsessively anti-German. Belloc's special contempt for Germany developed early in life. As a mere child he had escaped Paris with his family just as the Prussians were entering the city. Growing up in the atmosphere of French defeat permanently slanted his mind against Bismarck and everything Prussia represented. Thus, throughout his entire writing career, he considered Prussia (Belloc seldom used the term Germany) as the barbarous destroyer of Europe's democratic tradition and the repository of all evil. Belloc maintained his French citizenship even after the family moved to England, and ultimately fulfilled his required service in the French army before entering Oxford.

Belloc had a distinguished undergraduate career at Oxford, where he was widely respected as a public speaker, the president of the Oxford Union, and a student of history. One can gauge the influence of his views during those years by a publication in 1896 entitled *Essays in Liberalism*. This was a collection of discourses by Belloc and several colleagues who, as explained in the introduction, were primarily inspired and guided by Belloc's views on politics. The other contributors (including F.Y. Eccles, J.S. Phillimore, J.L. Hammond, J.A. Simon, and F.W. Hirst) came together again a few years later writing for *The Speaker* under Hammond's editorship.

Already, in this early collection of essays, Belloc demonstrated a fear of state power destroying individuality. The book's contributors recommended a return to the "fundamental principles of Liberalism" as a remedy to this looming problem. Belloc's notion of Liberalism, however, contained the anarchistic principle that no political association could command obedience unless each member of society played a part in the government he was to obey.[1] Belloc also insisted that a truly free citizen had to be politically and economically independent. To guarantee this he proposed a wider distribution of private ownership, as opposed to the socialist emphasis on state ownership of property. The ideas put forth in the book were so unorthodox that the *Isis* felt obliged to point out that they did not correspond to those of any recognized section of the Liberal Party.

Belloc's anti-Semitism, growing out of an opposition to Dreyfus, first appeared in his student days at Oxford.[2] Like the French right, Belloc opposed the reopening of the Dreyfus case both because he believed that it would weaken the French Army, and because he was convinced that the demand for a retrial was being directed by a small group of Jewish financiers. Belloc's anti-Semitism did not fade after the Dreyfus Affair receded from public attention. Nor did he ever forget the significance of the episode. He always maintained that the vindication of Dreyfus had destroyed the French Intelligence Bureau, a loss which permitted the German surprise at Mons and Charleroi in 1914 and served to prolong the great war. Throughout his literary career Belloc continued to assert that Jews were disproportionately prominent in French and English public life, and he steadfastly insisted that they controlled international finance.

Such views did much to damage his reputation as a political writer and philosopher.[3] Robert Speaight, Belloc's biographer, contended that Belloc's "exotic" anti-Semitism and overbearing personality were partly responsible for his rejection for a Fellowship at All Souls, whose dons felt that he was a little unbalanced. The rejection at Oxford was a blow from which he seems never to have recovered, always believing that he was turned down because of his militant Catholicism and radical political views.[4]

This cursory analysis shows that, from the beginning, Belloc had taken up a position on the fringe of English intellectual life. In addition, his French sympathies, reflected in his unusual defense of Danton and Robespierre, and the fact that he served in the French army (a claim no other Oxford student could make), made him an outcast amid the general Francophobic and pro-German mood which prevailed at the universities. Amongst both dons and students the ideas of Kant and Hegel were in vogue, Belloc's college, Balliol, being the center of Neo-idealism. In the area of popular journalism the *Daily Mail* (owned by Alfred Harmsworth) led the field in inflaming public opinion against France. Young Belloc never forgot its sensational and jingoistic policy, and during his years with the *New Witness* he singled out Harmsworth as a subversive and traitor to Britain. All of this precluded Belloc's acceptance by what one might call the British political establishment.

In order to appreciate fully the mind of Hilaire Belloc, it is worthwhile to consider those writers and traditions that had great influence upon him. In terms of cultural attitudes and literary style, Belloc was inspired by the classical writers, Homer, Theocritus, Anacreon, Catullus, and Virgil. His knowledge of classical literature was profound, most of which he read in the original Greek or Latin; and Belloc greatly admired good writing (e.g., he especially liked the crisp styles of Milton, Gibbon, and his own contemporary, Dean Inge, though completely disagreeing with their ideas).[5] It is more difficult to determine precisely which writers influenced Belloc's historical views. He never cited sources when writing history, and this damaged his reputation amongst professional historians. Those who knew Belloc claimed that he was a careful researcher who simply refused to flaunt his scholarship by copious footnotes.[6] Furthermore, Belloc had an errant contempt for academic convention (partly because it had rejected him).

On one crucial point, clearly, Belloc was open to severe historiographical criticism. He may have been a thorough researcher, and was certainly a masterful stylist, but he defied the most important tenet of the historian's craft by dismissing the necessity of objectivity. When asked by Father Philip Hughes why he refused to give references, he replied: "I am not a historian. I am a publicist."[7] The *modus operandi* of Belloc's historical methodology was more akin to that of Rousseau, a writer with whom he identified because of his ability to expound a fundamental dogma based not on the principle of reason but on faith.[8] To H.G. Wells, Belloc wrote that the historian who tried to write from a disinterested, objective viewpoint was condemned to sterility, because history required a flame of conviction comparable to that of religion.[9] Just as conviction made the good historian, so, believed Belloc, did the persuasion of personality mold the patterns of history. As opposed to the Marxist school of historiography, which highlights environment as the crucial historical determinant, Belloc seemed to believe in the great man idea. Most of his historical essays concerned personalities (Danton, Napoleon, Robespierre, Richelieu, among others) whose one or two "ideas" or convictions he supposed to have shaped the course of history.

Belloc never commented extensively on particular books he may have found helpful in reconstructing the past. Michelet, it seems, provided him with a certain appreciation of history. Robert Speaight contended that the French historian remained an inspiring model to Belloc by preaching that good historical writing was "a resurrection of the flesh."[10] Nearly all of Belloc's historical narratives possess a certain "eye-witness" quality. Yet Michelet does not seem to have contributed anything especially Catholic to Belloc's historiography. If anything, Belloc's rather unusual interpretation of the past, which highlighted European culture as fundamentally Catholic, sounds remarkably similar to that of the French Restoration writers, notably De Maistre, Chateaubriand, and Bonald. However, in one absolutely fundamental deviation, Belloc did not share the Restoration antipathy for the French Revolution.

Belloc did not give the great English Catholic historian, Lord Acton, a sympathetic reading. Nor did he pay very close attention to what Acton had to say about the multi-national state, which, in many ways, was quite similar to Belloc's conception of the "Imperium Christianum." For Belloc, Acton was probably too indulgent, and, above all, too Germanic. Of the English writers, John Henry Newman and William Cobbett seem to have been the only ones Belloc admired without reservation. Jonathan Swift also received high praise on occasion. Belloc wrote that he read and re-read *The Public Spirit of the Whigs*, not only because Swift was anti-Whig and satirized the sycophantic courtier (a latter-day parliamentary politician), but also because of its unrelenting assaults on lawyers, whom Belloc loathed because they hid behind a labyrinth of technical codes and made life miserable for the common man.[11]

As a young man Belloc had known and frequently called upon Cardinal H.E. Manning (a convert to Catholicism, somewhat narrow-minded and intensely Ultramontane in his convictions), and in later biographical essays he claimed that Manning was also a great influence on the formation of his thoughts.[12] Yet one finds very little of anything distinctly English in Belloc's Catholic polemics. Moreover, Robert Speaight claimed that he was never very familiar with the radical writers of contemporary French Catholicism, namely Léon Bloy, Charles Péguy, and Georges Bernanos. Belloc made no reference to these men in his writings; yet in several ways his reverence for the peasantry, whom writers like René Bazin, Paul Claudel, and Bloy regarded as the repository of tradition, patriotism, and the family, and his attacks on capitalism and the social irresponsibility it produced, were notably similar to the attitudes of these French writers. Like Bloy, Belloc also used the novel to dramatize his political grievances and attack his enemies. Though quite unlike these writers, who condemned other Catholics for trying to reconcile their religion with rationalism and democracy, Belloc was certainly no mystic and never anti-democratic.[13]

At first glance, Belloc's political ideas seem extraordinarily befuddled. He became an advocate of monarchism, appreciated the strong hand of dictatorship, yet called himself a democrat and a Republican. However, an examination of his historical views, especially those concerning the Church and the French Revolution, reveals a certain logic to these seemingly contradictory political stances. A thorough analysis of Belloc's historiography is rather difficult, not only because it grew in steps throughout his career, but also because it is nowhere developed philosophically in any one piece of writing. Again, however, it is important to appreciate that Belloc saw the world through the eyes of the Catholic Church. Catholicism was the good life itself—outside the Church was perdition. As he once told Dean Inge:

The Church is that within which is right order; outside, the puerilities and the despairs. . . . Within that household the human spirit has roof and hearth. Outside it, is the night.[14]

At the base of Belloc's historical views was an abiding admiration of Graeco-Roman civilization. The Romans civilized Europe by preserving the culture of Greece, and they brought political unity through language, laws, and civic institutions. Rome forged a variety of ethnic groups over disparate geographical areas into a single state. Just as the Roman Empire had kept alive the higher traditions of Greece, so, Belloc argued, had the Church, in the face of barbarian and Islamic invasion, preserved and revitalized the institutions of Rome. The civilization of Roman Catholic Europe reached its zenith in the High Middle Ages from the eleventh to the fourteenth century.

Belloc had a special loathing for Protestantism because it destroyed the Christian unity of Europe. The disruption of this unity brought men of wealth to power, an oligarchy which ruled not by law but by the force of money. In the long run Belloc saw Protestantism as the progenitor of all evil. Belloc believed that the Church not only maintained culture (a general rule of civilization, said he, is that a people is more civilized in proportion to its closeness to the Church), but that modern civilization went sour because men lost the faith. Thus man had not really progressed throughout the modern era, as the myth perpetuated by the Liberal-Whig historical tradition would have it; rather, life had deteriorated in both a qualitative and anti-democratic sense, because the single institution responsible for the rise of liberty (the Church) had been undermined by false doctrines.

Belloc's unorthodox interpretation of history was intended to counter the Whig bias in English historiography. He came to dislike the Gibbon-Macaulay historical thesis, which emphasized the development of parliamentary government and the curbing of monarchical prerogative, because it exalted the forces which destroyed Catholic universalism, downgraded the Middle Ages and eulogized an event (the abolition of the monasteries) that helped spawn a new class of predatory capitalists.[15] He even went so far as to argue that this historiographical tradition was the single most important factor preventing England's return to the Catholic fold.[16] Coupled with Belloc's detestation of Whig historiography was an intense abhorrence of the rich. He disliked the wealthy primarily because they were corruptors of politics and exploiters of the poor.[17] Belloc's attachment to what he defined as Republicanism seems to have grown directly out of this antipathy to the rich and privileged.

Unlike Burke, Carlyle, and most Catholic thinkers, great defenders of the ancien régime, Belloc was an admirer of the regicides of 1789. His consistent defense of the French Revolution is somewhat puzzling in light of the latter's assaults on the anti-democratic position of the Catholic Church. Belloc, however, was convinced that the Revolution was never the enemy of the Church, nor that there was anything intrinsically anti-democratic in Catholic theology. The conflict between the Revolutionaries and the Catholic establishment, Belloc argued, was due to a misunderstanding between personalities and to a climate of bitterness that had been generated by the eighteenth-century Gallican Church. Cut off from its titular leader and passing through a stage of decay and corruption, the Church in France had become identified with the sickness of the old regime. For these reasons the Church became the most visible object of attack, and when the government coffers went dry, the Church was the most accessible fund of wealth. Belloc, however, considered the Civil Constitution of the Clergy to have been the real source of conflict between the Revolutionaries and the Church. He believed that the Revolutionaries did not want to kill the Church, but only wanted it to have a safe funeral by controlling the hierarchy that had been bound up with the old society. However, they erred in thinking the faith moribund; their mistaken attack on the constitution of the Church had the effect of turning the small minority who were true Catholics against the Revolution.

To Belloc the French Revolution was essentially a violent return to conditions necessary for the health of any community. The old regime had decayed to the point that radical surgery was needed to save the life of the state. Simplicity and political flexibility, the main conditions of happiness in any community, had prevailed from the eleventh through the fourteenth century: "The king ruled, the knight fought, the peasant dug in his own ground, and the priest believed." But then came the Reformation, and the flexibility of Europe's institutions was stultified by the bonds of lawyers. By the seventeenth century the pedants were giving orders, the upper classes fought the princes, and the people were silent. With the coming of the century of revolution, the new rich class was maintaining its privileges by manipulating the ancient symbols of the faith: "They build ramparts of sacred tombs, and defend themselves with the bones of the Middle Ages, with the relics of the saint and the knight."[18] This, argued Belloc, determined the shape of the Revolution; this is why it seemed to take on the appearance of anti-Catholicism. Yet in reality it was the spirit of the faith that made the Revolution. The privileged men used the symbols of the Middle Ages because they thought it was dead, but suddenly the spirit became flesh: "the spirit of enthusiasm and of faith, the Crusade, came out of the tomb and routed them."[19]

Belloc saw the trend of revolution mainly in terms of forceful personalities who were moved by a vague sense of justice. Robespierre was singled out as a man with "heroic virtue," because he was sincerely attached to the conception of a Rousseauistic ideal of democracy and incorruptible in the pursuit of it. Belloc believed that the Terror was essential for saving the Revolution from its enemies, but he thought Carnot responsible for carrying it too far. Robespierre supported the Terror least, but was unjustly blamed for its excesses, simply because he was most identified with the popular clamor of the time.

Robert Speaight has explained Belloc's doctrine of Revolution in essentially Rousseauan terms. He believed that the sovereignty of a political community derived from what could be called a general will of its people. Possessed by a kind of revolutionary mystique, Belloc felt that power was the natural instrument by which the communal spirit manifested itself, and, for the highest point of efficiency, it was necessary for this to be centralized. This was especially the case in large communities where the presence of a strong ruler was required. Belloc defended Napoleon on the grounds that he substituted personal rule for oligarchy: he was the "incarnation of the community" in one man saving the Revolution from the special interests which always prey on the commonwealth where so-called "representative" parliamentary governments exist.[20] Dictators, oligarchs or monarchs exercising power in seeming defiance of the popular will could be excused by claiming that the true sense of community resides in its permanent institutions rather than in its occasional majorities. Belloc had no special fear of dictatorship, since he saw it as a public power and popular in its origins—i.e., despotism could be a manifestation of democracy. But the power generated by money was evil; it was a secret power, and hence the real enemy of the people.

Belloc's political attitudes, complementing his historiography, had a certain affinity with the French Right. Speaight has argued that most of what Belloc came to know of French politics was learned as a conscript with the batteries on the frontiers of Alsace-Lorraine and from reading Charles Maurras, the influential monarchist editor of *Action Française*.[21] On the other hand, Marie Belloc Lowndes has written that Belloc, as a young man, developed an enthusiasm for his family friend and neighbor, Paul Déroulède, and had even become a member of the latter's *Ligue des Patriotes*.[22] Déroulède had established the *Ligue* in order to rekindle patriotism and to propagandize for the recovery of Alsace-Lorraine. The founder, like Belloc, was basically a Jacobin Republican but opposed to the Third Republic because of its financial corruption, parliamentary instability, and its pusillanimous policy towards Germany. But a close study of Belloc's views suggests that Maurras probably remained his true mentor on the matter of French politics. Belloc frequently praised the French philosopher-journalist and read Maurras' newspaper *Action Française* whenever he could lay hands upon it.[23]

In general, Hilaire Belloc is a very difficult thinker to categorize. His great love for Republicanism and the radicals of the French Revolution certainly set him apart from much of the French Right. He was profoundly Catholic, yet outside conventional Church philosophy, and was never completely accepted by the official Catholic Social Movement.[24] He cannot be linked with the radical French Catholics, and he remained entirely outside English political conservatism in his later and more extremist years. Speaight relates a conversation he had with Belloc just before the latter's death. When Speaight asked him whether he thought the French Revolution had done more harm than good, Belloc replied: "It had to come; otherwise society would have just dried up."[25] And despite his later contempt for representative government, Belloc held to what might be called an anarchistic democratic ideal, which, like Rousseau's, asserted that democracy could only be realized in small unindustrialized communities. Belloc's Republicanism, like his love of democracy, was probably also an ideal. To him, Republicanism was a system of government which could operate effectively only after evil elements had been purged from the body politic.

Belloc's opposition to imperialism, like his political and historical attitudes, also derived from loyalty to the tradition of Rome. He considered Catholicism to be the mainspring of European culture—thus the meaning of his controversial phrase "Europe is the faith and the faith is Europe"—and he believed that Westerners could survive in the modern world only by returning to its principles. This view of history, unique in the English historiographical tradition, was the keystone of Belloc's world view. He always believed that Catholicism was more than just a religion. He considered it a culture, hence a temporal and spiritual loyalty to Rome were totally inseparable. Belloc felt a sense of belonging to European life, in its classical and medieval unity, only through the socio-cultural patterns of Roman and medieval history. The immense power of Belloc's writings convinced many of his readers that Catholicism had to mean a temporal and spiritual allegiance to Rome. Catholic ecclesiastical officials, theologians, and intellectuals (Jacques Maritain and Christopher Dawson in particular) for years were compelled to refute this mistaken assumption, though it meant challenging one of the most articulate writers in the English language. A Jesuit writing in 1925 pointed out (in reference to Belloc's theory that Roman civilization in Britain survived the Saxon invasions) the mistaken readiness of public opinion to believe that "what Mr. Belloc holds and defends is . . . the view of educated Catholics in general, and possibly . . . inspired by ecclesiastical authority."[26] Yet the impact of Belloc's thesis was so pervasive amongst some of his followers that it conditioned their political views, a factor in explaining why many later Distributists uncritically embraced Mussolini and empathized with fascism.[27] Belloc's feelings about Rome provide a key to understanding his position on the issue of European imperialism. He simply opposed anything which worked to destroy the unity of the Roman Church: thus his hatred of the Hohenzollerns, who, in his incorrect view, brought Protestantism to Germany; the Jews, who made money-making the *raison d'être* of life and work; and the entire development of capitalism, which destroyed imperial Rome as it was reborn in the cultural unity of medieval Christendom. He regarded imperialism as an extension of the money-grubbing which had destroyed the medieval social and political order.

Like most English Radicals, with whom he identified in his early career, Belloc believed that European international expansion was generated by capitalists seeking new areas for economic exploitation and financial investment. And like Déroulède and Maurras, he interpreted the financial root of British imperialism in the same fashion as French nationalists viewed the Panama scandal of 1892-93: it was a form of profiteering against the public good by a small clique of mainly Jewish cosmopolitan financiers.[28] Even worse, Belloc believed that the financial wire-pullers were essentially anonymous men who worked in secret, behind the scenes, by purchasing the favors of British politicians.

Belloc's repugnance for such activity was angrily dramatized in the novel *Emmanuel Burden* (1904). In this story the chief characters were meant to symbolize the social and economic forces that make up British politics. The source of corruptive power was a Mr. Barnett, a corpulent Jewish financier with a dark complexion and a foreign accent. Barnett's unsavory personal peculiarities make him stand out in stark contrast to the English environment in which he operated. But because of money and influence (Barnett owned several leading newspapers), he could wine and dine politicians whose cooperation was needed for a commercial undertaking in Africa. The protagonist was the respectably middle-class Emmanuel Burden, a pillar of the community who had worked honestly for his worldly success. Barnett needs Burden's cooperation so as to give his imperial venture commercial respectability. Barnett also seeks the help of Lord Benthrope, an important landed aristocrat with Parliamentary influence. Although Mr. Burden is skeptical about these plans and is mystified by Barnett's wheelings and dealings in the stock market, he is reluctantly drawn into the M'Korio Delta Development Company, an enterprise designed to exploit the riches of Africa. Ultimately Burden discovers that Barnett's men have sabotaged the business of a friend who has refused to join this venture, and he threatens to expose the affair in one of the newspapers that has not been bought off by the monied interests. Unfortunately the hero has made the discovery too late. Sickened by the skulduggery of the whole episode and with his spirits broken, Emmanuel Burden returns home to die.

Emmanuel Burden represents a vanishing breed, the honest Englishman who refuses to buckle under the machinations of the big swindle. However, his son, Cosmo, who inherits the family wealth, has recognized the wave of the future. Indeed, by working behind his father's back Cosmo has cooperated with Barnett all along and lives happily ever after by adjusting to the new system of financial manipulation. Lord Benthrope, the symbol of Britain's effete aristocracy, goes along with Barnett's intrigues, though he has not understood much of anything that has happened. In the end it is Cosmo, representative of an English middle class severed from its roots of commercial integrity, and Benthrope, an aristocratic politician owned by the Jews, who inherit the new Britain. The old virtues of honesty and hard work have been submerged by a cosmopolitan finance spawned from the ghettos of Eastern Europe.

Belloc's criticism of the secrecy that surrounded Jewish finance and its accompanying anti-Semitic tone was not untypical of his times. A general displeasure of plutocracy and its links with Jewish money was a common feature of Edwardian England, although explicit anti-Semitism was frowned upon in intellectual circles. Belloc was far more vitriolic and outspoken than his contemporaries on this subject. Indeed, parts of the original manuscript for *Emmanuel Burden* were considered so harsh on the Jews that the publisher, A.P. Watt and Son, suspected that Belloc might be accused of "Juden-hetze" (Jew-baiting). Belloc revised certain objectionable sections of the novel, but insisted that nothing so crude as Jew-baiting had ever appeared in his work. Admitting that *Emmanuel Burden* was clearly an attack on cosmopolitan finance, Belloc told his publisher that he doubted that this evil was uniquely Jewish.[29]

Mr. Barnett, the imperialist financier, made another significant appearance in Belloc's *Mr. Clutterbuck's Election* (1908). Barnett had now become Lord Lambeth (known by the nickname "Peabody Yid" amongst the younger members of his set), an august, indefatigable empire builder, though he still possessed that unfortunate accent and a strange oriental air about him. By now the aged and fleshy Barnett has had even greater successes: he has convinced the state to take over the M'Korio Delta Development Company (which went 17 years without paying a dividend) and makes a pile of money at the public's expense. For his efforts he is awarded a dukedom. By 1924, with the appearance of *Pongo and the Bull*, Lord Lambeth, now Duke of Battersea, has become the very fount of power in the Prime Minister's world and, for all practical purposes, controls the whole of British politics. The public had not been informed about any of this. Those good men who attempted to expose the corruption fail because of a wall of secrecy in Parliament and the media, a conspiracy forged through the connivance of international financiers.

This fictionalized world of alien financiers whose only concern is personal profit, mirrored Belloc's real feelings about what was wrong with Britain's political life. He believed that such destructive tendencies could be reversed only if the public were made aware of the problem.

*   *   *

G.K. Chesterton first encountered Hilaire Belloc through the agency of the *Speaker* group. The memorable relationship was christened with a bottle of Moulin à Vent at the Mont Blanc restaurant on Gerrard Street in Soho. Belloc and his friends were attracted to Chesterton because of his unusual radical views, though it seems that they were initially somewhat hesitant about reading his articles. G.K.'s friend and brother-in-law, Lucean Oldershaw, wrote that he had a difficult time getting his colleagues on *The Speaker* to read Chesterton's work. It seems that F.Y. Eccles (a close friend of Belloc's at Oxford) had decided that Chesterton's handwriting was that of a Jew, and this prejudiced Belloc against reading his articles. If Belloc had any suspicions about G.K., they certainly vanished in the course of their first meeting. Chesterton's description of the encounter makes it perfectly clear that Belloc was friendly, vivacious and tremendously inspiring:

He talked into the night, and left behind in it a glowing track of good things. When I have said that I mean things that are good, and certainly not merely *bons mots*, I have said all that can be said in the most serious aspect about the man who has made the greatest fight for good things of all the men of my time. . . . What he brought into our dream was this Roman appetite for reality and for reason in action, and when he came into the door there entered with him the smell of danger.[30]

It was Belloc's anti-establishment positions and the intensity of his convictions that Chesterton found appealing. Both writers also shared similar antipathies. Along with an anarchistic animosity towards the bureaucratic state was a common distaste for what the socialists and progressives called "modern." Belloc's chief philosophical concern was the reintegration of man with the tradition of Rome, which meant rescuing the individual from the rootlessness of modern industrial society. Detached from his Catholic origins, modern man was essentially a stranger lost in a wilderness of concrete pavements. Hence in 1890 Belloc helped found *The Paternoster*, a journal edited by Gilbert Ellis to oppose the *fin de siècle* chaos that Chesterton had also felt compelled to combat. *The Paternoster*, which declared open war on philosophical relativism, kept its pages open to young and unknown writers who did not have the reputation to have their views published elsewhere.

Besides their mutual aversion for imperialism and modern "progressivism," Chesterton and Belloc shared the same social views. Chesterton's love for the small and feelings about the sanctity of private property naturally meshed with Belloc's belief in the French social system of peasant proprietorship. From his childhood in France and Sussex, Belloc had been in close contact with a rural culture, which, by the end of the nineteenth century, still had not been marauded by urban capitalism. Belloc saw certain aeonian features of European culture being preserved in the lives of the French peasant proprietors. Above all there was a respect for tradition and communal cooperation that came from working one's own land. This produced a whole system of thought, a sense of rootedness, family organization, and a set of religious mores which served to give shape and coherence to the whole society of which the peasant was a part. This "Peasant State," as Belloc called it, was characterized by political freedom, an attachment to a locality and a concern with the produce of the soil. It was the existence of such an independent rural community, he believed, that provided a permanent model of good living to the "unstable, nomadic and creedless" creatures who inhabited the floating world of the cities.[31]

Chesterton's and Belloc's relationship blossomed into a lifetime journalistic assault on the ills of twentieth-century England. In the public eye the pair became known as the "Chesterbelloc," a label first coined by George Bernard Shaw in *The New Age*. Contrary to general belief, Shaw did not use the term to identify a common set of opinions on all subjects between Chesterton and Belloc. Instead, "Chesterbelloc" was meant to be a symbol of a pantomime elephant or unnatural beast representing the mistaken union of the two men. In using the label, Shaw was convinced that Chesterton, whom he called "a colossal genius," was following the lead of the lesser man. Despite their antithetical views on nearly every conceivable subject, Shaw and G.K.C. remained close friends throughout life; but Shaw objected to Chesterton's swallowing Belloc's socio-political views. "Chesterbellocisms," in Shaw's use of the term were opinions dictated by Belloc which Chesterton expressed without having discovered them for himself. Shaw was probably correct about much of what he criticized in the relationship, since Belloc was the dominant personality. Chesterton's biographer, Maisie Ward, has argued that G.K.C. took nearly all of his views on politics, sociology and history from Belloc.[32] Belloc himself told Hesketh Pearson and Hugh Kingsmill that Chesterton had taken all of his ideas—indeed, whole passages— from his books without realizing it, and had restated them for popular consumption.[33]

It is also true that Belloc and Gilbert Chesterton differed greatly in personality and artistic taste. Belloc, a strict classicist, found Chesterton's romantic and rather freewheeling style unpalatable and admitted at one time that he had read few of G.K.C.'s books. Even more obvious were the differences in personality and temperament. While G.K. was humble in combat, overflowing in friendliness and almost childlike in his humor, Belloc was vain, bitingly cynical and cantankerous in political debate.[34] Yet Chesterton, the romantic littérateur and social reformer, and Belloc, the historian and political analyst, seem to have made a pact to reform the world. A longtime admirer, Edward Collins S.J., saw the agreement defined in the last pages of *The Napoleon of Notting Hill*:

You and I, Auberon Quin, have both of us throughout our lives been again and again called mad. And we are mad. We are mad because we are not two but one man. We are mad because we are two lobes of the same brain, and that brain has been cloven in two. And if you ask for proof of it, it is not hard to find. It is not merely that you, the humorist, have been in these days stripped of the joy of gravity. It is not merely that I, the fanatic, have had to grope without humour. It is that, though we seem to be opposite in everything, we have been opposite like man and woman, aiming at the same practical thing. We are the father and mother of the Charter of Cities.[35]

It is by no means certain that Shaw was entirely correct in his interpretation of the Chesterbelloc. Even Shavian scholars have admitted that he never understood Chesterton. Nor should one regard the Chesterbelloc as an unnatural beast, and dismiss its socio-political program as mistaken nonsense. First of all, the relationship was not an artificial one. Both men had sound intellectual and emotional reasons for striking up a partnership. Secondly, the relationship was far from devoid of intellectual content.[36] The Chesterbelloc was solidly Thomistic in its philosophical orientation. In fact, the Dominican monthly, *Blackfriars*, considered Chesterton to be the precursor if not the originator of the entire neo-Thomistic revival in England.[37] This was no mean feat, considering that the Chesterbelloc did not draw on continental Catholic theology, which was simultaneously trying to work out a Thomistic approach to modern society. Lastly, the ideal of Distributism they subsequently developed was imaginative, influential, and perhaps most importantly, it almost completely absorbed the energies of two of England's finest literary talents. Those writers who have dismissed Distributism as unimportant have generally devoted their attention solely to the belletristic side of the Chesterbelloc. The outcome is a somewhat unbalanced picture of the phenomenon, since it ignores a sizeable portion of Shaw's beast.

III

Forming The Socio-Political Ideal

Chesterbelloc's social and political views gradually emerged in systematized fashion in the first decade of the twentieth century after a long series of journalistic debates with H.G. Wells, Shaw, Robert Blatchford, and other socialist writers, and after Belloc's personal experience of Parliament. At the base of their world view, which eventually earned the awkward term "Distributism," was Catholic philosophy—in particular the system of St. Thomas Aquinas—and Belloc's peculiar interpretation of English and European history. G.K.C. claimed that his move towards the Distributist ideal "was only a further sub-division of my Notting Hill romance, from the street to the house; but it was solidified by Belloc, his Irish friends and his French holidays."[1]

G.K.C. and Belloc were especially distressed at the drift towards socialism in England, since it threatened to sacrifice common man to the machinery of the state. Sidney Webb's comment that the fitting development of each individual was not necessarily the cultivation of his own personality, "but the filling . . . of his humble function in the great social machine," typified the cast of mind which the Chesterbelloc saw perverting English life.[2] The socialists, armed with collectivist ideas, were looking at the problem from the wrong perspective, that is, from the angle of the state and not that of man. Chesterton and Belloc did not believe that massive reforming schemes imposed from above could ever achieve lasting success, regardless of how well-intentioned and carefully planned. First, they argued that successful reform had to be supported by everyman; the people had to be committed to change, and they had to be involved individually in carrying out reforms that would affect their own personal lives. Reform from above was also wrong because it would stifle creativity and remove common man from a position of responsibility for his own affairs. Forcing change from outside the immediate community would have the further effect of compromising democracy, since the state would be taking the initiative in areas of local concern. Above all, the Chesterbelloc was convinced that in their constant emphasis on efficiency and central governmental control, the socialists were ignoring the nature of man.

In *What's Wrong with the World* (1910), a clear statement of Chesterton's sociological views, he argued that the family had to be the starting point for understanding man as a political animal. Only within the compass of family life were one's needs first satisfied; it was here that man learned to deal with the outside world. Chesterton deemed the state to be a contrivance of human wisdom to protect this basic social mechanism. And in his opinion, the integrity of the family could best be protected by the state's guaranteeing private property, which was recognized as the mainspring of liberty and the source of creativity. Socialists, on the other hand, were intent upon strengthening and renewing the state, the shell of society, but were not especially engaged in strengthening and renewing the family, the very substance of society. Nor were socialists concerned about basic familial relationships. Collectivism displayed no firm distinctive sense of one thing being in its nature private (family life) and another public (government). Nowhere was this better exemplified than in the call for turning private property over to the state, which, in Belloc's view, was a truly "novel proposal—to do something new and as yet untried by men of our descent with our inherited instincts and ways of looking at things."[3] A major problem in this proposal was that the socialists were confused about the importance of communal sharing, an oversight which stemmed from their inability to appreciate the private needs of man and family. Chesterton exposed their error:

Perhaps we ought to accept communal kitchens in the social crisis, just as we should accept communal cat's-meat in a siege. But the cultured Socialist . . . by no means in a siege, talks about communal kitchens as if they were the same thing as communal laundries. This shows that from the start he misunderstands human nature.[4]

In their emphasis on the importance of the family and private property, Chesterton and Belloc reveal themselves as philosophical moralists. Unlike the materialist thinkers, who developed in the tradition of La Mettrie, Condillac, and the more radical philosophers of the eighteenth century, Belloc and G.K.C. had an affinity with a more Rousseauan view of life, emphasizing the primacy of moral choice. They believed that the possession of property—above all the ownership of land—provided the kind of training required for a man to develop a sense of responsibility to himself, his family, and his community. Managing one's own property was a trial of intellectual and emotional choice and made one aware of the importance of law, civil morality, and communal cooperation. Through private ownership, man could become a shareholder in the great corporation of society; property would serve as the primary vehicle for moral instruction, which could only begin when men are forced to make choices.[5]

The Chesterbelloc attacked capitalism with the same ferocity as they did socialism. If the collectivists had overlooked the sanctity of property, capitalism had defiled property through greed. The Rothschilds and other tycoon capitalists had given a bad name to property because of their excesses. Thus they were the enemies of property—they were the enemies of their own limitations, for one could be creative only within clearly defined limits. Moreover, the capitalist entrepreneur and banker, spurred to action on the wings of the profit motive, were selfish and uncivil:

Now the Capitalist system . . . presumes that each side is bargaining with the other, and that neither is thinking primarily of the public . . . the only original case for Capitalism collapses entirely if we have to ask either party to go on for the good of the public.[6]

The practical groundwork for constructing an alternative to the twin ills of capitalism and socialism was prepared by Belloc's entry into politics as a Liberal M.P. Attacking the Education Act of 1902, Temperance Reform, and the question of Chinese labor in South Africa, Belloc was elected to Parliament in 1906 for the constituency of South Salford, a working-class suburb of Manchester.[7] He also made it a point to criticize those who were opposing Home Rule for Ireland, insisting that the real opposition to a National Council in Dublin came from those who held mortgages on Irish land and were afraid of losing them.[8] For him, this constituted yet another example of how money was influencing the course of political events.

Belloc's chief motive in entering politics was to fight the wealthy men who dominated Parliament and to expose corruption. Upon arriving at Westminster, he immediately fell afoul of the majority Liberal M.P.s. His first clash with the Liberal Party centered around the importation of Chinese labor to work for the Transvaal gold mines, a practice which the majority of Liberal candidates for Parliament vowed to eliminate if elected. The action outraged the pro-Boers and the supporters of labor within the Liberal Party, since it appeared that the mine owners and their Conservative colleagues were purposely undermining Transvaal wage scales to further their opportunities for profiteering. In his Albert Hall speech of December 21, 1905, Campbell-Bannerman announced that orders had been given to stop the recruitment and embarkation of coolies in China. This brought cries of joy from the audience and was understood to mean that no more Chinese would leave for the Transvaal. However, Belloc was greatly chagrined when the Liberal Cabinet reinterpreted Campbell-Bannerman's pledge, in accordance with the demands of financial practicability, simply stating that it meant that there would be no further recruitment of coolies. The businessmen who had already purchased licenses to import Chinese workers were allowed to continue the practice until their quota had been filled. Asquith had previously convinced the Cabinet that the revocation of import licenses already issued might have brought undue hardship to the mine owners and possible legal action for compensation against the government. Belloc was greatly disturbed over these developments, as he believed that the Liberals would put an end to all profiteering in South Africa. He became still more indignant when told by the Deputy Speaker that he could speak on the floor of the House only on condition that he not bring up the

Chinese labor question. He informed his constituency of this order, which aroused a great stir, although the Liberal Party officially denied the incident.[9] Outraged at the duplicity of his own party, Belloc ignored the order, demanding that the deportation of coolies commence within three months and that the entire cost of the operation be paid by the mine owners.[10]

Belloc was convinced that the Cabinet's refusal to reverse the Tory policy on coolie labor was dictated by certain rich men, with financial stakes in South Africa, who had contributed heavily to the Liberal Party's political fund. Consequently, he called for an audit of the party's secret war chest so that the public might know who these men were. The proposal proved highly embarrassing to Belloc's party, since many wealthy businessmen, like the South African Barny Barnato, had thrown much support to the Liberals on imperial issues. Although the House ignored Belloc's request, he knew who the guilty ones were: the money came from the pockets of the "Rand magnates" who had engineered the Boer War. In a bitingly satirical poem, he highlighted his disgust with such elements:

> We also know the sacred height
> Up on Tugela side,
> Where those three hundred fought with Beit
> And fair young Wernher died.
>
> The daybreak on the failing force,
> The final sabres drawn:
> Tall Goltman, silent on his horse,
> Superb against the dawn.
>
> The little mound where Eckstein stood
> And gallant Albu fell,
> And Oppenheim, half-blind with blood
> Went fording through the rising flood—
> My Lord, we know them well.[11]

From the moment he entered Parliament Belloc had few illusions as to what he might accomplish. As a governing body, he believed that the House of Commons had lost both its legislative power and its control of the executive. The only function it could still perform was that of publicity. Parliament still had the capacity to satisfy the

public's need to know. Amidst a national conspiracy to limit publicity (the financial plutocrats monopolized the press and controlled
the courts of law through their manipulation of judges), the only
break in the ring, albeit small, was the M.P.s' power of criticism. By
asking embarrassing questions in Commons and in a few "independent" newspapers, the M.P. might force the conspirators into the
public spotlight. It was primarily in this area that Belloc felt he
could succeed.

A major target of Belloc's attack was the Congo Reform Association, an organization formed in 1904 by E.D. Morel and Sir Roger
Casement, to secure British government intervention in the Congo
and to force the Belgians to treat the natives more humanely. Although the C.R.A. had the sympathy of the British public, Belloc's
suspicion was aroused by the massive support it received from
groups who usually were not interested in reformist causes. He also
sensed a note of anti-Catholicism in the C.R.A.'s charges against
Belgium, a Catholic state. Most important, however, was Belloc's
concern that Germany might move into the Congo if the Belgian
position were seriously weakened. In fact, Morel had proposed that
the Germans, being efficient and resourceful colonizers, be allowed
to purchase most of the Belgian Congo as well as Angola. For these
reasons Belloc publicly called for an investigation of Morel and the
C.R.A. In a series of articles in *The New Age* he charged that Morel's
background and interests were purposely kept secret (the implica-
tion being that he was an untrustworthy Jew with foreign money
connections) and that those who financed his association (he demanded that their names be published) were less interested in humanitarian causes than in destroying Leopold's monopoly, so that they
themselves might make a fortune in the Congo rubber trade.[12]
Belloc's acerbic campaign against the C.R.A., his personal attacks
on E.D. Morel, and finally his Germanophobia served to separate
him further from the Radical elements within the Liberal Party.

Belloc also clashed with the large nonconformist element within
his party. Although he campaigned against the power of the brewing monopoly, a highly popular stand amongst teetotaling nonconformists, Belloc's hostility towards the brewers was never based on
standard temperance grounds. He was instead motivated by sympathy for the independent publicans, who he believed were being

run out of business by a small and wealthy clique of monopolistic brewers.

Belloc's differences with his nonconformist colleagues were intensified during the government's efforts to pass a Licensing Bill. The Liberals introduced a proposal in 1908 which aimed at advancing temperance by closing 32,000 public drinking houses, with compensation to be provided by a special tax on drink. Belloc supported the measure, despite some reservations, because he saw it as the first attempt "in our industrial generation . . . to tackle one of the great monopolies."[13] That monopoly was the brewing industry, which had controlled most of the public drinking places by means of the "tied-house" system. Although the House of Lords defeated the Liberal Licensing Bill, Belloc had become convinced that it had been purposely undermined by the cabinet itself. He felt that the government could have steered a more popular bill eliminating the tied-house system. But instead the "intensely and deservedly unpopular" bill was directed at restricting the use of fermented liquors. Once again, the only explanation Belloc could find for such action was the government's desire to cater to what he called "the principle force in politics"—those who contributed to the secret party funds.[14]

Belloc's growing distaste for both the Liberals and the entire party system intensified in the 1909-1910 session of Parliament. In Belloc's mind, the earlier defeat of the Licensing Bill had suggested the existence of a secret clique of plutocrats who were rapidly replacing the traditional aristocratic gentlemen as the arbiters of English politics. Belloc's final disillusionment with Parliament grew out of the Liberals' efforts to reform the House of Lords. In a letter to *The Times* on February 14, 1910, he voiced suspicions that the proposals to curb the Lords' veto power would go the same way as the Licensing Bill. He believed that the government would allow the legislation to become complicated by amendments and lengthy debates, thus losing sight of the initial objective and confusing the voters. The Lords would consequently reject the altered legislation and another general election would be called, though it would not be fought on the clear-cut issue of reforming the House of Lords. Belloc insisted that, if this were the case, it would signify "a deliberate intention to shelve the whole question of the House of

Lords . . . the determination of the professional politicians to keep up the worst unrealities of an outworn system." He believed that the Liberals were intent on "preventing the democratic reform upon which the great majority of this people are certainly determined."[15]

The unexpected death of King Edward VII on May 7, 1910, forced a postponement of a resolution of the House of Lords question. Instead of asking the new and inexperienced King to pack the Upper House, thus guaranteeing the passage of the Reform Bill, the Liberals opted for a conference with the opposition leaders in order to reach a compromise on the issue. The conference failed, however, and it was decided to call another general election to settle the matter. Yet Belloc remained convinced that this was just a ploy to postpone reform further. Just as in the Chinese labor question, no real consequence would result from a proposed election and Liberal victory, because the leaders of both parties were only responsible to the secret plutocratic governing class rather than the elected House of Commons. The only alternative was for the Prime Minister to get assurance from the King that additional peers would be created if the Lords vetoed reform. If that failed, an appropriate action would be the resignation of the Liberal government, allowing the opposition the chance of trying to form a cabinet without a majority in Commons. Since the mechanics of party politics precluded this alternative, Belloc refused to play the party game and announced that he would not stand for reelection.[16]

Belloc's political battles now shifted from the arid atmosphere of the House of Commons to the more audacious world of journalism. The new attack was spearheaded by *The Party System* (1911), a book written by Belloc and Cecil Chesterton outlining the plutocratic conspiracy which had turned parliamentary government into a sham fight between the two major political parties.

Belloc's co-author was in many ways as original a character as Belloc himself. Cecil Chesterton, who had a youthful reputation as a Bohemian, was a mixture of Tory and socialist. In 1901 Cecil became active in the Fabian Society and the Christian Social Union and during these years fell under the influence of the Reverend Conrad Noel, who combined High Church theology with radical socialism. In 1906 Cecil Chesterton, Noel, and others left the Church Socialist Union and joined the new Christian Socialist League. As spokesman for the militant wing of this league, Cecil called for the nationalization of the land and of the means of production and exchange. Not surprisingly, Cecil was soon condemned by the Anglican bishops as a dangerous man. Cecil became close friends with fellow Fabian Hubert Bland, a socialist Roman Catholic and one of the Society's founders. Brocard Sewell, Cecil's biographer, claims that, as a young man, he was more influenced by Bland than anybody else and became one of the Fabian Society's most dynamic polemicists. In April 1904 he was elected to the Fabian Executive Committee and by 1905 was chosen to be an official speaker for the Society along with G.B. Shaw and S.G. Hobson.

Cecil Chesterton was not an easy man to get along with. Leonard Woolf, who knew him briefly at St. Paul's School, said that he had a fanatical streak of intolerance that was fueled not by convictions but by personal animosities. Cecil's volatile personality, in conjunction with the curious intellectual mixture of conservatism and radicalism, made things increasingly difficult for him within the confines of the Fabian Society. In 1907 he lost his bid for reelection to the Executive Committee. Thereafter he joined forces with Holbrook Jackson and A.R. Orage and served *The New Age* as assistant editor. In his early days as a journalist, Cecil opposed the pusillanimous politicians in the Labor movement as well as the anti-socialist diatribes of his brother and Belloc.[17] However, Cecil gradually lost his socialist convictions and by 1911, against all his earlier beliefs, he became convinced that the Chesterbelloc's arguments were correct. But even before this, Cecil's intrinsic conservatism and his suspicions about party politics were drawing him closer to Belloc. As early as February 1908, Cecil applauded Belloc's attack on the party funds.[18] In July 1910 he began a series of articles on the evils of parliamentary politics, a collection of arguments with a Bellocian ring to them, asserting that the party system was a hoax and that Britain was under the control of wealthy plutocrats.[19] In that same year Cecil set out his views more clearly in an anti-Whig polemic entitled *Party and People: A Criticism of the Recent Elections and their Consequences*. The book contended that the party system was a game engineered by the rich to dupe the public and concluded with numerous but rather woolly proposals for eliminating political parties and restoring "true democracy" to British politics.

Belloc and Cecil Chesterton became fast friends after 1910. Cecil wrote that he was ultimately attracted to Belloc because of the latter's principled reformism and his view of the world "as continually slipping back from the simplicity and sanity at which men were always aiming."[20] The two men joined together in 1911 to launch a career in muckraking journalism.

The Party System (1911) was a detailed exposé of how power within the House of Commons had shifted to "the Front Benches" which directed politics without reference to the British electorate. The authors told how this select body of men was chosen from among the rich politicians and their descendants by a process of cooptation, forming, in reality, a single organ operating as despotically as an Asian tyrant. The existence of this coterie of men rendered the old differences between the Tory and Liberal parties meaningless, though a division continued in form so as to fool the public into believing that real differences still prevailed. Parliament was arbitrarily divided into two teams, each of which by mutual understanding took turns running the government. Cecil and Belloc called this "the sham game," a process by which manufactured issues were raised periodically by the politicians "in order to give semblance of reality to their empty competition." This "Party System" rendered the House of Commons null and the people of Britain impotent without a voice in political affairs.[21]

In effect, Belloc and Cecil Chesterton had simply noticed the increasing Cabinet control over the House of Commons and the corresponding decline in influence of the private members. Other political commentators had recognized this tendency, though it was as yet unknown to the general public. *The Party System* differed from these other observations in that it alleged outright political conspiracy. The bogus party fight could be explained by "a united plutocracy, a homogeneous mass of the rich, commercial and territorial, into whose hands practically all power, political as well as economic, has now passed."[22] The authors were also forthright in their allegations and criticisms: the plutocratic chiefs were identified by name, and a detailed genealogical survey was provided showing how many of these men were related by birth or marriage. These familial ties were compared cleverly with the relationships of the Montagues and Capulets in *Romeo and Juliet*:

We were not surprised at Romeo loving Juliet, though he is a Montague and she a Capulet. But if we found in addition that Lady Capulet was by birth a Montague, that Lady Montague was the first cousin of old Capulet, that Mercutio was at once the nephew of Capulet and the brother-in-law of a Montague, that Count Paris was related on his father's side to one house and on his mother's side to the other, that Tybalt was Romeo's uncle's stepson and that the Friar who married Romeo and Juliet was Juliet's uncle and Romeo's first cousin once removed, we should probably conclude that the feud between the two houses was kept up mainly for the dramatic entertainment of the people of Verona.[23]

Numerous references were also made to what Belloc had witnessed as a participant in the party game. As might be expected, the Chinese labor question was singled out as a classical case of the system in operation. The politicians paid no attention to the election mandate against importing coolies to South Africa. Instead, the leaders of the two front benches consulted with the South African Jews as to what would best suit their convenience; they in turn felt they would lose money unless the Chinese were left to work out their contracts.

The Party System proposed two specific reforms. The first was a mandatory auditing of the party funds. The funds were secret and used for financing the election campaigns for men selected by the local party organizations. The existence of this source of money naturally raised questions as to the identity of the contributors and possible rewards that might have been expected by contributors for services rendered. Belloc and Cecil Chesterton considered the role of the "secret funds" and the efforts to satisfy the contributors as "the most important fact about English politics."[24] Both knew the sale of peerages and other such honors were used to replenish the party funds, but even more insidious was the fact that many wealthy men contributed to the funds in order to gain a measure of control over Parliament. As a member of Parliament Belloc had called for public disclosure of those who contributed to the party funds; he felt certain that such disclosures would make it more difficult for the wealthy to call politicians to heel for money. The struggle over the Licensing

Bill was a clear example of the way in which the party funds were influencing the course of legislation. Belloc believed that the Unionists had opposed reform of the drink trade because of the support they received from the brewers, whereas the Liberals sought to placate the moral sensitivities of their nonconformist adherents.[25]

The second reform proposal was a call for legislation to limit the duration of Parliament to a short fixed period (four years at the very most), during which the House could not be dissolved. Belloc and Cecil felt that this reform would immediately modify the course of politics: a vote of censure against the government would not bring the expense of a general election for those who passed it, thus containing the further influence of the party funds, which were used mainly for floating election campaigns. The book ended on a note of hope, explaining the *raison d'être* of the Chesterbelloc's decision to enter the world of journalism. There was no need to supplant the present political system:

All we have to do is make the party system impossible, and that will result when a sufficient number of men are instructed in its hypocrisies and follies and when men begin to ask for an opportunity to express their opinions at the polls. . . . Light on the nasty thing and an exposure of it are all that is necessary.[26]

The Party System was a clarion call to battle and remained the essential foundation from which the Chesterbelloc circle would snipe at the political establishment through the first decade of the century and throughout the inter-war years.

The publication of *The Servile State* in 1912, Belloc's single most important work and considered by some to be the most prophetic book of the twentieth century, proposed the alternative which came to be called Distributism. This brilliant social thesis first appeared in the pages of *The New Age*. From the journal's inception in 1907 through 1909, Wells, Shaw, Belloc, Cecil and G.K. Chesterton conducted a running debate on the merits of socialism. G.K. Chesterton's and Belloc's concern about the necessity of individual freedom protected by private property made them natural enemies of the collectivist ideas of the socialists. In the pages of *The New Age*, Chesterton frequently emphasized the loss of dignity and human creativity in state-directed socialism. Belloc, for his part, developed a criticism of socialist reform programs on the basis that they inevitably led to a servile society. Hence when David Lloyd George introduced his Insurance Bill of 1911, Belloc immediately took up arms against the advent of what he called "the Servile State." From the outset, Belloc was suspicious of the insurance scheme because it was a principle first invented in heathen Prussia. Thereafter Lloyd George was singled out for special contempt—"the man George," as Belloc called him—being regarded as the chief instrument for importing the principles of German state-welfare into English life.

The first part of *The Servile State* explained Belloc's own curious analysis of European and English history. Throughout early pagan times men had lived in a servile society—a society of slaves. Gradually, by the end of the Middle Ages, there emerged a new society of peasant proprietors, who were no longer slaves or serfs but free agents secure in their possessions through the ownership of property. According to Belloc, Europe at this point was a Christian agglomeration of families with varying degrees of wealth, most owning the means of production. This was also a period of great stability. Social relationships and the distribution of goods were guaranteed by cooperative bodies binding together men of the same craft or village. The small artisans and merchants, organized into guilds, were ensured against the loss of their economic independence and protected from unreasonable competition. The various guilds assured the stability of this "distributive system" by regulating competition and inheritance, and by placing legal restrictions on usury. Although these were obvious restraints on individual conduct, Belloc felt that they were necessary in order to preserve liberty, for they prevented the "growth of an oligarchy which could exploit the rest of the community."[27] Every action of this Christian medieval society was directed towards the establishment of a state in which men would be economically free through the possession of capital and land. Belloc called this society of well-distributed property the first "Distributive State." He insisted that the rise of capitalism, with its emphasis on profit, brought about the downfall of the Distributive State; it was the urge for monetary gain that inspired the Enclosure movements and the monastic confiscations of the English Reformation.

Although Belloc believed that the industrial revolution was beneficial to man, he felt that it could have taken on a cooperative form if it had developed initially where people were economically free. Coming as it did on a people who had already lost their freedom (due to the decline of the guilds), industrialism at its very origin assumed a capitalist form. Yet England could have industrialized from a well-distributed basis of property. The corporations of small owners, with their parcels of combined wealth, would have furnished the capitalization required for new technological methods, and the total wealth of the community could have grown without disturbing the balance of distribution. As it was, since the small owners had disappeared, the new industries had no choice but to turn to the big capitalists. Instead of enhancing the wealth of all, capitalist industrialization worsened the condition of the dispossessed, further concentrating wealth in the hands of the few. In a manner somewhat reminiscent of Marxism, Belloc explained how every circumstance of that post-Reformation society—"the forms in which the laws that governed ownership and profit were cast, the obligations of partners, the relationship between master and man"—directly made for the indefinite expansion of a subject class controlled by a small body of owners whom he called "the English landlord-mercantile plutocracy."[28] He traced their origin to those families enriched by Henry VIII's confiscation of the monastic lands. Through rack-renting, enclosing the common lands, and monopolizing the courts and Parliament, this early clique of magnates amassed fortunes and eventually merged with the men of commercial wealth created by the industrial revolution. They took the English state out of the hands of a powerful monarchy capable of working for the common man and delivered it to a plutocracy riding roughshod over the masses in search of larger profits. The Distributive State had given way to the Capitalist State.

Belloc believed that the Capitalist State was inherently unstable. According to his analysis, its economic system was subject to two forces which increased in direct proportion to the rate at which society became capitalized. The first of these tensions developed out of a divergence between the moral theories upon which the state reposed (capitalism purports to be founded upon a society of free citizens) and the social facts to which these theories were applied. The second strain arose from the insecurity which capitalism created amongst those who must serve it as wage earners. A combination of these tensions would eventually destroy the capitalist system. Belloc believed that the capitalists had recognized this danger, since the logical outcome of their social arrangement would be the outright starvation of the dispossessed. It was in the capitalist's own interest to prevent this occurrence, because the demise of the wage earner would destroy the economic engine of the state. Thus for years the capitalists had employed noncapitalist methods (such as the organization of poor relief) to keep the system functioning.

Belloc felt that there were only two solutions to such a state of affairs: the government must either redistribute the means of production, i.e., Distributism; or property would have to be placed in the hands of the state, i.e., completely negate the whole notion of private property. This latter alternative would also mean the total denial of freedom to everyone. Belloc believed that the first solution of redistributing the means of production was flatly rejected by those who ran the capitalist system. Instead, the chosen model for reform was collectivism. Yet, he was convinced that the capitalists would ultimately fail in this endeavor. As early as 1911 in a debate with Ramsay MacDonald, he had pointed out that the political action of the collectivists was not leading to true socialism: "There has been no advance towards that primary action, that vile thing, without which Socialism is worthless—confiscation." Belloc told MacDonald that the socialists were instead approaching a system of economic servility where the proletariat would be given security, yet be "permanently dispossessed of the means of production."[29] In other words, the Capitalist State was breeding a collectivist theory which would produce not socialism but the "Servile State." This was defined as a condition in which the mass of men were constrained by law to work for the profit of a minority; as the price of such constraint, the workers would be given a security which capitalism could not provide. Belloc was convinced that this would happen because the reformers would not have the courage to confiscate the means of production, since that would cause a complete breakdown of the economic system. The reformers would rather settle for devices which, while giving them control, would also provide security and sufficiency for the proletariat. Yet all of this guaranteed to the ownership class continued control of the means of production.

Both Chesterton and Belloc had no doubt that the common man desired the Distributist alternative to the Servile State. Moreover, the real possibility of a totalitarian alliance between the capitalist and socialist thoroughly convinced them that a return to an order of widely distributed property was the only means of saving modern society. Belloc's historical description of the medieval distributive state soon became the model for the kind of society the Chesterbelloc desired for England.

It is important to emphasize that Belloc arrived at the Distributist position through his religion. In particular, he had been swayed by Pope Leo XIII's 1891 social encyclical *De Rerum Novarum*, a classical document for twentieth-century Catholicism's ideas on private property. In it the Pope voiced concern about the inherent danger that capitalist industrialism would undermine the social and family life of the Catholic working class. The workers were thought to be especially susceptible to the dictatorial control of callous employers. Yet the Pope condemned socialism as a means for battling the excesses of capitalism because it was inimical to the natural rights of man. Instead, the "stable and permanent possession" of individual property was seen as absolutely necessary if man were to be a fully responsible Christian. This was particularly important for the preservation of family life (the "true 'society,' anterior to every kind of State or nation"), which the Church was anxious to protect from the intrusion of the state. *De Rerum Novarum* tended to regard the role of the state in a largely negative light; the organs of government were to be used primarily for protecting individual rights and preventing injustices, rather than promulgating any positive programs of social welfare. In this respect the state's most important function should be the safeguarding of private property and guaranteeing a reasonable wage for labor. Yet even in this latter requirement the Pope was anxious lest the state exercise undue influence; for this reason, he looked to workers' unions as the better vehicle for improving conditions. Finally, the encyclical recommended that the laws of the land not only favor ownership but also be constituted to induce as many people as possible to become owners. This would have the effect of narrowing the gap between the wealth of the few and the impoverished masses.[30]

The Church's views on property and government partially explain Belloc's animus towards socialism. But one should not regard Distributism as merely imitative. Belloc instead turned the theory adumbrated in *De Rerum Novarum* into a complete system of practical economics and social planning. There can be little doubt that *De Rerum Novarum* inspired Distributism; the Chesterbelloc frequently admitted as much, and many people followed their program because it was so close to Catholic social teaching. Yet there always remained one very important difference between the Chesterbelloc and the official Catholic Social Movement: unlike the majority of other early twentieth-century English reformers, the Distributists proposed revolution to attain their aims. The immediate objective was the destruction of the capitalist establishment. Chesterton himself did not shrink from advocating violent measures to accomplish this goal, though he cautioned his readers that the destruction of capitalism and socialism was only part of the problem.[31] Considering himself a democrat, Chesterton felt that the dignity and freedom of the citizen, on the basis established by the French Revolution, were of greater importance than material welfare. Thus overthrowing the system and winning a greater distribution of wealth was never to be achieved through the sacrifice of liberty, an argument some of his later followers overlooked.

Distributism was frequently criticized for being an unrealistic, medieval solution to social problems. Yet it must be pointed out that Chesterton and Belloc never called for a return to medieval society. They simply used the Middle Ages as an example of a society that had achieved a reasonable balance between spiritual and materialistic values, in which men employed their creative faculties to the fullest. Unlike the modern factory employee who spends his entire life turning screws in the production of a machine he might never see, the medieval craftsman was seen to be a true artist who created a special object of art. The medieval peasant, guildsman, and consumer were parts of an organic whole, one dependent upon the other— there was no "immense distance between the craftsman and the crowd."[32] Like that of Carlyle, Cobbett, and William Morris, Gilbert Chesterton's particular brand of medievalism was a longing for a society in which human relationships had not been destroyed by the "cash nexus." G.K.C. and Belloc never made a cult of the Middle Ages. Both were convinced that their ideal would never become reality until the economic bases of modern society were completely destroyed.

A strong and dynamic Catholicism was the unifying thread of all Chesterton's and Belloc's views. This pervasive quality permeated every page of their writing and shaped all their thoughts. Convinced of the Church's constructive impact on medieval society, they believed that a revived activist type of Catholicism could take the lead in changing the social and political life of Britain. After having worked out these socio-political attitudes, the Chesterbelloc were prepared to take their battles into the public eye through the medium of muckraking journalism.

CHAPTER IV

Journalism: The First Phase

On June 22, 1911, Belloc and Cecil Chesterton launched the first number of their independent weekly, the *Eye-Witness*. The journal was organized under Belloc's editorship, with the financial backing of Charles Granville. Its purpose was to expose the fraudulence of the party system, to fight against all measures which served to undermine the freedom of the individual and to expose corruption. This was the Chesterbelloc's declaration of war on the British political establishment, an ongoing journalistic crusade that would be maintained with varying degrees of intensity and under different newspaper titles for nearly forty years.

The weekly, blessed with an impressive list of contributors and supporters, had immediate success. Essays and poems by Maurice Baring, H.G. Wells, Algernon Blackwood, Desmond MacCarthy, and Wilfrid Blunt appeared in the first number, and Shaw, H.A.L. Fisher, E.C. Bentley, and G.K. C., among others, contributed regularly thereafter. The *Eye-Witness* maintained a high standard of intelligence, seriousness and good taste. Although it was ignored by a large number of the better-known newspapers, the journal was read and quoted by a number of respectable political and literary pundits. After just six months of publication its circulation was larger than any other weekly except the *Spectator*. Belloc wished to maintain a completely independent journal; for this reason, he tried not to rely on the sale of advertising. This remained a policy of the Chesterbelloc papers, though it also meant that Belloc and the

Chestertons were often in or on the verge of debt in the attempt to keep their papers running. In fact, G.K.C. ran his own weekly for ten years without taking a salary.

The notable list of literary contributors was only meant to provide a respectable packaging for the real purpose of the *Eye-Witness*, which was muckraking and defending the freedoms of everyman. For purposes of the latter, Belloc's paper included a section called "Lex versus the Poor," in which the editor compiled stories of various governmental and industrial bureaucrats who were increasing their powers and oppressing the poor. It was in this column that the men attacked such laws as the Mentally Deficient Bill, which allowed the state to place "mentally unfit" children in institutions against their parents' will.

The *Eye-Witness*'s first major campaign was against Lloyd George's National Unemployment and Health Insurance Bill. Since coming to power in 1906, the Liberal Party, in the hopes of winning Labor support, had compiled an impressive record of social reform. Those supportive of the Labor movement generally approved this legislation (the Coal Mines Act, the Workingman's Compensation Act, etc.), but the National Insurance Bill, though it was supported by the bulk of trade unionists, was hotly denounced by many socialists, either because it did not go far enough, or, on the Bellocian premise, because it would produce a regimented or servile working class in Britain. Lloyd George's Insurance Bill brought about an inevitable split in the Labor movement between socialist and Liberal ideas about reform. Above all, a growing minority of younger and more radical trade unionists and intellectuals began to demand that Labor sever its alliance with the Liberal Party altogether and strike out on its own. Cecil Chesterton and Belloc had long been aware of the fundamental difference in policy between Liberals and the Labor movement. In attacking the Insurance Bill, the *Eye-Witness* hoped to lay bare the perfidy of the Liberals and, at the same time, convince the trade unionists and others in the Labor ranks to take their struggle beyond the halls of Parliament.

Lloyd George presented his Insurance Bill at a time of considerable working-class distress. The plethora of strikes that occurred throughout Britain from 1909 through 1914 were partly the result of union political disappointments. The election of 1906 had brought four years of Liberal-Labor domination (the so-called "Lib-Lab" pact) in Parliament, but no real economic gains for workers. Earlier wage increases were wiped out after 1908, and amidst a staggering increase in living costs and unemployment, the average British worker came to the conclusion that he was getting little help from his government.

The *Eye-Witness*, along with Orage's *The New Age*, and the militant *Daily Herald*, sought to capture this reaction against the failures of orthodox trade unionism and parliamentary politics and to direct it into distinctly revolutionary channels. Most importantly, the *Eye-Witness* hoped that opposition to the National Insurance Bill would unite all segments of labor into a revolutionary confrontation with the ruling classes. The *Eye-Witness*'s resistance to the Bill was based on essentially Radical and anarchist grounds. The fact that the scheme was mandatory for all workers male and female between the ages 16 to 70, and was to be supervised from above by national insurance commissioners, meant that the entire working force in Britain would be controlled by state bureaucracy. Not only would the proposal compromise the liberty and dignity of the worker, but would also place servile conditions upon those who were forced to receive unemployment benefits. The Bill allowed management to deny coverage to workers discharged for misconduct, and it completely denied benefits to men on strike. This was naturally regarded as an irrevocable step towards the coercion of labor and as a denial of the employee's freedom, especially since determination of benefit eligibility was to be decided by a special "court of referees." Even more unpalatable were the Bill's stipulations regulating the administration of union benefits, in particular the requirement that they could not use their unemployment assistance funds for militant purposes. Indeed, the *Eye-Witness* was convinced that the real motive of Lloyd George's Bill, like that of the Taff Vale Decision and the Osborne Judgement, was the destruction of the economic power of the trade unions.[1] Finally, the proposal was condemned both because it ignored the most needy, irregularly employed, and poorly-paid workers, and because it failed to provide death benefits for widows and orphans.

Belloc offered an alternative to Lloyd George's plan. His scheme called for a voluntary insurance program which would require employers to foot the entire bill through a tax paid directly to the state. Priority for benefits would be given to the lowest income families in the nation—whom he estimated to number three million —whereas only the remaining funds generated by the tax would be distributed to the trade unions and friendly societies. There would be no compulsion under this system. In Belloc's plan the neediest would be helped first, workers would be free to choose their own insurance societies and doctors, and there would be no state official to interfere between them and their freedom. The genius of this scheme was that there would be no opportunity for capitalists to regiment the workers, while the finance of the plan would come from those most able to afford it—"The million of well-to-do who were above the income tax limits."[2]

Belloc and the Chestertons concluded that the Labour Party's support of Lloyd George's Unemployment and Health Insurance Bill was the inevitable result of parliamentary corruption. The plutocrats of Commons had co-opted the Labor M.P.; he had been absorbed into the party system and henceforth would no longer represent working-class interests. In the view of Cecil Chesterton a new type of trade union official had emerged: the Labor M.P. "perorates in Parliament, tours the country, sits in a big London office two or three hundred miles away from the nearest workman and conducts negotiations with politicians and capitalists whom he finds to be nice fellows, meanwhile he is out of touch with the men he is supposed to represent."[3] Cecil claimed that the average worker had recognized all of this; it was the workingman's disgust with his leadership that was behind the plethora of strikes afflicting Britain. They would continue, argued Cecil, until union officials returned to their proper trade of organizing workers. Time for "political action" would arrive when the workers were organized industrially, realized the treachery of the politician and set out not to cooperate with him, but to smash him.

This antipathy for bureaucracy and trade union officials also appeared in G.K.C.'s writings at the time. Chesterton cautioned the workers:

Committing property to any officials, even guild officials, was like having to leave one's legs in the cloakroom along with one's stick or umbrella. The point is that a man may want his legs at any minute, to kick a man or to dance with a lady; and recovering them may be postponed by any hitch, from the loss of the ticket to the criminal flight of the official. So in a social crisis, such as a strike, a man must be ready to act without officials who may hamper or betray him.[4]

The *Eye-Witness* was quite specific about what the workers could do in their war against capital. In its leader of August 17, 1911, in support of Tom Mann and the railway and dockers' strike, the paper called on the trade union membership to reject their parliamentary representatives completely (a thoroughly middle-class set of men divorced from the populace) and develop the power to organize "from below." By this the editors meant that the workers, in anarchist fashion, should choose their own delegates from the grass-roots level, thereby electing officials who would be union "servants" and more in tune with the intimate feelings and needs of the rank and file. Cecil, writing in *The New Age*, insisted that the workers should throw moderation and their leaders to the winds and initiate an economic struggle in the industrial sphere. The full emancipation of the laboring classes would never come about until the workers "absorbed every shilling of surplus value." This required more than a fight for a minimum wage; it called for a class struggle and a direct attack on rent and interest "undisturbed by the clutterings and flutterings of the politicians."[5]

The government tried to promote a settlement of the strikes and lock-outs by getting the disputants to work out their differences in arbitration and conciliation committees. The whole idea of "forced" conciliation and arbitration, which was contained in the government's Labour Disputes Bill, was repugnant to the Chestertons and Belloc. The *Eye-Witness* attacked the Bill on the grounds that it was, in reality, a strike-breaking device, since it denied workmen the right to refuse work. There was no guarantee that the rank and file could express their interests, while compulsory conciliation before work stoppages would take away the power of surprise strikes, an extremely important weapon for the workingman. The *Eye-Witness* also criticized the government's efforts to secure workers "the power to earn a reasonable minimum wage." This was seen as a cheap substitute for what labor really needed—ownership of the means of production. In short, the Labour Disputes Bill was management's Trojan horse: it was contrived to deflect labor's fight for ownership and ultimately enslave it to a state bureaucracy. The *Eye-Witness* warned that all such proposals involving "compulsion" clauses had to be defeated. Since the workers of Britain could not rely on violence to overthrow their oppressors (capitalists controlled the police and army), their only hope was the strike; the workers must be able to do it "suddenly" and "secretly."[6] The *Eye-Witness*'s advocacy of "direct action" tactics throughout the near-revolutionary series of rail, coal, and dock strikes of 1910, 1911, and 1912 was sufficiently radical to have earned its editors a syndicalist image.[7]

*   *   *

In June of 1912, Belloc, seeking a respite from the rigors of journalism and from the responsibilities of managing a newspaper which he had never enjoyed, resigned as editor of the *Eye-Witness* and sold his shares to Cecil Chesterton. By the autumn of that year the paper began to experience difficulties (the fate of nearly all the so-called independent periodicals which avoided advertisements), and in November Granville was no longer able to provide financial support. The *Eye-Witness* collapsed altogether in November of 1912; however, Cecil was able to scrape together enough money from his father to reacquire the paper under the title of the *New Witness*. This new weekly continued the tradition of its predecessor, though Cecil was forced to cut operating costs to a bare minimum. The struggling *New Witness* was obliged to pay contributors three guineas per article "or nothing—depending on the state of the exchequer."[8] Belloc still contributed and Cecil's wife-to-be, Ada Jones, helped him run the enterprise as his chief assistant. Various sympathizers were solicited for funds, and several well-known men came to the rescue. A notable supporter and contributor (besides Shaw, Wells, Ernest Newman, and Alice Meynell) was the conductor, Sir Thomas Beecham.

Cecil Chesterton's chief journalistic concern was to help clean up the mess of government, and in this endeavor the *New Witness* made some progress toward ameliorating political abuse. A group of *New*

Witness supporters formed a society called "The League for Clean Government," organized along nonparty lines, to promote the candidacy of independent MPs in by-elections and to campaign against party "place men." The organization concerned itself with all kinds of objectionable practices ranging from abusive health laws to food scandals. One of the most vivid episodes in its history was the exposure of a firm which imported diseased Australian meat for slum consumption in London's East End. This particular scandal turned into an even greater drama when the *New Witness* discovered that the same tainted meat was also being sold to the British Army from a wharf in the Borough of Southwark.

Cecil's wife claimed that the idea of establishing a League caught on immediately. It appealed to people of varying backgrounds, centralizing all kinds of warring factions into a common cause. At its first meeting the leaders openly declared war on the sale of honors, "which at the time were being sold like pigs and pumpkins."[9] Since only a small section of the public was familiar with this practice, those attending that first League meeting were shocked upon hearing the charges. But surprises can generate excitement and enthusiasm. Mrs. Cecil Chesterton wrote that meetings were held all over the country and that membership grew in leaps and bounds, especially during by-elections when the League organized heckling parties. The greatest indignation was always produced when the League explained that the money raised by the annual sale of honors went into the funds of the party in power and not to the state.[10]

One might conclude that the reforming efforts of the League, in a general sense, were successful. It generated a needed enthusiasm for cleaning up what seemed wrong in politics, and it served as a vehicle for winning and holding converts to the Chesterbelloc reformist movement. One must also give the Clean Government League credit for effecting certain changes in Britain's health laws. The organization opposed all types of legislation which undermined human rights and dignity, and it rightfully claimed credit for defeating the sterility provisions of the Mental Deficiency Bill. Mrs. Cecil Chesterton also claimed that the League's spirited campaign against the proposal to give compulsory powers to Health Visitors (who were to

have the right of entry into the homes of the poor) created such a stir
that the suggestion was never legalized.[11]

In April 1918 the League for Clean Government was resurrected
under the title of the *"New Witness* League." The new organization
expanded its operations to include propaganda work for Britain's
war effort. It also developed an affiliation with the "Mothers' Defense League," a society, like the *New Witness* group, that concerned itself with the protection of mothers' rights and the home
against state control. A major cause of concern for the League, and
an evil that the Chesterbelloc would battle well into the post war
years, was the eugenists' campaign for birth control. There were
many disturbing aspects to eugenist arguments (namely their implicit racism and proposals for mandatory sterilization and even
outright elimination of the poor and mentally deficient), and the
followers of Chesterton and Belloc did great service in exposing the
totalitarian overtones of these positions.[12] Unfortunately, the
League's attack on the eugenist movement was marred by crude
anti-Semitism. The *New Witness* charged that the eugenists were
supported by Jewish financiers who, along with the Germans,
hoped to decrease British population and deliberately sap the foundations of common morality by destroying the home.[13] The *New
Witness* League was also concerned about the abrogation of personal liberties during the war. Although it recognized that some of these
wartime controls were necessary, the League vowed that it would
fight to have all laws restricting personal freedoms rescinded after
the peace settlement.

Unfortunately, the literary and intellectual standards of Cecil's
paper were far below those of the old *Eye-Witness*. Under his editorship the *New Witness* became increasingly shrill, and monomaniacal in its political muckraking. The acerbic tone of the journal owed much to Cecil's temperament. He had a fierce polemical
style which would be unleashed on anyone suspected of disingenu-
ous conduct. Many distinguished contributors to the *New Witness*
were so antagonized by Cecil's violent style that they ceased to write
for the paper altogether.[14] Some of the most venomous language was
used on the unfortunate C.F.G. Masterman, an old friend who
entered Parliament with Belloc in 1906. Masterman climbed within

the party ranks, and since in the process he changed some of his backbench opinions, Cecil Chesterton and Belloc accused him of betraying his principles for political mileage. The men never forgave Masterman for this. Indeed, Cecil asked his readers "to tear Masterman in pieces," and under his personal direction friends of the *New Witness* mounted an organized campaign to defeat Masterman every time he ran for reelection to Parliament.[15]

Cecil was candid about the ultimate purpose of his discourteous polemics. Writing open letters in the *Eye-Witness* under the signature "Junius," he had told his readers that he would pay no attention whatever to "what is called 'the Law of Libel.' " There was no law anyway, explained "Junius," it was simply what someone who serves the politicians decides it is and is then stretched to include anyone who embarrasses his employers. "What you have to consider is this: is the man you are attacking likely to be prepared to face the ordeal of cross-examination in the witness box?"[16]

Hence Cecil was perfectly willing to flirt with libel in an honest attempt to get what he called "truth" into the spotlight. The first need of a democracy, he explained, was the continual watching and sharp criticism of rulers by the ruled. Like his friend Belloc, Cecil had an obsession about the depravity of mankind. The first postulate of the Christian faith, said he, "is that no man, however rich and powerful, is exempt from sin or from the normal temptations of cruelty, hypocrisy and covetousness which all men find in their hearts."[17]

The early *Eye-Witness* was also scrappy and abrasive in its attempts to expose corruption, but unlike Cecil's paper it was reasonably well-informed about what it chose to attack, because Belloc had friends like George Wyndham who apprised him of the inside business of government. The *New Witness* could make no claim to such inside information, and, because of a lack of money to pay investigators, the alleged facts it publicized were not always sufficiently verified. All of this, in conjunction with Cecil's proclivity for indulging in *ad hominem* attacks, gave even Belloc cause for alarm. By late 1912 the pugnacity of the *New Witness* reached scurrilous proportions as Cecil prepared its readers for his assault on the so-called "Marconi men."

The struggle to expose the culpability of those involved in what became known as the Marconi affair proved to be a watershed in the history of Chesterbellocian journalism, for which this financial controversy was final proof of the venal and plutocratic character of British politics. In the words of Cecil it was the fulfillment of a prophecy and therefore the justification of a hypothesis.[18] The *New Witness* and its successors, *G.K.'s Weekly* and the *Weekly Review* cited the scandal as conclusive evidence for demonstrating the machinations of the party system. G.K. Chesterton believed that historians would eventually consider the Marconi scandal as one of the turning points in the history of England and possibly the world. The Marconi question was an obsession of G.K.C.'s and of monumental importance in the hardening of his political attitudes. Whereas most men spoke of the early twentieth century in terms of pre war and post war conditions, Chesterton divided political history into pre-Marconi and post-Marconi days:

It was during the agitations upon that affair that the ordinary English citizen lost his invincible ignorance; or in ordinary language, his innocence.[19]

Only a brief outline of the Marconi affair is necessary to explain its impact on the Chesterbelloc. The Imperial Conference of 1911 had approved a plan for the construction of state-owned radio stations throughout the British Empire. After briefly considering various systems, the Post Office, under the direction of Herbert Samuel, accepted a tender for building a chain of stations from the Marconi Wireless Telegraph Company of London. The actual contract for the work, subject to parliamentary ratification, was to be drawn up later. A postponement of the contract and a call for inquiry resulted from increasing public suspicion over the circumstances surrounding the grant to the Marconi Company. The managing director of the company was Godfrey Isaacs, a brother of the Attorney-General, Sir Rufus Isaacs, who as Lord Reading was later to become Lord Chief Justice and Viceroy of India. Godfrey Isaacs was also managing director of the separate American Marconi Company. After arriving in New York to drum up business for the Marconi invention, Godfrey learned that his company's chief American competitor, the United Wireless Company, had gone into liquidation. He then bought up the tangible assets of that company and decided to reissue new shares for the Marconi American subsidiary at a higher cost. Godfrey then told his brothers, Harry and Rufus, of the prospective contract with the British government and the stock reissue arrangements—all of which had not yet been made known to the public. Harry purchased 50,000 of American Marconi shares from Godfrey at the face value of 21 shillings, 3 pence, and on April 17, Rufus Isaacs bought 10,000 shares at two pounds. Of these shares, Rufus immediately sold 1,000 to Lloyd George, the Chancellor of the Exchequer, and an equal number to the Master of Elibank, Chief Whip of the Liberal Party. Yet no money was passed in any of these transactions, and there is no evidence to suggest that the stocks were not just gifts. All of this transpired before the American Marconi Company authorized the issue of new capital and before Parliament had completed the English Marconi Company contract.

In April Lloyd George and Elibank sold a portion of their shares at a considerable profit, since the price they were supposed to pay for the shares was lower than what the American company charged for its stock on the open market. Rumors soon circulated to the effect that ministerial officials were gambling in the shares of a corporation negotiating with the government. Called before the special investigating committee, the men in question (with the exception of Elibank, who was in South America at the time) denied having speculated in the shares of the Marconi Wireless Telegraph Company of London, though they carefully avoided mentioning their involvement in American Marconi shares. It was only some time later that the men admitted their connection with the American company, which they insisted had nothing to do with the London organization. The parliamentary committee voted on straight party lines, exonerating all the individuals involved. A minority report emphasized that the men had acted with impropriety, since the American company was indirectly interested in the contract. The report was never placed on record because it was rejected by a vote in the full House.

The *Eye* and *New Witness*, along with the *Outlook* and the *National Review*, led the field in exposing the so-called "facts" surrounding the affair. Cecil Chesterton's paper was the most outspoken and careless in assaulting the ministers concerned. An example of Cecil's distinctive style can be seen in a satirical piece on Rufus Isaacs, whom he detested because of his role in the persecution of Tom Mann and what Cecil considered to be his overreaction to the syndicalism business.[20] Pointing out that Isaacs was a Jew who could not be expected to understand the subtle workings of a Christian conscience, Cecil wrote, in facetious defense of the man, that he should not be tried in England: "He is an alien, a nomad, an Asiatic, the heir of a religious and racial tradition wholly alien from ours. He is amongst us: he is not of us."[21]

On August 8, Cecil launched his major attack on the "Marconi men." He accused the Isaacs and Herbert Samuel of theft and "swindling" the English public, although it was never made clear how the Postmaster-General was implicated in these events. However, Cecil claimed that he had evidence of corruption in the placing of the Marconi contract.[22] The *New Witness* pointed out that before the boom Marconi shares were quoted at not more than 13 shillings or 14 shillings, while after negotiations with the government the shares rose to 9 pounds, ten shillings, while the public was being told nothing. Cecil further charged that Godfrey would have been prosecuted over numerous other shady transactions had not the Attorney-General been his brother. These were very serious charges. The fact that the ministers concerned failed to respond to them only increased public suspicions, and Cecil Chesterton, who admitted that he was shooting in the dark, was further encouraged in his invective. Finally, on January 9, 1913, after months of scurrilous personal attacks on the Isaacs, Lloyd George, and Samuel, Cecil wrote an article listing some twenty bankrupt companies of which Godfrey Isaacs had been promoter or director. Should such a person be given one of the largest government contracts ever awarded, he asked. On the same day, some over-zealous administrator at the *New Witness* dispatched sandwichmen to Isaacs' office with placards advertising his "ghastly failures." Both the article and the sandwichmen prompted Godfrey to prosecute Cecil Chesterton for criminal libel.

When the attacks first began, Samuel had recommended against suing the *Eye-Witness* for libel, because he feared it would only increase its notoriety and bring adverse publicity to the Jewish community. The Prime Minister, Asquith, also argued against prosecution for similar reasons, believing that the *Eye-Witness*'s circulation was meager and its opinions therefore unimportant. It probably would have been better for the accused to have brought the case to court immediately, thereby silencing their accusers, for despite the *Eye-Witness*'s small circulation, it was read by influential people. By the time Godfrey Isaacs decided to sue for libel, the case had already become a *cause célèbre*.

Cecil and his supporters insisted that they had deliberately sought a libel suit as the only way to smoke out one of the culprits and subject him to cross-examination on the docket. Under heavy questioning in court, Cecil withdrew his charges of corruption against the ministers he had attacked in the *Eye* and *New Witness*. The jury found him guilty. The judge issued a stern lecture on journalistic responsibility, emphasizing the danger of Cecil's general ignorance of business practices and his racial prejudices, and fined the defendant 100 pounds. Cecil Chesterton's supporters applauded the verdict, considering the sentence a moral victory for having brought the affair further into the public eye.

The whole episode certainly captured public attention, but Cecil and his supporters did not seem to understand the seriousness of the jury's guilty verdict. Cecil's charges were not that the ministers had gambled but that they were corrupt in arranging the contract. After making a series of gratuitous accusations based on inane assumptions, Cecil had no choice but to withdraw his charges. It was only Cecil's respectable background that prevented the judge from putting him in prison. He and his friends assumed from the outset that the judge was prejudiced against Cecil because he had attacked public officials. Belloc went so far as to claim that the government had arranged to have the jury deliver a guilty verdict.[23]

The trial seemed to have invigorated Cecil. Exposure brought an increase in circulation for his paper, and it strengthened the premise for launching more attacks on the party system. Belloc and the Chestertons could now point to further proof of parliamentary chicanery. The fact that the ministers involved escaped without condemnation and later rose to more prominent positions in the government clearly demonstrated, in the Chesterbelloc mind, the insidious power of anonymous wire-pullers. Moreover, because the special parliamentary committee of inquiry had acquitted the suspects along straight party lines, the *New Witness*'s supporters could argue that the procedure followed the exact pattern that Cecil and Belloc had outlined in *The Party System*. As Reginald Jebb explained:

The inter-Party front bench clique decided that exposure of the Ministers was to be avoided at all costs, for that would have struck a fatal blow at the prestige of Parliamentary government throughout the country. The thing was on too big a scale to be dealt with by selecting a scapegoat. Therefore the Ministers must be whitewashed, and this was done quite simply by ensuring that the government supporters, always in a majority, should back up their leaders.[24]

Even more evidence appeared to support the Chesterbelloc accusations. In June of 1913 a trustee appointed to handle the affairs of a London stockbroker who had absconded, discovered that the departed agent had acted for the still-absent Elibank. It was revealed that the Liberal Whip had ordered the broker to purchase a total of 3,000 shares in American Marconi, the profits from which were to be used for the funds of the Liberal Party.

Although the ministers' actions in the Marconi affair were not illegal, there is enough evidence to suggest that they acted in an improper manner. The Isaacs brothers, Lloyd George, and Elibank had either purchased shares, or were given gifts, from the managing director of a company seeking to win a contract with the government they served. Although they had purchased shares from the American company, it was obvious that their stock would have declined in value if the English Marconi contract had been rejected. The incident became even more galling to Belloc and G.K.C. when two of the men in question, Lloyd George and Rufus Isaacs, acceded to some of the highest offices in the land, while Elibank gained a reputation for carrying the sale of honors to an unprecedented height in his efforts to bloat the Liberal Party funds.

The Marconi affair and Cecil's prosecution for criminal libel greatly shocked G.K. Chesterton. The trial was his first encounter with the hard realities of the political world, and the experience had the effect of embittering him towards politics, the powers of high finance, and in some ways, also towards Jews, forever after. The fact that the Isaacs brothers were Jews, who preferred, in Belloc's opinion, conferring loyalty upon "their kind" rather than upon the nation, did much to harden the Chesterbelloc's anti-Semitism. This was particularly true with respect to G.K.C., who had not been noticeably anti-Semitic until this juncture.

G.K.'s angriest feelings were reserved for Rufus Isaacs. His wrath, the bitterest of his writing career, was vented in 1918 (following Cecil's death in the war) when he dispatched an open letter to Isaacs in the *New Witness*. G.K. accused the Jews of destroying England's dignity and called Rufus Isaacs (who by then had become Lord Reading) nothing but a blot on the national landscape.[25] For the remainder of his journalistic days, Chesterton's rare personal attacks were reserved for the Jews, politicians, and moneyed-groups who were either directly involved in the Marconi incident or had supported the Liberal government during the parliamentary investigation. This change in G.K.C.'s gentle style appeared immediately after his brother's conviction, and in the few months following that event his writing became more recklessly violent than at any period in his career. His first response was to break off a twelve-year-long affiliation with the *Daily News*, a newspaper which supported the government throughout the Marconi crisis. The resignation was marked by a bitingly cynical poem in the *New Witness* against the paper's owner:

> Tea, although an Oriental,
> Is a gentleman at least;
> Cocoa is a cad and coward,
> Cocoa is a vulgar beast,
> Cocoa is a dull, disloyal,
> Lying, crawling cad and clown. . . .[26]

Everyone on Fleet Street understood the meaning of Chesterton's barb—George Cadbury's *Daily News* was universally known as part of the "Cocoa Press."

During this period G.K.C. also began to question the efficacy of parliamentary government. Cecil's attack on the party system made him doubt that the machinery of popular suffrage was expressing the true desires of the people. Not only could the voters easily be swayed by the well-financed and keenly orchestrated propaganda campaigns, but it seemed clear that politicians elected to serve the nation were generally working against the best interests of the public as a whole. In fact, Chesterton began to feel that the various Reform Acts were simply tricks to make everyman think he could exercise political power; whereas in practice his vote could be bought with propaganda and his representatives completely ignored in Parliament because of the power of the "Marconi men" who controlled the front benches and party funds. The people of England were being ruled by "brutes who refuse them bread, by liars who refuse them news and by fools who cannot govern and therefore wish to enslave."[27] The foregoing statements remind one of an outraged Cecil Chesterton or Hilaire Belloc. The bitterness was uncharacteristic of Gilbert Chesterton; fortunately after a few years it disappeared from his writing.

*   *   *

The Marconi experience also transformed the Chesterbelloc's latent anti-Semitism into a more conspicuous feature of their journalism. From the beginning of the affair the *New Witness* continually emphasized that the Isaacs brothers and Samuel were Jews who had close links with their brothers in international finance. Their journals would always remain hostile to "international Jewry," though under Cecil's editorship the *New Witness* was rampantly anti-Semitic. Regular Jew-baiting was generally the forte of F. Hugh O'Donnell, who worked up his venom on a weekly section entitled "Twenty Years Later." His political and social commentaries closely resembled Maurras' articles in *Action française*, a journal which O'Donnell regularly singled out for the highest praise. The Third Republic was frequently scorned for its Marconi-type scandals and weak-kneed foreign policy. O'Donnell particularly objected to French Republicanism because of its Jewish connections. The "constant element" in the development of French Republicanism since the Revolution was seen to be a "Jewish Directory," "Traitorous, corrupt and decadent." Jews were behind the Panama Canal scandal, while Leon Gambetta (whom O'Donnell called an Italian Jew) and his "Jew attorney-general" engineered the destruction of the Union Générale. The great fraud engulfed the fortunes and estates of some of France's best families; Frenchmen were ruined while "every Semitic cutpurse on the Bourse stole a château in the scramble."[28]

This outlandish anti-Semitism seriously undermined the *New Witness*'s public image. Theodore Maynard, reminiscing on his days with the *New Witness*, praised Cecil as one of the greatest editors on Fleet Street and eulogized what he considered the high literary standards of the paper. Yet, he admitted that the *New Witness*'s reputation was compromised by its attacks on Jews.[29] Even Belloc was distressed at the *New Witness*'s anti-Semitism. In various letters to his friend, Maurice Baring, Belloc voiced chagrin at the newspaper's blind personal attacks on Jews, believing that the continuation of such policy would destroy the *New Witness*'s credibility.[30]

Chesterbelloc admirers have traditionally played down this anti-Semitism.[31] Yet it cannot be swept under the carpet; their writings displayed a certain motif of anti-Semitism, and to ignore it is to overlook a dimension of the Chesterbelloc world view. Fortunately, after the demise of the *New Witness* their anti-Semitism became less malicious. The post-*New Witness* position on the subject is best summed up in G.K.C.'s *The New Jerusalem* (1920) and Belloc's book entitled *The Jews* (1922).

According to Belloc's analysis, the Jews and Gentiles associated together under conditions of deplorable racial tension, caused mainly by Jews living as disguised aliens in other people's countries. He repeatedly argued that these tensions would have to be eased or the "tragic cycle" of persecution, exile, and even massacre would befall the Jews as it had in earlier centuries. The worst possible approach to this dilemma, in Belloc's opinion, was to ignore completely that the Jews were a problem. This would only serve to camouflage the "true anti-Semite," who had to be exposed because he could inflict physical damage on Jews. In short, Westerners must be made aware of this foreign element in their midst in order that they may learn to deal with it in a humane fashion:

The problem is the problem of reducing or accommodating the strain produced by the presence of an alien body within an organism. The alien body sets up strains, or . . . produces a friction, which is evil both to itself and to the organism which it inhabits. The problem is, how to relax those strains for good and to set things permanently at their ease. There are two ways to such a desirable end. The first is by the elimination of what is alien. The second is by its segregation. There is no other way.[32]

Belloc championed the second alternative, though in most of his writing he preferred to use the word "recognition" in place of "segregation."

For the purposes of highlighting "the Jewish problem," Belloc detailed the steady and insidious manner by which Jews reached positions of world leadership. Throughout the 1870s and 1880s Jews rose to prominent positions by infiltrating the world's political parties, international news agencies (Reuters being the most prominent example), the organs of freemasonry, and the world's great banking corporations. By the end of the century, Jews were represented in the governing institutions of Europe fifty to one hundred times more than was due their numbers. Belloc explained that this overrepresentation in finance, government, and the press, together with Jewish responsibility for the Boer War and the Marconi and Panama scandals, directly produced the outbreak of late nineteenth-century anti-Semitism.

Belloc also asserted that the Jews were creating immeasurable damage to European life because of their anti-nationalist bias—they were natural cosmopolitans. Jews could never become patriotic Frenchmen or Englishmen, since they were outsiders, whose first loyalties were to religion and family and to a culture that was fundamentally Eastern. In Belloc's opinion, the best example of this inherent Jewish inability to become patriotic was their link to international socialism and communism. Enlarging on the fact that Marx, Trotsky, and several of the early Bolsheviks were Jewish, Belloc insisted that Jews engineered the Russian Revolution of 1917, and that their secret international organizations were the cement which held the communist movement together throughout the world. Furthermore, Belloc believed that the Western nations did nothing to thwart the Bolshevik Revolution and the spread of communism, because the Jews, who controlled European governments, were in sympathy with their revolutionary relatives: "It is this which explains the half-heartedness of the defense against Bolshevism—especially in Westminster."[33]

It was further explained that the Jew was ideally suited to direct international communism, since the movement aimed to bring about something contrary to the natural instinct of European nationals. The Communist Revolution endeavored to destroy the concept of private property. The Jews could engineer this drive because they were unable to sympathize with the central core of European civic instincts. The Jew was free to destroy capitalism, because he had "neither the political instinct for the sanctity of property in his national tradition nor a religious doctrine supporting and expressing such an interest." Abhorrent as the excesses of capitalism might be, that other great international organization—the Roman Church—could not destroy the system, inasmuch as it believed in the sanctity of private property. The Jews, on the other hand, had certain advantages preparing them for this unique revolutionary role. The Jew could conceptualize without respect to national boundaries, since he did not possess the European sense of patriotism. His patriotism was of a different complexion, for he lacked traditions rooted in a common soil. This Jewish Bolshevism was yet another unfortunate force bringing out anti-Semitism in Europe.

Strange as it may seem, Belloc's *The Jews* was not meant to attack Jews. The essay was dedicated to his Jewish secretary and concluded with the words, "Peace be to Israel." In order to mitigate the inherent dangers of anti-Semitism, Belloc had proposed that the Jews be recognized as a different people and be given a national homeland of their own; or, if this were impossible, he felt that Jews should live under special protective laws in the countries of their domicile. Belloc could not recognize the implications of his opinions, yet he was clearly calling for a policy of ethnic separation. Neither he nor Chesterton believed that the Jew could ever be absorbed into the European community.[34]

G.K. Chesterton's attitudes towards Jews appear to have been influenced considerably by his brother Cecil and Hilaire Belloc. It is not clear how much these two colored G.K.'s views, but his proclivity for picking up their political assumptions uncritically would lead one to suspect that Cecil's and Belloc's anti-Semitism had a telling impact on him. One finds little if anything anti-Semitic in Chesterton's writings before the Marconi scandal. However, in *The Wisdom of Father Brown* and *The Flying Inn*, both published in 1914, Jews are described in rather nasty terms, though this was not the case in earlier books. Whereas the Dreyfus case was the catalyst for Belloc's anti-Semitism, the Marconi episode, which impugned his brother's personal honor, would seem to have triggered G.K.'s hostility.

Chesterton was never as rancorous as Cecil or as obsessive as Belloc on the subject of Jews, but his postwar work was laced with insensitive passages concerning Jewish financiers and politicians. The Jews in G.K.'s novels have many of the unsavory characteristics as those who appear in Belloc's fiction, and they generally seem responsible for inflicting the same sort of evils on the world. In *What I Saw in America* (1922) and *Four Faultless Felons* (1930), for example, Chesterton suggests that Jews are the moving forces behind both communism and capitalism. G.K. unquestionably accepted the notion that there was an international money power which was largely Jewish and that it aimed to control the governments and societies of European states. The themes of *The New Jerusalem* (1920) have a discernable Bellocian ring to them. Chesterton, without any reservations, proclaimed that the Jew could not share in the mystical passion of the soil with his fellow citizens: "That problem has its proof . . . in the history of the Jew, and the fact that he came from the East." The Jew intensified the problem by trying to hide his "strangeness" through the irritating habit of changing his name. Chesterton wanted the Jew to come out and identify himself:

Let all literal and legal civic equality stand; let a Jew occupy any political or social position which he can gain in open competition; let us not listen for a moment to any suggestions of reactionary restrictions or racial privilege. Let a Jew be Lord Chief Justice. . . . But let there be one single-clause bill; one simple and sweeping law about Jews; and no other. Be it enacted . . . that every Jew be dressed like an arab. . . . The Point is that we should know where we are; and he would know where he is, which is in a foreign land.[35]

The Jew could not be a loyal Englishman, because he lacked that vital tie to the fatherland: "If England had sunk in the Atlantic, Disraeli would not have sunk with her, but easily floated to America to stand for the presidency."[36] *The New Jerusalem* supported the Zionist solution; Gilbert Chesterton recommended that Jews be given a home of their own in Palestine.[37]

Another permanent feature of the *New Witness*'s journalism was a furious anti-Prussianism. The personality of Cecil Chesterton and his capacity to hate were chiefly responsible for this attitude, which the paper carried to heights of reckless extremism. By the beginning of World War I this malignant anti-German obsession had fully engulfed G.K.C., who was able to carry on the tradition in good stead while his brother was in the army. As in its attack on the Marconi men, the *New Witness*'s war propaganda was also carelessly exaggerated.

Cecil Chesterton took up Belloc's anti-Prussianism with unbridled enthusiasm after the Marconi affair, in part, it seems, because of his conversion to Catholicism. Between the time he was remanded for libel at Bow Street and his Old Bailey trial, Cecil was received into the Roman Catholic Church. Cecil never publicly explained his reasons for doing this, though his wife wrote that he joined the Church to gain a working philosophy of life.

The German violation of Belgian neutrality in 1914 ushered in Belloc's prognostication of a life-and-death struggle between the forces of culture and barbarism. Prussia, naturally, was seen as the force of darkness, and, as a modern Carthage, she had to be destroyed if Europe were to live. Even before the war Belloc wrote of the threatening Prussian character:

It is already half mad. Before long we shall see it run amok. And if we do not kill it, it will kill us.[38]

Cecil Chesterton's *New Witness* sustained a blistering tirade on the perils of Prussia throughout the war, acting as a self-appointed watchdog for English patriotism.[39] The paper did its utmost to ferret out citizens of German descent holding sensitive positions in the government and military. So-called Prussian sympathizers, pacifists, and war profiteers were also regularly exposed as internal enemies of the state. Pacifists and men of international finance (meaning Jews) were considered to be a special problem, since they could prevent what Cecil Chesterton considered to be a final solution to the German problem.

Both Chestertons and Belloc steadfastly insisted that World War I was at bottom a religious conflict, since the Catholic force which had defined European culture was being challenged by "Protestant-atheist" Prussia. Cecil explained that all the other nations of Europe had been the product of generations of men, whereas Prussia was created by one man—the atheist and pervert, Frederick II. Frederick "the Mad" had forged obedience into the Prussian nation, not through law based on democratic principles of right and justice but through the military power of the Prussian army. Cecil did not feel that Frederick could have established this militarist state with such ease in a land that had known freedom. But since Prussia had not been conquered by Roman legions and was peopled by "a mongrel Slavonic stock" (originally ruled by a small German aristocracy), the faith had reached her soil rather late and had not the time to penetrate the barbarian character. Hence the Prussians became Protestant simply through the will of their aristocratic overlords.

The *New Witness* warned its readers, even before the war, that the Prussian spirit was a cancer sapping the vitality of European culture. As in its anti-Semitism, the journal's attitudes on the German problem closely paralleled *Action française*, which depicted Prussia as the scourge of nations and firmly asserted that Prussia would have to be destroyed if Europe were to survive.[40] As the war raged on, Cecil, like Maurras, managed to link together the German danger with international Jewry. In the issue of March 30, 1916, he claimed that Germany had become a special enclave of the insidious Jew:

The fact is that there is no country in Europe—not even this one—where the Jews are more predominant in all directions. . . . They have in their hands finance to a considerable extent, journalism to an unprecedented extent, and, as everywhere else in Europe, pornography to the extent of a virtual monopoly. . . .[41]

The Prussian threat seemed so severe that one might wonder why Britain and Europe had ever tolerated that state's existence. Cecil

Chesterton's answer was that it had been allowed to flourish because of the pervasive influence of un-Christian pacifism, which had made significant inroads into British government and public opinion by the close of the nineteenth century. Considered by him essentially materialistic, pacifist ideology had as its sole objectives the avoidance of pain and death (hence war) and increasing material wealth. Since the Chesterbelloc saw the party system lubricated by "Quaker and Jewish" money, it naturally followed that the pacifist views of those two groups would prevail as the British government tended more and more towards pure plutocracy. Quakers and Jews had selfish reasons for practicing pacifism—war would jeopardize their major objective, money-making. Yet this particular British tendency towards peacemongering was compounded by the enormous increase in the power of international finance. The Chesterbelloc believed that the men who controlled the world's money markets were primarily de-nationalized Jews who, although in favor of small wars for profit, dreaded the dislocations in international trade and finance if there were worldwide war. Consequently, neither international finance nor those who controlled the party system were willing to go all the way towards stopping the Prussian menace. Both forces tolerated belligerent German foreign policy, because they feared that international war would damage profits.

Cecil Chesterton's solution to "the German problem" was the complete destruction of Prussia as an independent state and the dismantling of the German Empire. In the *Perils of Peace* (1916), Cecil suggested that France could be given Alsace-Lorraine and the whole west bank of the Rhine as far as the Dutch border. The old kingdom of Hanover with Westphalia might be resurrected under Franco-British protection, and Poland could be given Silesia and reconstituted as an independent kingdom. Finally, he recommended that Prussia be treated "as the Americans treated Indian territory"— a reserve of barbarism where the infidels could live under the Hohenzollerns but closely watched, forbidden to arm and completely isolated from the civilized world community. Austria could then be the focal point for a Catholic South German nation.[42]

The plutocracy fought against this ideal solution—so went the argument—because it would have the effect of damaging profits gained from trading with a unified German Empire. Cecil and

Belloc believed that the capitalists would prevent total victory by either suing for peace or by breaking England's will to fight through their control of the press. In the opinion of the *New Witness*, the "official press" (that owned by the governing plutocracy) was systematically publishing misinformation and distressing battlefront news in order to weaken the British people's resolve to carry on to the final victory. The weekly went so far as to call some of these wealthy newspaper owners "traitors" to Britain. Lord Northcliffe (who owned and operated the *Evening News, Daily Mail, Daily Mirror*, and controlled *The Times*) was singled out for special criticism in nearly every issue because of his wealth and influence in the highest offices of government. On September 30, 1915, Belloc intimated that Northcliffe was a traitor and demanded that the government take action against his newspapers for confusing, agitating, and frightening public opinion, all of which, he argued, were calculated to shake the nation's confidence in achieving victory. Despite his outrage, Belloc seems to have enjoyed needling Northcliffe. "I'm going to keep him worried, dancing round and round at the end of his rope. He is in a panic and likely to go mad with it."[43] Belloc was quite right—Northcliffe became livid. The Harmsworth press never publicly addressed itself to the *New Witness's* attacks, but Northcliffe did not forgive the Chesterbelloc for their outspoken criticism of his newspapers.[44] The Chestertons, Belloc and every journalist who regularly wrote for their papers were boycotted by the Harmsworth press: never would one of their books receive a favorable review. Lord Northcliffe's action was followed some years later by the Beaverbrook press. On March 4, 1927, Beaverbrook sent Lord Rothermere (Alfred Harmsworth's brother and successor) a note explaining that G.K. Chesterton and Belloc would be permanently blacklisted by his newspapers because of their abusive articles.[45]

Another target of the *New Witness's* patriotic campaign was Alfred Mond. Mond was accused of treason by the paper's correspondent, Perceval Smith, for trading with the Germans. Smith argued that the Mond Nickel Company had continued to trade with the enemy after the declaration of war. According to act of Parliament, this was illegal. After making numerous charges to this effect, and after personally writing to the Public Prosecutor, Smith discovered that the company had received special permission from the government to carry on these transactions. Since this would have been a crime for an ordinary citizen, the *New Witness* assumed that Mond had bribed the government for special favors, or, even worse, was given permission after the fact by the government in order to protect a contributor to the Party Funds. Since Mond was a Jew, a friend of Lloyd George (whom the paper also accused of treason), and because his paper, the *Westminster Gazette,* favored lenience towards Germans suspected of espionage, the *New Witness* concluded that both German and Jewish finance were influencing British political policy. Writing a series of articles on "Our Gold Lords" in the *New Witness,* Smith demanded that Mond and the directors of his company (he claimed that the majority of its shares were owned by German Jews) be brought to trial for treason.

The *New Witness's* intrepid journalism only served to alienate those of moderate political persuasion. Beginning with the outbreak of World War I, the major political figures of the day considered the Chesterbelloc dangerous extremists, and, as such, refused to give them any serious consideration. This situation became even more unfortunate as the major newspapers systematically ignored their books and journals.

The struggle of world war brought personal anguish to Chesterton and Belloc and left an indelible mark on their journalism. Of course Britain and her Allies had defeated the Germans, but both men were convinced that the Allied Powers had lost the peace settlement. And on a more personal level, both had incurred deep family losses: Belloc's son had been killed in the fighting and G.K.'s brother, Cecil, died of influenza in Wimereux, near Boulogne, soon after the armistice was signed. Some of Cecil's friends at the *New Witness* never accepted the army's official explanation for his death, that the two years' service in Flanders broke down his health. They insisted that Cecil died as the result of a conspiracy by someone in the government who arranged to have him undertake a long march when his health was already weakened.[46] This was a traumatic loss for G.K., but he vowed to carry forward Cecil's struggle for freedom against the powers of plutocracy. It was for the memory of Cecil that he decided to continue the *New Witness* and to devote the rest of his life to journalism:

Every instinct and nerve of intelligence I have tells me that this is a time when it must not be abandoned . . . though I can never be as good as my brother, I will see if I can be better than myself. . . . We are now divided between those who care and those who don't. . . . I know that this great nation is governed by sneaks and swindlers, by venal and vulgar adventurers and every other sort of worthless men.[47]

The Chesterbelloc had long insisted that only the removal of Prussia from Germany could save Europe from ultimate chaos. But since both the American and English delegations at Versailles were "ignorant of Europe," such required policy went unheeded. Chesterton considered Wilson a narrow political doctrinaire; a man who could envision a Europe "which was not there" in the form of the League of Nations, but not the real nations of Italy and Poland. As for Lloyd George, the Chesterbelloc considered him a puppet of the plutocracy (the creation of the Harmsworth press) dancing to the tune of Jewish finance. The *New Witness* told its readers that the League was simply a creation of international finance to garner the support of international pacifism. The Treaty of Versailles was a paper peace. Too many states were left aggrieved. Belloc warned that the peace settlement would be the parent of many future wars. The soldiers (the people) had won a victory, but the politicians had thrown the whole thing away; in the long run it would be a defeat snatched from the jaws of victory.

Belloc published *Europe and the Faith* in 1921 in order to explain the meaning of the Great War. The work also made a plea for Europe to return to the traditions of the Roman Church. In it he described World War I as the logical but unfortunate extension of the Protestant Reformation. The war was seen as a clash between the forces of materialism (Prussia) and the central forces of both European and Christian civilization as embodied in the nation of France. This struggle was inevitable, given the peculiar Protestant type of society created by the sixteenth-century religious rebellion.[48]

In Belloc's thinking the principal product of the Reformation was the isolation of the soul, lost from its unity with the Mother Church. He felt that this isolation was extremely dangerous, for it could lead to unhappiness and ultimate destruction. The loss of soul meant the loss of corporate sustenance:

In the first place . . . the isolation of the soul releases in society a furious new accession of force. The break-up of any stable system in physics, as in society, makes actual a prodigious reserve of potential energy. It transforms the power that was keeping things together with a power driving separately each component part; the effect is an explosion. This is why the Reformation launched the whole series of material advance, but launched it chaotically and on divergent lines which would only end in disaster.[49]

This isolation compelled the soul to wild wandering and searching. The soul could not remain in a void; it could not be bound and limited.[50] For Belloc the repressed soul was tending towards perversion due to the dissolution of the corporate sense formerly created by Catholicism. Because the soul had lost its corporate religion, it set up successive temporary idols to satisfy its need for worship. The highest but most perverted form of its expression was a compulsion back to some form of corporate life, which took shape in the excessive worship of nationality. This constituted a form of perverted pride, and, as far as Belloc was concerned, it had led directly to World War I. Prussia, being the state most stricken with the sin of overweening pride (which took the form of patriotism), sought to dominate all of Europe.

All the ills presently affecting Europe—from excessive capitalist exploitation to communism—were seen to have arisen directly from the isolation of the soul; or putting it another way, Europe's problems stemmed directly from the Reformation. Belloc considered World War I absolutely justifiable, indeed obligatory, as a Catholic crusade against the false idols of Protestantism.[51]

Europe and the Faith concluded by calling for a return to the classical culture of the Catholic Church. Belloc demanded that Europe accept historical truth and not deny her past. European culture, built on the foundations of classical Greek and Roman antiquity, was shaped and perpetuated through the ages by the institutions of the Catholic Church. Europe would have to return to this tradition or perish: "The Faith is Europe. And Europe is the Faith."[52]

*   *   *

Despite the enthusiasm, colorful skirmishes with the establishment, and the many long months of hard work, the *Eye* and *New*

Witness crusade largely failed in its endeavors to stop the onslaught of plutocracy and the servile state. The *New Witness* itself plodded along with great difficulty under G.K.C.'s editorship and finally collapsed in May 1923. The more optimistic supporters could point to the glorious days of the Clean Government League, the *New Witness*'s exposure of the Marconi affair, and breaking the conspiracy of silence about Jewish finance as solid achievements of the Chesterbelloc campaign against government corruption. Yet, in a very practical sense, the plutocratic leviathan had increased its powers over the English people, and the great Christian battle against Germany had not destroyed the spirit of Antichrist on the continent. The futility of such efforts eventually convinced Chesterton and Belloc that they would have to reevaluate their belief in Parliament's ability to reform British politics.

Immediately after the Marconi affair G.K.C. had started to question the entire tradition of English parliamentary democracy. The extension of the suffrage and the reforms of Parliament were seen as charades calculated to fool the people into thinking that they had a representative government. The same sense of betrayal appeared in Belloc's writing as well. In the preface to Cecil Chesterton's *The Perils of Peace* (1916), Belloc pointed out that under aristocratic conditions the Marconi conspirators would have been severely punished. In 1920 Belloc publicly announced his preference for a vague type of monarchism in a book entitled *The House of Commons and Monarchy*.

It must be emphasized that Belloc was never fully convinced that democracy could work in modern Britain (democratic government being practicable in only very small countries). Consequently, he never considered the House of Commons to have been a true representative body, nor did he believe it could ever become one in a state as large as Britain. Belloc argued that the House of Commons had always been the governing organ of a select coterie which had seized power in the seventeenth century. Since that time the state of Britain had been fashioned by an aristocracy (those who had seized power) working through Parliament, which governed effectively only because of the moral authority conferred upon it by public respect. Belloc called this governmental condition the "aristocratic state," defining aristocracy as "an oligarchy enjoying the popular worship of its fellow citizens."[53] This oligarchical type of government functioned properly only when the citizenry possessed the instinct for nobility.

By 1920 Belloc had decided that the requisite instinct for aristocracy had disappeared, and, for that reason, Parliament could no longer meet the needs of the day. The continuity of the aristocratic tradition of decency and prestige had been broken, and the old parliamentary oligarchy could not carry on without it. The loss of aristocratic spirit was manifest within the very governing elite, where there was an obvious decline in morality. In Belloc's mind, this change in standards was leading to a wholesale cultural decline in the arts, literature, and public taste. Wealth was now being divorced from manners and all was being "accepted and sought for at the expense of dignity."[54] The appetite for aristocratic government was also failing common man. A clear example of this was the growing inability of the masses to distinguish the old type of public servant: "The gesture of the gentleman was no longer recognized as a special thing." Belloc seems to have seen this as a special sickness of the cities. The urban masses could only see distinctions in wealth; outside traditional rural society there was no distinction between good and bad breeding. Popular thought in the cities only concerned itself with "wages or . . . the rights and privileges of trade organizations, the question of prices, or the demands for the 'nationalization' of this or that."[55] The nation was passing through an interlude of materialism and decadence, and no positive direction was replacing this negation of the old aristocratic order.

Unfortunately for Britain the men of new wealth, who were assimilated into the governing class, had not the virtue of being able to imitate the dignified manners of the old guard. Nor was the new elite in communion with common man. Unlike the squirearchy, the capitalist class did not live with their underlings, for they immediately fled the soot and slums of the city for the solitude of the countryside. This new industrial wealth, by merging with a modified aristocracy of land and commerce, had completed the final phase of the capitalist dynamic. Since this loss of desire for true aristocratic government had also left the people, the former institution of oligarchic government—Parliament—was completely bereft of moral authority. Belloc concluded that it was absolutely impossible to reform the House of Commons from within, because aristocratic leadership (encompassing a particular political spirit) was incapable of self-regeneration. It could function only through popular deference and respect:

The continuity of tradition is the condition of its existence; when the continuity is broken the principle disappears. Once broken the thing dies and it cannot be restored.[56]

Belloc was never convinced that the English people wanted it this way. The decline of parliamentary authority was not desired by common man—he still wished to continue his old allegiance to the aristocratic institution. Instead, parliamentary government was made impossible by the new elite's calculated refusal to punish personal corruption. The habitual practice of blackmail in the course of personal intrigue for power (which, in his opinion, had become an accepted policy between the politicians and newspaper owners by the middle of World War I) had made it impossible to restore the prestige of Parliament to English political life.

Belloc could see that trade unions and the various corporations (legal, medical, teaching, army and domestic guilds) were rapidly beginning to fill the power vacuum created by the destruction of Parliament's authority. Yet these autonomous bodies were incapable of exercising sovereignty in their own right. Instead, they needed to be regulated for the sake of national unity, and Belloc believed that the monarchy was the one organ in English political life capable of imposing this needed discipline. Belloc's monarchical alternative was to take the form of a benevolent dictatorship. The leading function of the sovereign was to protect the weak against the strong, to prohibit the accumulation of wealth at the expense of the commonweal, and to prevent the corruption of justice and the sources of public opinion. Monarchical rule had the virtue of being the most responsible form of government for a society of great numbers, since one man could be held accountable for its conduct. On the other hand, a Parliament which was not aristocratic could not easily be held accountable and it could never be fully responsible, for it had forsaken a moral code for immediate material gain:

Oligarchy that is not aristocratic is never really responsible. You cannot attack it; you can hardly define it. Each individual in such an amorphous executive does harm with impunity because he can always say that it was not he that did it. No Parliamentarian, since aristocracy failed in England, has gone to prison for a bribe taken or given.[57]

In growing Procrustean fashion, Belloc was insisting that monarchy was the only alternative to England's governmental ills: without such a transformation England would perish, just as Europe would fail without returning to the faith. In Belloc's mind there was no alternative.

Thus, by the beginning of the 1920s, the Chesterbelloc had moved considerably further towards the reactionary Right. Indeed, they had become, for all practical purposes, upholders of revolutionary doctrines. Their goal was to overturn the social and political framework of British life. We shall now shift our focus to those who fell under the sway of their forceful arguments.

CHAPTER V

The Emergence Of The First Distributist Circle

The lugubrious procession of economists, welfare workers, mother Grundies and busybodies was held up by a circus. The *Flying Inn*, the *Eye-Witness*, the Chester-Belloc partnership, the Marconi Scandal broke the spell. The dull drama of Reform turned into a joyous harlequinade, we had escaped the Fabian. We ceased to recite statistics and sang songs, good fellows romped on a stage set for inspectors, freedom eluded the officials and the cow jumped over the moon.
                    -H.D.C. Pepler, *Blackfriars*, August 1936

Maurice Reckitt wrote that by 1911 Chesterton and Belloc were reaping the benefits of a great intellectual blacklash against the "progressivist superstition" of Fabian socialism. This reaction provided them with a ready-made audience, not merely for their assaults on the party system, but also for their more fundamental sociological critique of British society. The Marconi episode gave the *New Witness* a sensational libel suit, but Reckitt explained that he and his friends felt such thrills superficial compared with the shock delivered to their political complacency by the publication of Belloc's book, *The Servile State*. Reckitt could scarcely overestimate its impact on his young mind and, in stating this, claimed that he was but symptomatic of thousands of others who passed through a similar phase. Not certain as to whether Belloc's thesis included "all ye know on earth, and all ye need to know," Reckitt at least was convinced that it contained enough to blow the "New Liberalism" sky-high.[1] This enthusiasm was by no means unusual. Countless young men everywhere in Britain devoured Belloc's book with the avidity of religious zealots.

Chesterton and Belloc, as a team, first gathered together a group of like-minded supporters while writing for A.R. Orage's *The New Age* before the war. As editor of *The New Age,* Orage had become one of the most influential literary forces of his day. He arrived in London, relatively unknown, after having spent several years teaching elementary school in Leeds. Despite this intellectually unprepossessing background, Orage had developed a comprehensive knowledge of politics, philosophy, and literature. His career was a mercurial one. Starting as a Theosophist, Orage moved from Fabianism through guild socialism and Distributism, eventually ending his life in a spiritual quest under the influence of the Russian mystic, George Gurdjieff.

The New Age was purchased with the help of G.B. Shaw in 1907 and was, at that time, edited jointly by Orage and Holbrook Jackson.[2] Jackson left in 1908 and until 1922 the paper was controlled by Orage. Under his editorship, *The New Age* quickly became one of the premier cultural and political journals of the first two decades of the twentieth century. Orage's tolerant editorial policy enabled writers of diverse political stances to air their views. In the early years of the weekly, Shaw, Wells, the Chestertons, Belloc, Arnold Bennett, and S.G. Hobson were regular contributors. Several writers who contributed in successive years, though not well-known at the time, became major literary figures: Ezra Pound, T.E. Hulme, Wyndham Lewis, Katherine Mansfield, and Herbert Read, among others. *The New Age* also did much to introduce the British public to continental philosophy (in particular the writings of Nietzsche, Bergson, and Sorel) and to new developments in the artistic world by reproducing and commenting on the works of Gaudier-Brzeska, Epstein, Wyndham Lewis, and Picasso. As was the case with the other independent literary and political journals of the day—*The Nation, The Commentator, The New Statesman, et al.*—Orage's paper had a modest circulation (probably under 3,000) and generally operated at a loss.[3] It appears as though *The New Age*'s readers were of widely different classes. Orage claimed his audience came from what Matthew Arnold called the "fourth class," namely socially-conscious individuals who had overcome their class prejudices.[4]

From the outset, several of those who wrote in *The New Age* shared Chesterton's and Belloc's feelings about the nature of man and the evils of modern industrial society. Many of these regular contributors seem to have developed their social and political criticism out of a strong impression that man was a fallen creature, perpetually burdened by the stain of original sin. Orage, A.J. Penty, and the self-proclaimed "reactionary conservatives," F.M. Kennedy, T.E. Hulme, and Romain de Maeztu, among others, had a common antipathy towards what they defined as Fabian socialism, materialism, and liberal notions of progress. In particular, these men generally condemned British socialism because of its strictly materialistic aims and lack of spiritual values.

It was only natural that Belloc and Chesterton would get a sympathetic hearing amongst these writers. Indeed, not only did Orage accept Belloc's views on the servile state completely, but *The New Age* came down on many of the major social and political issues of the day on nearly the same grounds as the *Eye* and *New Witness*. Orage severely criticized the government's growing intervention in the lives of the working class, especially as exemplified by Lloyd George's Insurance Act (1911), which he called "the most dangerous legislative proposal ever seriously made against the liberties of the poor."[5] Like Chesterton's and Belloc's papers, *The New Age* repudiated the official Labour Party and encouraged the syndicalist-flavored strikes of 1910-1913. In its editorial of September 1, 1910, *The New Age* urged the trade unionists to undertake a more radical approach to industrial and political problems, recommending the tactic of the general strike. Writers for *The New Age* also considered the Great War necessary for the preservation of European civilization, and, much like the Chesterbelloc, condemned the Russian Revolution of 1917 as the onslaught of tyranny under the guise of a classless society. Nearly all of the other Radical journals praised the Bolshevik revolution as a great victory for democracy and socialism. In fact, there seemed to be a certain philosophical affinity and sense of mission tying *The New Age* and the Chesterbelloc papers together.

Between 1911 and 1919, Orage and *The New Age* preached the theory of guild socialism. Belloc's *Servile State* was an important force behind the enthusiasm for guild socialism. Belloc's and Chesterton's involvement with the idea did much to clarify their attitudes on trade unionism and on the problems of industrialism. After helping to formulate the early principles of guild socialism, Belloc remained a proponent of the guild idea, incorporating it as an integral part of his theories on Distributism.[6] In addition, many of those who were involved in the debates on guild socialism readily accepted Distributism and later became enthusiastic supporters of Chesterton's paper, *G.K.'s Weekly,* and the Distributist League. Thus, Orage's journal and the various discussions on the guild issue served as a fertile breeding ground for a genuine Distributist movement.

Throughout the first decade of the twentieth century, Orage searched for a scheme which might counter some of the ill effects of modern industrialism, especially its destruction of skilled craftsmanship and the humanity of the worker. In order to attenuate the oppressive consequences of the factory system, Orage, S.G. Hobson, Belloc, and several others who would later write for *The New Age,* were demanding that labor be given a share in the control and perhaps even the ownership of industry. Orage eventually discovered that England's labor and economic problems could best be resolved by reorganizing industry along the lines of the medieval guilds.

This solution was first proposed by A.J. Penty. It was Penty, "a shaggy-looking architect with a fearful stammer," who brought the guild idea and the word itself into modern English social thinking.[7] Penty had been a Fabian but left the society because of its intellectual vapidity, its excessive materialism, and lack of concern for anything aesthetic. According to Penty's own testimony, he quit the Fabians altogether when he discovered that its executives had selected the plans for the home of the London School of Economics by the sheer statistical principle of measuring the floor space of all designs submitted and awarding the prize to the architect whose classrooms added up to the highest total of square feet.[8] Penty devoted his life to a variety of causes, not the least of which was fighting philistinism in English architecture and city planning.

Penty, who soon became an enthusiastic supporter of Distributism, claimed that he had arrived at the guild idea through hard
times. Distressed at the late nineteenth-century economic recession
that was undermining the financial prosperity of that section of the
middle class which had given him work as an architect, Penty wrote:
"In such circumstances my mind naturally turned to economics, to
the problem of finding ways and means of recovering my position."[9]
Ultimately Penty penetrated the problem: the middle classes, he
discovered, were being victimized by the spread of limited-liability
companies and the growth of big business. These two evils, he
explained, were spawned by the unrestricted use of machinery, since
it was the need of large capital investments for the acquisition of
machinery that had created the demand for corporative business
organization. He traced the origins of Britain's economic instability
(the immediate cause of which was the unrestricted use of machinery) back to the disappearance of the medieval guilds, which, under
the auspices of the Church, had been established to regulate prices
and to restrain the unlimited growth of economic individualism.

Penty believed that the early guilds had existed primarily to
promote economic equity. In order to ensure fairness, the medieval
guild legislators had purposely regulated currency, since unregulat-
ed money supply could be manipulated for private profit. Consequently, the guild masters restricted money to use as a medium of
exchange and enforced a system of fixed prices. To further assure
equity, it was necessary for the guilds to sustain certain standards of
quality. The authority for regulating standards was the responsibility of the guild masters (who were workers), and a consensus
amongst them constituted the final court of appeal for all matters
concerning production.[10] Hence, according to Penty's analysis, the
medieval guilds were guarantors of economic stability through their
regulation of currency and craft production.

In *The Restoration of the Gild System* (1906), which first proposed the guild principle for modern England, Penty made a plea
for returning to the standards of medieval craftsmanship and to the
guild traditions of self-regulation and self-government in the various occupations. The book charged that the breakdown of the early
guild system had permanently weakened the socio-economic fabric
of the state by unleashing the rapacious and egocentric side of man's

natural character. The medieval guilds, the writer insisted, had succeeded as agencies of social control only by exercising strict discipline over their individual members. As the guilds lost this power, profit became the object of all social action. The inevitable result of this breakdown in social regulation, so Penty argued, was the appearance of a godless, soul-destroying machine age.

As opposed to the collectivists, who were mainly interested in the distribution of wealth, Penty saw the chief social problem growing out of the modern factory system. He believed that a new pride in workmanship and better overall craft production would automatically ensue if the guilds were reestablished along medieval lines. The guild was seen as a new advance towards sound social reconstruction, an approach "from the point of view of qualities rather than quantities, of personality and aesthetics rather than external material conditions." In short, a restoration of the guilds would bring modern man back to Christian principles, which recognized the heart and mind of man as the active creative forces in society.

Penty's aesthetics, his repugnance for the growing materialism of industrial society, and his condemnation of machine production were strongly influenced by William Morris and John Ruskin. Throughout *The Restoration of the Gild System* (Penty preferred the medieval spelling of guild), Penty drew heavily on their ideas, as he did upon those of Matthew Arnold and Thomas Carlyle, though perhaps most obvious was the influence of Morris's theories concerning hand-production and the central importance of the craftsman. Unlike his mentors, however, who at least recognized the efficacy of some machine production, Penty saw machines to be an unmitigated evil. Modern society, he believed, would be much better without machines altogether.

Although Penty never developed a religious affiliation, his social views rested firmly on religious grounds. He always believed in the intrinsic sinfulness of man and in the necessity of perceiving a higher spiritual end for man's earthly existence. Unless the individual were willing to acknowledge and serve some principle higher than that dictated by sensuous appetite, there could be for him no hope of social salvation.[11] Penty first became interested in Distributism because of what he saw as its clear insight into these fundamental social requirements. He also appreciated the Chesterbelloc critique of socialism. Socialism was criticized because of its psychological failings and its crass materialism. Penty fully concurred, since he felt that socialism ignored the fundamental value upon which society reposed, namely the individual man. In his opinion, this ignorance explained why the Fabians blindly proposed the abolition of private property for the furtherance of impersonal public bureaucracy.[12]

Penty's guild thesis remained popular with Chesterton and Belloc and the "arts and crafts" people, but it soon lost its appeal for many of those socialists who had bolted the Fabian Society.[13] It became increasingly obvious to the latter group, including Orage, that Penty's medieval ideal was impracticable for modern society. Rejecting Penty's medievalism, but keeping the idea that workers should have more control over the standards and conditions of their labor, S.G. Hobson, writing a series of unsigned articles in *The New Age*, developed a more moderate program which came to be called "guild socialism." Hobson's proposal, which was subsequently elaborated by Orage and G.D.H. Cole, was essentially a synthesis of political socialism and industrial syndicalism. The proponents of guild socialism recommended the organization of all workers in a given occupation into a single fellowship or guild. They believed that this type of "national" guild arrangement could be facilitated by making use of the present trade union structure. Each guild was to be controlled exclusively and completely by the workers of a given industry. In this way, the guilds would supplant the capitalist class by eliminating the wage system; and they, instead of the state, would assume complete responsibility for the material welfare of their members. The national guilds were not meant to replace the state, as the anarcho-syndicalists intended but, instead, would share in the management of society with the state. Ownership would be in the hands of the state, which would provide capital while the workers delivered the goods. The guild socialists envisioned a popularly elected government, whose function would be to regulate the guilds, to enact national legislation, and to conduct relations with foreign governments. In this manner, it was believed that the goals of traditional socialism could be secured without the ills of bureaucratic collectivism.[14]

Penty, Chesterton, Belloc, and others who favored Distributism initially broke with the guild socialists because of the latter's willingness to accept the modern factory system. Belloc had long predicted the collapse of large-scale capitalist industrialism. For this reason, he was not willing to superimpose an alternative scheme of production on an "abnormal" economic structure, which carried the seeds of its own destruction. The guild socialists, on the other hand, acted out of the conviction that the large-scale factory system would remain a permanent feature of economic life and thus insisted that the guild institutions be grafted onto the existing industrial structure. Consequently, they favored the introduction of national guilds (and became known as the "national guildsmen"), arguing that these forms would be more efficient in production and distribution.

Essentially, the Distributists and guild socialists were at odds over the purpose of guilds. Penty claimed that the national guild idea emphasized primarily the importance of industrial organization on an entirely self-governing basis, but without any admixture of private interests, whereas he and other Distributists believed that this was only a half-way measure to solving the ills of working class alienation. Belloc, for his part, felt that the national guild propaganda might be valuable in organizing resistance to the servile state, but saw guild principles as indecisive and completely worthless unless they were founded upon the dogma of private property. The central core of the Distributist medieval idea was that the guild should act as a "court of appeal," whose chief function would be to maintain the discipline of members in a given industry.

Penty also feared that the guild socialists, by grafting their organization onto the large-scale industrial system, would place ultimate authority in the hands of the employers. Most importantly, Penty, Belloc, and G.K.C. objected to the large-scale organizational objectives of the guild socialists. In Penty's view, one insuperable obstacle stood in the path of this approach: all the guild's activities would become choked by the necessity of working through a multiplicity of bureaucracies. Because the average committeeman would get lost in the complexity of details, there would be a natural tendency for power to migrate into the hands of professional bureaucrats. Thus, the guild movement could ultimately develop into an inverted form of the bureaucratic monster it initially set out to destroy. To guard against the evil of bureaucracy, Penty, in the anarchist tradition, insisted upon the utilization of small, self-governing guilds, exercising control on the local level:

The units of their organization must be as small as is consonant with the function they are required to perform. And if for such purposes as those of finance and the buying of material a larger unit is found desirable, then the larger unit must consist of federated groups. . . .[15]

The Penty-Belloc position on the guild question was given support in academic circles by the Rota Club, established by James Harrington at Oxford just before the war. The group published a collection of essays dedicated to Belloc in 1913 entitled *The Real Democracy*. The Rota Club recommended what it called the "Associative State" of well-distributed property. This was to be a society of integrated but autonomous property-owning guilds of associated producers, which would have responsibility for the material welfare of the whole citizen body. Each guild as a corporation would own a portion of its capital, and members would be remunerated either by salaries and wages or by dividends. Guild standards would be enforced by the state, and the guilds themselves would form the determining type of government for economic production.

The Real Democracy received a critical review in *The New Age*. The criticisms triggered a lengthy exchange in that journal between the followers of Belloc and the National Guildsmen from the summer through December of 1913. In the process of responding to Orage's group, Belloc managed to elaborate more clearly than ever before his own ideas on the weaknesses and virtues of guild socialism. Although Orage admitted that *The Real Democracy* writers were close to *The New Age* position, it became clear in the ensuing debates that the two groups were split irrevocably on questions concerning the state and private ownership. Belloc's anarchistic phobia of state power led him to reject *The New Age*'s idea of a guild-government partnership (which he labeled the "communal" guild solution—i.e., a corporation of laborers controlling the instruments with which it works) on the basis that it inevitably would lead to control by politicians.[16] Like Penty, Belloc also feared that *The New Age* scheme would bind workers to industrial bodies too large for them to control: "You'll have 'leaders' and 'parliamentary committees' and the rest of the rubbish."[17] This would mean that the administration of the guild, though nominally subject to its members, would ultimately fall into the hands of some caucus or machine.

Both the National Guildsmen and Belloc's group rejected the wage system, but for different reasons. The Rota writers attacked the idea of wages because it degraded the worker and vitiated the principle of democracy; but *The New Age* group felt that the poorer workers had no appetite for personal ownership of the means of production and believed that the mere elimination of wages in itself would be enough to guarantee working-class freedom. Of course, Belloc and the Rota writers considered this to be a faulty assumption. Belloc argued that *The New Age*'s attempt to transform trade unionism (which was essentially a "proletarian" guild in that it worked along with but was subordinate to capitalist ownership) into a "communal" guild was doomed to failure. The problem with this approach, explained Belloc in almost Marxian fashion, was that it was impossible to move from proletarian to communal guilds until the workers themselves developed a sense of corporate grievance or consciousness which would force them to demand revolution. This sense of corporation and its corollary—the overthrow of the capitalists—could never emerge with people who were accustomed to wages alone and ignorant of the principle of private ownership. Belloc's group insisted that working-class independence could come about only by transforming the laborer into a self-regulating economic and political unit. In place of the communal guild solution of *The New Age*, which might give workers political freedom but perpetuate economic servility, Belloc proposed what he called "free" guilds of separate owners. Under his system the workers and their families, as shareholders in small corporations, would own the means of production. The necessary transfer of property to the laboring classes could be brought about, not by loans, which would put workers under the heel of finance, but by revenue expropriated from the capitalists in the form of direct taxation.[18]

In the long run, Penty's theories on the guilds were ultimately joined with the more conservative sociological ideas of the Chesterbelloc. Penty did not agree with them on all issues; for a long while there were debates over the question of authority, small property holdings, and the use of machinery. Unlike Chesterton and Belloc, who essentially opposed capitalism because of its emphasis on competition and profit, Penty, for a long while, was against industrialism *per se*, which he hoped to destroy through the revival of agriculture and handicrafts. Yet, on the general socio-political issues of the day, Penty supported the Distributist positions. He also became an ardent supporter of Chesterton's application of Thomism to modern British society. This approach was later outlined in *G.K.'s Weekly* and in Chesterton's book, *The Outline of Sanity* (1926), which further expanded upon the principles of Distributism. It was St. Thomas' arguments for social self-sufficiency, as explained in *De Regimine Principum*, that convinced Penty of the supreme necessity of abandoning the industrial commercial society. Aquinas decried the growth of "cosmopolitanism" as detrimental to fostering a stable life based on one's own social environment. In accepting the Thomistic criticism of commercial capitalism, Penty's entire philosophy came very close to one of the strongest traditions of Catholic social thinking, namely, the emphasis on the efficacy of the self-contained organic community. This also helps explain Penty's interest in the back-to-the-land movements. In agricultural theory, Penty greatly influenced Montague Fordham, a supporter of Distributism and the moving spirit of the Rural Reconstruction Association.

Two other early converts to the Distributist movement were Maurice Reckitt and W.R. Titterton. Both men helped run *G.K.'s Weekly*, the chief propaganda organ of the Distributist position. G.K. Chesterton was probably the single most important influence on Reckitt's career as a writer and leader of the Christian Socialist Movement. Reckitt admitted that if he did not owe his faith to Chesterton, he at least owed to him the beginnings of a capacity to relate that faith to the affairs of real life.[19] Above all, G.K.C. gave Reckitt a sense of social direction. For Reckitt, Distributism was a viable alternative to the worn-out socialism and liberalism of the prewar years. Although he clung to Fabianism for a time, since that seemed to be the only decent thing to do, Reckitt gradually drifted into the Distributist camp while a student at Oxford.[20] Many others followed. Reckitt claimed that Distributism took great numbers of young people away from the Oxford Fabian Society in the years before the Great War. The young Reckitt was naturally receptive to the Chesterbelloc's social views. As an undergraduate, he had been introduced by Professor Herbert Fisher to the functional society of the medieval world, which in Reckitt's mind contrasted sharply in its emphasis on personal relationships with the impersonal collectivist programs of the Fabians.

Reckitt played a very important part in the history of Distributism because of his link with the Anglo-Catholic wing of the Church of England.[21] It was primarily through Reckitt's influence that various Anglo-Catholic associations took up Distributist positions. Before their conversion to the Church of Rome (Cecil in 1913; G.K. in 1922), Cecil and Gilbert Chesterton had been active in the Anglo-Catholic Christian Socialist movement and had a close interest in and wrote for *The Commonwealth* and the *Church Socialist Quarterly*, journals devoted to expounding the views of the Christian Socialist League. The League was established in 1906 by a group of Anglo-Catholic clergy from the north of England. The main aim of the group was to establish a "democratic commonwealth in which the community shall own the land and capital collectively, and use them co-operatively for the good of all."[22] Those who were active in the movement, people like P.E.T. Widdrington, George Lansbury, Edgerton Swann, Reckitt, and Cecil Chesterton, had become impatient with the Anglican establishment's hostility to socialism and its refusal to do anything constructive about industrial problems. After its birth in 1906, the League immediately threw itself into the working-class struggle, organizing demonstrations, taking part in agitations and publishing radical manifestoes. By linking itself with working-class problems, the League did much to counteract the notion that the Anglican Church was a reactionary institution.

Under Widdrington's leadership, the Christian Socialist League, in a fashion paralleling the Chesterbelloc papers and *The New Age*, turned against party politics and prepared to examine new ways to bring a Christian sociology to industrial life. Chesterton's and Belloc's exposure of the religious problems inherent in collectivism made considerable impact on the Christian Socialists, and the servile state theme helped push the League towards guild socialism.

Widdrington's followers saw in the guild alternative many of the virtues that had appealed to the Chesterbelloc and *The New Age* circle, namely the proposition that guilds promised to allow the worker a greater voice in running the national economy as well as preserving individual freedoms from bureaucratic centralization. Reckitt believed that the guild would blaze the path to Morris' craftsmen democracy and protect all men against Belloc's servile state. However, Reckitt adhered to *The New Age* scheme, and under his influence the League became one of the first societies to endorse the principles of national guilds.

Although Reckitt greatly admired G.K.C., his commitment to Distributism was never complete. He would always differ with Chesterton and Belloc on the guild issue, and he had numerous objections to the Distributist League because of its refusal to modify its doctrines by the addition of certain ideas on social credit. Nevertheless, Reckitt regarded Distributism as an important part of his social theory, and, although not a true believer, he remained deeply loyal to what he considered to be Chesterton's real ideals.

W.R. Titterton was perhaps Chesterton's most loyal supporter. An excellent journalist, Titterton joined forces with Belloc and Chesterton on the *Eye-Witness* and later served as assistant editor of the *New Witness* and *G.K.'s Weekly*. It was G.K.C., more than any other man, who persuaded Titterton to become a Catholic; and it was Chesterton, more than Belloc, who turned him from a socialist to a Distributist. Before joining the *New Witness*, Titterton, along with Cecil Chesterton and G.K.C., wrote for *Everyman*. The three of them used the paper as a kind of soap box for preaching early, only partly hatched, Distributist ideas. After the *New Witness* folded in May, 1923, Titterton founded his own paper, *The Englishman*, a journal intended primarily for amusement and the raising of eyebrows. Although it extolled the virtues of Distributism, the paper's policy was mainly "a bit of truth torn out of its context and done big." Its bit of truth was that England should be governed by Englishmen and all alien influences suppressed, beginning with the influence of Scots, Jews, Welshmen, and Irishmen, all of whom were to be deported.[23]

Gilbert Chesterton always remained a model for Titterton, who admitted to a strong hope that Chesterton would one day be declared a saint. His journalism and poetry were laced with a Chestertonian blend of simple humor, romanticism, and paradox. In many respects, he was Chesterton's alter ego, though he differed from G.K.C. in temperament. Although lively and full of good humor, Titterton was somewhat vain, sensitive to criticism, and more uncompromising than Chesterton. Like the mercurial Cecil Chesterton, Titterton had a reputation for being an extravagant journalist and was sometimes rather careless in his polemics.[24]

Aside from Chesterton and Belloc, the most eccentric but influential members of the Distributist circle were Father Vincent McNabb and the radical sculptor-craftsman, Eric Gill. As was the case with many other Distributists, Gill became attached to Chesterton through an interest in Catholicism. Gill was widely known as an innovator in the arts of engraving and sculpture, and his radical social and aesthetic views had considerable impact on artists and certain sections of the working classes. Gill's robust approach to life, and his ideas on art grew directly out of an intense commitment to Catholicism.

As a young man, Gill first recognized the connection between religion and social problems while serving as an architect's apprentice in London. He was deeply disturbed at the ugliness of the city, its slums and the decadent morals of those who lived there. Even more distressing, in his view, was the failure of the Church of England to do anything constructive to alter the situation. Although Gill had regularly attended church services (his father was an ordained minister and his brother an Anglican missionary), the traumatic experience of trying to cope with London life convinced him that it was necessary to forsake what he considered a meaningless ritual. Leaving the Anglican Church was not easy for a minister's son, but as Gill later explained:

. . . religion in St. Saviour's, Clapham, and irreligion in the architect's office were unequally matched. Nothing in the outward sign of that Christianity could possibly hold me—the frightful church, the frightful music, the apparently empty conventionality of the congregation. And nothing that the parson ever said seemed to imply any realization that the Church of England was in any way responsible for the intellectual and moral and physical state of London.[25]

The Anglican ecclesiastics preached morality but did nothing to protect their congregation from the rapaciousness of landlords and commercial magnates; nor did they assume any responsibility for cleaning up the ugliness and squalor of urban living.

Out of a sense of frustration, Gill became an agnostic and a socialist. As a youth he had read Carlyle and Ruskin, and, after encountering the work of William Morris, came to believe in the absolute necessity of art and the artist serving the practical needs of society. He also accepted Morris's socialism, though with his own qualifications. Gill insisted that his socialism was a revolt against the intellectual degradation of the factory workers and the ugliness produced by capitalist-industrialism. It was not a reaction against economic exploitation and the poverty of the worker as a class, but a revolt against a system that maligned the dignity of working men. Gill volunteered to associate with the Fabians on these terms. However, this was a marriage of convenience, since Gill accepted Fabian economics only on the condition that they accept his concern for humanity. The honeymoon with socialism did not last long. Like Penty, Gill discovered that the Fabians ignored individual man and his spiritual needs. It was a profound disillusionment with both Anglicanism and socialism that caused Gill to turn to Catholicism.

Like Reckitt, Penty and countless other intellectuals who embraced an essentially conservative social philosophy, Gill was vitally concerned about the rootlessness and loss of traditional values in modern society. Throughout his long career as an artist and writer, Gill constantly emphasized the terribly corrosive effects of secularism on modern life, arguing that only a restoration of religion could restore a sense of humanity, direction, and wholesomeness in worldly affairs. In a letter to William Rothenstein, Gill asserted that all the ills of modern industrialism had resulted from a loss of religion and the powerlessness of religious organizations:

The fact is I think the Church should rule the world like a government. If there were no Church it would be necessary to create one. The desirability or necessity of membership in the Church is a political matter.[26]

Gill considered it a personal duty to become a Roman Catholic. "If there be God," explained Gill, it would be unwise to go against him.

"If there be God, the whole world must be ruled in his name." For Gill, Christianity was in the nature of a love affair. As he told his friend, Rayner Heppenstall, joining the Church was not like taking up membership in the I.L.P. or the Third International: "It's like getting married and, speaking analogically, we are f——d by Christ, and bear children to him—or we don't."[27] But a true religion had to be Catholic, argued Gill, and since the Roman Church was the only church which professed to rule the world, it had to be the only true religion. Echoing Belloc, Gill also insisted that the Roman Church was necessary for culture:

Outside the Church, in spite of the presence of individual bright sparks, there is only barbarism, disorder, uncertainty, commercial insubordination, and vulgarity in word and work.[28]

In January of 1912, Gill wrote the only Catholic he personally knew, Everard Meynell, and asked for the necessary information and guidance for conversion. Meanwhile, before "taking the leap," he attended mass regularly and began reading Chesterton's *Orthodoxy*, and Frances Cornford's *Philosophy of Foundations in Religion*. On February 22, 1913, Gill and his wife, Mary, were received into the Catholic Church. Soon after that the Gills purchased a home with two acres of land at Ditchling, where Eric planned to expand further upon his newly discovered faith, while becoming self-sufficient by living off the soil.

Gill's presence at Ditchling and his exemplary life style, completely independent of modern industrial society, soon attracted several other artist-craftsmen who wanted to live and work in the purity of the countryside. This group of like-minded men eventually formed a loosely knit commune or craft guild at Ditchling with each family living in separate houses. Gill, it seems, was chiefly responsible for setting the pristine tone of the commune's life style, though there were no pressures brought to bear upon anyone who chose to live differently. Gill's clothes were always handmade, and, since he wore a beard, a cloth smock and a round, flat-topped cap, he generally had the appearance of an Arab or Cossack. The same penchant for simplicity was evident in his eating and living habits. At Ditchling, the Gills avoided using anything produced by modern commercialism. Gill failed to see the need for a bathroom; water was drawn from a hand-pump. He refused to use a typewriter or ride in a car. No custard powder was allowed (one had to use fresh eggs), all cooking was done over an open fire, and the family maintained a self-sufficiency in food by growing their own vegetables and raising animals.[29] Ditchling was a step towards Gill's major goal in life: to create "a cell of good living" in the form of small, self-governing communities completely independent from government and modern industrialism.[30]

Several men who later became stalwart members of Chesterton's Distributist League joined this community at Ditchling. Those at Ditchling not only subscribed to Gill's ideas on society and the arts, but many were either Catholics or were soon converted to that religion. The most notable figures associated with the guild were Vincent McNabb (a radical Dominican and part-founder of *Blackfriars*), Desmond Chute, Hilary Pepler, and Father John O'Connor, the man upon whom Chesterton patterned the Father Brown stories.[31] Under the guidance of McNabb and O'Connor, two men who became what Gill called his "spiritual father and mother," the Ditchling group decided to become Dominican tertiaries.[32] This religious order, called the "Blackfriars," was an association of lay people, originally founded in the Middle Ages, whose members were to follow a private rule of life under the direction of the Dominican friars. As a group, the Ditchling Guild devoted many of their leisure hours to the study of the ideas of St. Thomas. Chesterton's writings were helpful in this endeavor, since it was he who first began to apply the philosophy of St. Thomas to modern English society. It was St. Thomas's clarity of style and his philosophical common sense that first attracted Gill to his writings. For Gill, Thomism provided a ready-made battering ram with which to beat against the political and industrial structure of modern England. Indeed, this seems to have been the main purpose of the Ditchling Guild: Gill's group hoped to demonstrate how the material basis of twentieth-century civilization was fundamentally incompatible not only with Christianity but also with man's natural needs and desires.

In articles which appeared in *The Game*, an occasional magazine (Oct. 1916-Jan. 1923) which served as a forum for voicing Distributist ideas on art and society, and in several subsequently published books, Gill developed a Thomistic critique of modern society and the factory system along much the same lines as Chesterton and Penty. Yet, he tended to emphasize the "holiness" of work, the aesthetic aspects of craftsmanship and the ideal of "Christian poverty" to a greater extent than did the other Distributists. He was chiefly opposed to modern industrialism because it tended to make work a form of drudgery and demeaned the craftsmanship of the laborer, who then lost pride in his work and no longer produced objects of beauty. The methods of industrialism, Gill explained, reduced the worker to a condition of intellectual irresponsibility:

. . . it makes good mechanics, good machine minders, but men and women who in every other respect are morons, cretins, for whom crossword puzzles, football games, watered beer, sham half-timbered bungalows and shimmering film stars are the highest form of amusement.[33]

It must be emphasized, however, that Gill's anti-industrialism was never directed against machines as such, but at a social and industrial set-up which made the acquisition of leisure time, mechanical devices, and money-making the objectives of living. Like the Chesterbelloc and Penty, he was accused of being a machine-breaking medievalist. This was not the case. Gill never suggested that modern man give up his mechanical conveniences, nor did he call for a return to a life of the middle ages. Like Chesterton and Belloc, Gill simply proposed that his contemporaries return to the higher spiritual values of Christianity, which were best expressed in the hierarchical guild society of medieval times. In 1934, when there was an outcry against the construction of telephone pylons across the South Downs, Gill wrote in *The Times*:

An attachment to 'nature,' which goes with a refusal to see beauty in engineering and making money by it, is fundamentally sentimental and romantic and hypocritical. Let the modern world abandon such an attachment, or let it abandon its use of electric power.[34]

In short, Gill did not object to machines and the material advantages of modern living, but to the evils of the system that produced them.

Gill's essential criticism of the modern industrial system first appeared in *The Game* in 1918, and was later published posthumously in a compilation of essays on philosophy and art entitled, *It All Goes Together* (1944). Industrialism, as Gill saw it, was chiefly responsible for separating the artist from the laborer. It effected a fundamental change in the nature of work in the minds of men, producing a world in which the artist created solely to express himself, without relating to society, while the working man, being dispossessed of the tools of production, was denied the only means by which he could express himself. In a word, the factory system was evil because it was unchristian: it deprived the working man of responsibility for his work and perverted Christian values by placing the making of money before the making of goods. The system undermined the worker's own personal sense of dignity and worth, and promoted the notion that "leisured time" was the object of all laboring endeavor, since "work time" in the factory was insufferably tedious. It led to the uglification of Britain, with its soot and smokestacks and "damnable advertisements" covering the land. The factory system put a premium on mechanical dexterity and discounted intellectual ability in the workman. It also corroded the family as the basic social unit (it "destroyed home work and home life"), and, finally, industrialism promoted wars by destroying local markets and making trade dependent upon "world markets" and international financial magnates. Overproduction was an inevitable result of such trends, and this, Gill explained, would be followed by a world struggle for fresh markets.[35]

Gill's life at Ditchling Common and the outstanding quality of his artistic production brought him considerable national attention. In part, he left the Guild of St. Joseph and St. Dominic for the Welsh mountains because of the publicity and the crowds of people who flocked to see him at Ditchling.[36] Gill had also managed to generate a great deal of enthusiasm for Distributism during lecture tours with Hilary Pepler. The Gill-Pepler lectures dealt with everything "from Marriage to the conditions prevailing in jam factories," but, in general, they attempted to chart out the path for a large-scale return to guild craftsmanship and subsistence farming.[37] Indeed, the Ditchling Guild lectures marked the beginning of the plans for a back-to-the-land movement, which finally materialized in the early 1930s. Gill and Pepler essentially recommended a revival of the Penty-type medieval guilds functioning within the enclosed domestic economy of the village. They felt that the village could serve as the basic economic unit in a new Christian national economy.

Gill had a reputation as an honest and pious man of the highest order, and, like his friend Chesterton, he was a constant defender of the common man. Much of his writing on aesthetics was directed towards the average person who knew nothing about art. The artist, in Gill's view, should not be some distinct sort of man, removed from the common things of life, but "every man should be a special kind of artist," since art was simply "the making well what needed making." As Gill saw it, the "special artist" came into existence because of the misplaced priorities of industrial civilization, which had eliminated an art form that used to be the expression of the mind of all the people. Because of the factory system, the ordinary things used by man were produced by machinery, and since these were no longer beautiful, people wanted distinct items of elegance (paintings, sculpture, and jewelry). Thus a new class of people called "artists" came into being. Yet these "artists" were special people cut off from the ordinary needs of life:

and so they become very eccentric and more and
    more peculiar
and their works become more and more expensive
and so they are bought only by very rich people
and so artists have become like hot-house
    flowers, or lap-dogs
and so their works are more and more as peculiar
    as themselves
and so we have all the new kinds of "art movements"
and so what we call Art (with a large A) is now
    simply a sort
        of psychological
        self-exhibitionism.[38]

Gill's egalitarian aesthetics and his sincere concern for the ordinary man were very appealing to the average workingman.[39] His influence spread into Catholic intellectual circles as well. Gerald Vann, the eminent Thomist theologian, seems to have been affected deeply by Gill's work: Walter Shewring wrote that much of Vann's writing appeared to be a spiritual elaboration of Gill's general thesis, though it was tempered by a "missionary consciousness" that Gill did not possess.[40] Gill's art and crafts ideas were also an important influence on Peter Maurin, founder of the American *Catholic Worker*. Distributist ideas in America, especially in the New England area, were popularized by Gill's close friend, Graham Carey, a Boston resident. Carey had discovered Gill by way of *G.K.'s Weekly*, and through Gill he was naturally drawn to the ideas of G.K.C., Belloc, and Penty.[41]

In addition to O'Connor, Father Vincent McNabb was a major spiritual force behind Ditchling, and the man who most influenced Gill's views on the importance of returning to the land. McNabb was probably one of the best known Catholic personalities in Britain. He was an indefatigable writer and public speaker, the first Dominican priest to become an official lecturer of the University of London Extension scheme, and a remarkable inspiration to Distributism, the back-to-the-land movements, and the Catholic Social Movement. McNabb's influence also went beyond strictly Catholic groups.[42] Like his friend, Eric Gill, McNabb also practiced the virtues of living the simple life. Indeed, McNabb (the "Mahatma Gandhi of Kentishtown," as his brethren called him) was the quintessential Distributist. Himself a practicing farmer, McNabb claimed that only a wholesale return to the land could provide the social and economic sustenance needed for a true Christian life. McNabb had been called the leader of the "left wing" of the Distributist League. Although he was a close and lifelong friend of Belloc, he always felt that both Belloc and Chesterton were too moderate in their criticism of modern society. McNabb was against all machinery on principle, and, as part of his protest against these devil's devices, he wore handwoven clothes, refused to use a typewriter, and traveled nearly everywhere on foot.[43] Unlike most of England's proponents of land reform, he opposed the mechanization of agriculture and probably would have desired a return to conditions as they prevailed in the thirteenth and fourteenth centuries. Those who loved McNabb— and there were many—hailed him as a prophet born before his time, while others, upset with his radicalism, simply considered him a harmless crank. McNabb's social philosophy was largely shaped by Leo XIII's *De Rerum Novarum*, and by his reading of Belloc's works. In many respects, Belloc and McNabb seemed stamped from the same intellectual mold. Both were militant Catholics, unyielding in their opinions, fearless in controversy, and articulate and dogmatic with the pen. McNabb was attracted to Ditchling Common through the Gill-Pepler lectures at Hawkesyard Priory. While acting as Prior of Hawkesyard, McNabb had already started to work the soil, in part as a means of venting his sheer physical energy. Farming eventually helped him draw a closer association between his own spiritual life and his social teaching, which he had been slowly developing since writing with Belloc on the *Eye* and *New Witness*. For McNabb, Gill's guild experiment completed the link between the needs of the spirit and social necessity. McNabb's acceptance of Ditchling enabled him to form a constructive social philosophy from what had formerly been only a general statement of social principles. Ditchling was McNabb's *Turmerlebnis*; there he met Nazareth, a spiritual vision "in which his soul rather than his mind had found the security it had all-unconsciously been seeking."[44]

Like Eric Gill and the Chesterbelloc, McNabb's social philosophy, as it emerged out of his Ditchling days, had a distinctly anarchistic tinge to it. The central point of his teaching, a principle which dominated all McNabb's public acts, was a hatred of "the big thing."[45] Never was he more indignant than when attacking social and political reformers who emphasized the nation over the family, the city over the village, and central planning over parental authority. Thus, McNabb called for Englishmen to turn their backs on industrialism and the city and to return to the land:

There is no hope for England's salvation except on the land. But it must be the land cultivated on a land basis and not on an industrial basis. Nothing but religion will solve the land question. And nothing but a religious order seeking not wealth but God will pioneer the movement from town to land. O that I could make religious men and women see what I see.[46]

One other Ditchling personality deserving mention is Commander Herbert Shove, a retired naval officer who became a leading spirit in the Distributist League. Like Pepler and Gill, Shove was another convert to Catholicism, and, along with McNabb, he provided an additional component of color to the community. A big bearded man, usually dressed in disheveled old clothes and a formless felt hat, Shove had the habit of wandering over the countryside playing strange airs on a homemade bamboo flute. A man of catholic interests (distilling, bee-keeping, silversmithing, farming, and studying economics, among others), Shove ultimately took up mysticism and the occult and became an interpreter of the works of St. John of the Cross and Montague Summers.[47]

Another important early convert to the Distributist position was Sir Henry Slesser. Slesser had a distinguished legal career as an expert on labor relations. He also spent many years in politics, first as an executive officer of the Fabian Society and later as a Labour Member of Parliament. Slesser finally left active political life in 1929 in order to assume a position as Judge on the Royal Court of Appeal. As with many others who were eventually attracted to Chesterton and Belloc, Slesser's early political experience centered around the Fabian Society. In the years before World War I, he had frequently debated with Belloc on socialism (supporting the Fabian position) in the columns of *The New Age*. At that time Slesser was a committed Fabian, a firm believer in what he called the "organistic" argument of physical being, a theory which regarded man as so many "molecules, atoms and subatoms" making up one unit in the higher organism of the state. "Brought up without any specific theological outlook," wrote Slesser, "there was everywhere about me that atmosphere of predestined betterment which harmonized well with gratifying statistics of increasing national revenue, trade returns, railway mileage, mineral exploitation and general statistical prosperity."[48] World War I forced Slesser to reevaluate some of these basic assumptions. In general, the war convinced him of the necessity of returning to a closer study of philosophy and religion. It was at this juncture that he began to doubt many of his Fabian presuppositions, especially his belief in the cosmic necessity of human progress. Tiring of politics, Slesser withdrew to private life and began to study the social criticisms of Chesterton and Belloc, in whose writing he finally discovered how the Fabians had erred. The Fabians, as Slesser learned from the Chesterbelloc, lacked historical perspective and were profoundly ignorant of human psychology. He and his Fabian fellows assumed, wrote Slesser, that man could be educated to reasonableness, just as the systematic application of science to

society would automatically bring happiness and material plenitude:

The world in which I and my contemporaries believed was one potentially
good . . . we were eschatologists, waiting for the Kingdom; we saw it
close at hand, in the chaste form of a garden city.[49]

Beyond the walls of Slesser's garden city lay the end of Fabian ideals.
The contestants in the Fabian Society had not anticipated the advent
of a world war and the unavoidable aftermath of spiritual decay.
Only after recognizing the spiritual implications of the Great War
did Slesser come to grasp the import of the Chesterbelloc socio-
political critique.

By October 1921, when he made his appearance on the Church
Congress platform to read a paper on property, Slesser had clearly
been converted to the Chesterbelloc position. Slesser later wrote that
he came to admire Belloc because of his insistence that religion was
the most important of man's activities and that man's fate would
ultimately be determined by his theology; while G.K.C., a neighbor
and close friend, demonstrated to Slesser that property was a necessary means for the expression of personality. It was probably his
appreciation of the values of medieval Catholic society, more than
anything else, that brought Slesser into the Distributist circle. Slesser sincerely believed that an almost ideal type of human society was
in the process of being achieved in medieval times, and he did not
feel that nobler ideals of social justice could ever be discovered.

After the breakup of the Coalition Government in 1922, Slesser
ran for Parliament for the Labour Party at Central Leeds. He
conducted his campaign on religious lines, appealing to the early
Church Fathers and St. Thomas for support in condemning the rule
of the "plutocratic" governing elite, and, much to the surprise of his
more stalwart socialist supporters, called for a redistribution of
property rather than for its nationalization. He polled second. In
subsequent elections he conducted his campaigns on straight
Distributist platforms: he adhered to medieval economic principles
and distributive social justice; he supported a return to the medieval-
type guild; and, in good Thomist fashion, called for the implementation of the "just price," while roundly condemning usury and the

pecuniary avarice of modern industrial society. While running on Labour Party tickets, Slesser publicly declared that he was not a socialist. He was ultimately elected to Parliament in 1924 by supporting the Labour Party on Catholic principles, rather than those of Marx or even the Fabians. Slesser served the Labour Party because he felt that it was the only major party fighting for social justice. As an M.P., he was a tireless proponent of the Chesterbelloc thesis, and he faithfully opposed all government and opposition proposals which encroached upon individual rights. In these years of active politics, before he left public life to serve as a judge, all Slesser's energies were devoted to the exposition of two themes: the need for the nation to regain an appreciation of the value of freedom (which could be fully achieved only through a redistribution of property) and the necessity of restoring England's social values to Catholic belief.[50]

Slesser completes what one might consider to be the early Distributist circle. Despite disagreements which arose on occasion amongst these men, they all shared a distinctly anarchistic social philosophy which opposed Britain's collectivist-plutocratic drift into the twentieth century. Certain beliefs about the nature of man and society held these writers and artists together as a special group. First of all, there was a general belief in the efficacy of widely distributed private property, together with a certain yearning for a return to the land and to the guilds of old. These people keenly felt the need for authority in a rootless and directionless society. Rootlessness was seen as the modern disease stemming from the secularism of an industrial society which emphasized quantity and efficiency at the expense of aesthetics, individuals, and spiritual values. There were also certain religious beliefs which these men held in common. Although they were not all Catholics, the group was what one might call "orthodox" (in the Chestertonian sense) in their approach to Christianity; that is to say, they felt that modern society had to return to basic spiritual principles that were fundamentally Catholic (Thomist) in nature. Finally, they were writers and artists in flight from Fabianism, in full revolt against the failures of liberalism and socialism. The alternative they discovered was not daring, experimental, or even innovative, but it was something they felt had worked effectively in the past. History and Christianity became their guides to the future, Distributism their social and political philosophy. This group would provide a crucial bulwark of support for the next and most important phase in the drama of Distributism, the launching of Chesterton's independent journal, *G.K.'s Weekly*.

CHAPTER

VI

Battling The Servile State: The Politics Of G.K.'s Weekly And The Distributist League

The first edition of *G.K.'s Weekly* appeared in March of 1925. The journal was inspired by Chesterton's commitment to continue his brother's battle against the prevailing social and political system and by his own desire to have a vehicle with which to express freely his own social philosophy. By the 1920s both Chesterton and Belloc had been effectively boycotted by the popular press; without a paper of their own, they could not have gotten their views across to the public. In a letter to Maurice Baring (in which G.K. asked his friend to serve on the journal's board of directors), Chesterton explained how important it was to carry on the struggle for Distributism:

. . . I believe that what is wanted in this promising moment of transition is a paper to fight every week for Catholic ethics and economics as the *New Statesman* does for Socialist ethics and economics, only in a livelier and more entertaining fashion. . . . There is nobody to say a single word for the family, or the true case for property, or the proper understanding of the religious peasantries, while the whole press is full of every sort of sophistry to smooth the way of divorce, of birth control, of mere State expediency and all the rest.[1]

G.K.'s Weekly was to fight for both Distributism and Catholic principles, though it could not be labeled a Catholic paper. Still, the religious concern was especially significant, since many in the English Catholic hierarchy were purposely avoiding religious and political controversy in their official publishing organs, all of which annoyed Catholic Distributists greatly. This became an even greater source of irritation in the inter-war years because of a marked revival of attacks on Catholicism on the part of some Anglicans and so-called "modernists."[2] Those few Catholic writers who did see the need for engaging in social and political debate were generally disappointed by the lethargy and general reluctance to discuss controversial issues within the English Catholic lay community. E.J. Oldmeadow, editor of *The Tablet* (a major Catholic monthly), made a concerted effort to champion the controversial approach but claimed that his readers grew bored with it all. In fact, many Catholics were resentful of Belloc's polemical militancy, regarding it as excessive and potentially damaging to Catholic respectability. Arnold Lunn, a proponent of Belloc's ideas, wrote that Catholics had forgotten that the Church was cradled in controversy from its origins and that if Catholics had been more familiar with the disputations of St. Augustine and St. Thomas More, they would have been less ready to accuse modern controversialists of undue militancy.[3]

Eric Gill was the angriest of all—the clergy gave Ditchling little support—and on numerous occasions lashed out at the Catholic hierarchy for not being in touch with the problems of industrial society. In his view, the clergy lacked the intrepidity and energy to apply the principles of Catholic social teaching to the life of the times.[4]

G.K.'s Weekly was launched amidst enthusiastic cheers from the *Eye* and *New Witness* crowd. The new journal followed the format of the other Chesterbelloc papers, though with more emphasis on G.K.C. and Distributism, and it also managed to recruit many old friends to contribute articles and reviews (e.g., Shaw, Wells, Compton Mackenzie, Gill, H.D.C. Pepler, Maurice Baring). Belloc contributed by writing on current affairs and foreign relations, and Chesterton wrote a weekly leading article and a middle spread ("Straws in the Wind"), each of which generally exceeded 1,500 words. Reckitt joined the editorial board at the end of 1924, and

Cecil's wife, Ada, and W.R. Titterton (who acted as assistant editor) helped get the operation started.

Chesterton's journal was a unique publishing venture, for it was one of the last postwar English reviews operating independently of advertising subsidies. G.K. edited and wrote for the paper without taking a salary. His weekly workload was astounding. At the beginning he wrote nearly everything that got into the frames, an output that approximated 10,000 words per week. He also read letters and answered them in "The Cockpit" (the correspondence section), and even managed to write the book reviews.[5] Soon, however, Chesterton slackened his pace and Titterton and others took on a greater share of this work. Owing to Chesterton's poor business sense, the paper suffered innumerable financial difficulties. *G.K.'s Weekly* had a circulation of only 5,000 after its first publication and probably would have collapsed in late 1926 had not the Distributist League been organized to keep it in operation. The League recruited a sizable body of supporters to promote the paper, and with a reduction in price its circulation rose considerably, remaining finally at a consistent 8,000 copies per week. Chesterton also put an enormous amount of his own time and money into the venture—as much as 5,000 pounds.[6] This obviously taxed his capacities, for after 1925 he devoted nearly all of his energies to Distributist propaganda and Father Brown stories, the latter of which were churned out on an irregular basis simply to earn enough money to keep the paper in operation.

W.R. Titterton claimed that it was he who first suggested the idea of establishing a Distributist League. Titterton had hoped that such an organization could be used as a means for raising a "fighting fund" to increase the circulation of Chesterton's paper.[7] Throughout 1925 various readers of *G.K.'s Weekly* had also suggested that Distributists form a special society. Encouraged by Slesser's discovery that some of his Labour colleagues mistrusted MacDonald and had strong sympathies with the Chesterbelloc position, the editors of *G.K.'s Weekly* even suggested that the Distributists might consider forming a party in Parliament.

It was Captain H.S.D. Went, a retired officer of the Royal Marines, who developed the actual organizational plans for the Distributist League. Went was convinced that it was necessary for Chesterton's followers to unite in local branches across Britain so that the principles of Distributism could be put into action. According to his plan, *G.K.'s Weekly* was to act as the society's unifying element by keeping all the Distributist groups in contact with one another.

After a considerable amount of advance publicity, the Distributist League ("a fellowship of beer and board," as Reckitt called it) held its inaugural meeting in Essex Hall, London, on September 17, 1926. The turnout was even larger than expected; a cheering multitude of Distributists from all over Britain overflowed the lesser Essex Hall, which became so congested that the proceedings had to be moved into a larger part of the building. Chesterton bounded onto the stage, welcomed the enthusiastic crowd and set the appropriate Distributist tone by explaining that the people who ran his "funny little paper":

. . . believed in the very simple social idea that a man felt happier, more dignified, and more like the image of God, when the hat he is wearing is his own hat; and not only his hat, but his house, the ground he trod on, and various other things. There might be people who preferred to have their hats leased out to them every week, or wear their neighbour's hats in rotation to express the idea of comradeship, or possibly to crowd under one very large hat to represent an even larger cosmic conception; but most of them felt that something was added to the dignity of men when they put on their own hats.[8]

G.K.C.'s witty introduction drew thunders of laughter. The Distributist idea simply was to restore private property, for property "was like muck . . . good only if it be spread."[9] The Essex Hall crowd went wild with enthusiasm. Everyone "was on fire with hope and zeal;" Belloc, William Blackie, and Reckitt delivered fiery speeches and G.K.C. was proudly proclaimed President of the Distributist League. Chesterton later wrote that he had been astonished and overwhelmed:

Had we anything to do with the making of this ardent, eager, indefatigable creature? The answer is, of course, that though we had something to do with the shaping of the body, we had nothing to do with the birth of the soul. That was a miracle, a miracle we had hoped for, and which yet, when it happened, overwhelmed us.[10]

Went's idea of organizing local Distributist societies caught on very quickly and within three months branches were established in London (this was the Central Branch which met at the Devereux, a tavern near Fleet Street), Birmingham, Manchester, Chatham, Liverpool, Oxford, Glasgow, and Edinburgh. Within the next few years dozens of additional branches were established in England, Scotland, Wales, Australia, South Africa, and Canada. Each branch organization usually met on a weekly basis, set up reading and discussion circles, and at regular intervals Titterton, acting for the Central Branch, scheduled public lectures and debates, all of which provided G.K.C. with a platform for personal appearances and the League with a healthy profit. These special meetings were tremendously popular and served to keep Distributism in the public eye. Chesterton had a sufficient reputation to attract large crowds to the Distributist public debates. This was especially true when he crossed swords with George Bernard Shaw, although their 1928 debate "Do We Agree?" resulted in a near riot.

Titterton, J. Desmond Glesson, and Father Brocard Sewell have written rather interesting accounts of what went on at Distributist gatherings. After an evening of serious social and political discussions, Leaguers at the Central Branch would frequently retreat to Titterton's flat for drink and song. Glesson claimed that the Distributists were probably the last people in England to make up their own songs: "The lyric outburst was not without merit, the songs had individuality and character and the rhythm was sometimes not far short of poetry."[11] The songs must have been good, for Titterton promptly collected them for publication. Singing was an essential part of the mission, explained Titterton, for Distributism was more than an economic theory: it was a whole way of life.

Immediately after the inaugural meeting, the Distributists published a short pamphlet explaining the purpose of their new organization, which initially took the clumsy but pointed title "The League for the Preservation of Liberty by the Restoration of Property." The organization's two primary objectives were: (1) the preservation of property, in order that the liberty of the individual and family could be independent of oppressive systems, and (2) the better distribution of capital by individual ownership of the means and instruments of production, which was the only way to preserve private property. The latter objective, it was declared, could only be accomplished by the wholesale destruction of plutocracy and capitalism. The League declared that it would fight for:

Small Shops and Shopkeepers against multiple shops and trusts. Individual Craftsmanship and Cooperation in industrial enterprise. (Every worker should own a share in the Assets and Control of the business in which he works.) The Small Holder and Yeoman Farmer against monopolists of large inadequately farmed estates. And the Maximum, instead of the minimum, initiative on the part of the citizen.

This statement appeared each week on a special page of *G.K.'s Weekly* devoted to League activity. The League section of the paper carried the latest news from the various branches, announced important League meetings and debates and listed books pertinent to Distributism. This part of the paper also contained a curious department entitled "Work for Leaguers," where members were asked to do such things as: leave handbills, leaflets, and copies of *G.K.'s Weekly* in suitable places, such as clubs, libraries, and bars; ask for *G.K.'s Weekly* at all libraries and bookstalls where it should be stocked—"and always carry your own copy with the title showing outside;" write letters to the local press on issues relating to League principles; and so on.

The men who gathered each week at the Central Branch took an immediate interest in rectifying the financial difficulties of *G.K.'s Weekly*, which, according to Captain Went, was supposed to act as the special mouthpiece for the Distributist League. Many of the London Distributists had business training and a good understanding of what would be required financially to run a newspaper. The professional journalists on Chesterton's staff (mainly the older Distributists) resented this group's steady intrusion into the affairs of the paper. In the end the old crowd was obliged to give way to the suggestions for reorganization and austerity, since the journal was on the threshold of collapse. G.K.C. reluctantly decided to relinquish business control to a new editorial board made up of these young "revolutionary" men from the Devereux, for it was important to him that Cecil's work be continued.

Titterton and Edward J. Macdonald, the brother of Gregory Macdonald and a man in tune with the more zealous and proselytiz-

ing Devereux group, became the new assistant editors. After the new
business agreement, *G.K.'s Weekly* and the Distributist League were
practically inseparable entities, especially since those at the Central
Branch, who rescued the paper, were now members of the new
editorial board. Along with the change in management came new
writers. Among these were the satirist, A.M. Currie, Keston Clarke,
who also wrote under a pseudonym for the *Evening News* and was
well known as a Lecturer in literature at Morley College, and Ted
Kavanagh, the man who later made the Tommy Handley radio
program ("It's That Man Again") famous. Probably the most forceful writer of the new group was Gregory Macdonald, a foreign
affairs journalist who had considerable knowledge of Poland. Macdonald's political temperament and his views on international
affairs were similar to those of Belloc. He eventually became Director of the Central European Service of the B.B.C.

The new editorial board cut the operating costs of *G.K.'s Weekly*
to the barest minimum, and, with the hard work of Edward Macdonald (becoming the link with Chesterton, who spent most of his time
in Beaconsfield), the paper became reasonably well-managed despite financial problems. Chesterton continued to use his own funds
to pay bills. Staff salaries were low and contributors were not paid.
But the continued existence of the journal was now secure. Beginning November 6, 1926, *G.K.'s Weekly* was reduced to half its former
size and the selling price dropped from 6 to 2 pence per copy. The
next year the paper broke even for the first and perhaps last time.[12]
From then on, the paper shifted its main emphasis from literary
concerns to social issues. The editors promptly announced that
since *G.K.'s Weekly* had initiated the Distributist League, that body
would take responsibility for circulating the paper. However, Chesterton assured his readers that *G.K.'s Weekly* would be every bit as
radical as its predecessors, the *Eye* and *New Witness*:

Our purpose is revolution. We do not want to tinker with the capitalist
system, we want to destroy it. We are, in fact . . . the only revolutionary
body in England. . . . We do not propose to blow it [Parliament] up with
T.N.T., but with argument at first and then by means of cooperation of the
weak versus the strong.[13]

A major priority of *G.K.'s Weekly* was to defend the individual against the encroachment of both big government and big business. This developed into a domestic struggle on two fronts, against socialism as well as against monopolistic capitalism. Both were accused of bringing on the oppressive servile state. In the name of liberty, *G.K.'s Weekly* consistently opposed the extension of state welfare, corporate monopolies, and government efforts to control education.

Essentially, Chesterton's paper was intended to appeal to what he called the "small men," those who were independently employed, such as shopkeepers, small businessmen, and farmers. In order to warn the small man against the peril of industrial monopoly, each issue of *G.K.'s Weekly* contained a story of the latest business mergers, and several articles explained how well-known trusts and combines were managed by interlocking directorates. In November, 1926, for example, *G.K.'s Weekly* outlined the methods and means by which the "Berry-Rothermere-Beaverbrook combines" were buying up and cornering the London newspaper market. Chesterton pointed out that these newspaper magnates, along with a few powerful capitalist entrepreneurs, notably Alfred Mond and Lord Ashfield, were systematically carving out monopolies for themselves in the British chemical, transportation, and entertainment industries. In fact, within a few years of Chesterton's warnings (1931) the Amalgamated Press Limited, a Harmsworth company, had extended its control over some one hundred weekly and monthly periodicals, and through a pact with the Berry Brothers acquired a monopoly of the entire provincial press. Furthermore, the Amalgamated Press was assured of a continuous supply of resources independent of paper merchants, since Northcliffe (the "Napoleon of Fleet Street") owned mills in Canada which provided nearly all the group's needs, including paper for many other leading newspapers and periodicals in London and in the provinces. Unlike Northcliffe, his brother and successor, Lord Rothermere, carried his activities well beyond journalism, reaching out from newspapers to cattle-raising and agriculture.

One issue that aroused the wrath of Distributists was the London omnibus "war." Chesterton's followers came out in droves to defend independent bus owners as they waged a furious battle for survival against the buses of Lord Ashfield's London General Omnibus Transportation Company. The scenario could have been lifted from a prewar Chesterton novel. Drab London streets were a blaze of color and moving life as privately owned omnibuses, distinctively painted in greens, scarlets and blues, with special names indicating the proprietor's history and outlook on life (e.g., the "Vanguard," "Pro Bono Publico," the "Silver Bell," and "Mountain Daisy") raced against the double-decked "Generals" for public fares. To the Distributists they looked like "laughing children" harassing the sterile "workhouse red" buses used by the baffled omnibus combine.[14]

Lord Ashfield, who was appointed to the Board of Trade by Lloyd George in 1916, hoped to solve London's transportation problem in the best interests of his own bus company. In order to corner the market completely and bring some needed order to the city's traffic system, the London General Omnibus Company (L.G.O.C.), along with the Bank of England and the Transport and General Workers' Union (T.G.W.U.), pooled their resources to secure a government transportation monopoly. Ashfield, with the full backing of the Beaverbrook papers, argued that only the L.G.O.C. had the funds and the experience adequate to meet the city's transportation needs. London traffic was clearly in a mess, and the lively competition between the combine buses (the "Generals") and the independents—"pirates," as they were called—was becoming a public safety hazard. Chesterton and the Distributists rushed to the rescue of the enterprising private bus companies, most of which were owned and operated by ex-soldiers who had used government loans from the King's Fund to launch themselves in business. The Distributists realized that London's streets were becoming too crowded and recognized the need for an overall regulation of London bus traffic. The position adopted by *G.K.'s Weekly*, however, was that the government only needed to set up a special body to issue rules and regulations for motor-vehicle transportation in the same fashion that it did for railway and ship traffic, not to centralize ownership.

On March 10, 1926, Chesterton chaired a meeting in the Great Hall at the Commons Street Hotel to protest the government's decision to grant an omnibus monopoly to the L.G.O.C. The government's policy was clearly unpopular: more than a million London passengers signed a petition in favor of keeping the private companies. Chesterton, of course, considered the intense struggle of the independent busmen convincing proof that Englishmen desired proprietorship. Believing that such feelings were inherent in all men, he hoped that the plight of the independents would act as a stimulus to Distributist instincts. As G.K.C. explained it, the colorful London traffic "pirates" could be "a beacon for guidance to Distributism."[15] The readers of *G.K.'s Weekly* were asked to boycott the monopoly buses, tube trains, and trams. Lord Ashfield, an associate of Alfred Mond in the Chemical Combine and Beaverbrook's partner in the film industry, was depicted in Chesterton's newspaper as an "American exploiter of the worst type," a great transportation octopus strangling the freedoms of London's street travelers. *G.K.'s Weekly* also informed its readers that the great monopolists were foreigners: Ashfield came from Detroit, Beaverbrook from Canada, and Mond from Palestine.

The independents ultimately lost their fight with the L.G.O.C. Most of the private companies were eventually bought out by Ashfield's corporation after the government placed a limit on the number of buses which could legally operate on any given route. In the spring of 1933 Parliament passed the London Passenger Transportation Act, which provided for the establishment of a complete monopoly of all passenger transport in the London area. The London Passenger Transportation Board, with Lord Ashfield as Chairman, was put in charge of pooling the city's public transportation, including railways, the various underground lines, tramways, and the L.G.O.C.

Undaunted by defeat at the hands of London's transportation magnates, Distributists continued the struggle to preserve the liberties of everyman and family life against corporate monopolies and big government. One item of abiding concern, for example, was the government's reconstruction schemes for education (plans for increased state aid, tighter centralized control, and increasing the school leaving age to 15), which Distributists felt would increase the powers of bureaucracy, exalt the state above the school, and deprive the family of its influence over the intellectual and moral growth of its children. State-controlled education was considered one of the greatest threats to individual liberties; Chesterton even went so far as to claim that such a scheme caused the Great War:

The theories that exalted Germany as a Super-Nation didn't grow out of the Catholic home or school, or from Munich beer halls and drinking songs, but instead was imposed entirely, exclusively and forcibly, by the huge modern machine of universal instruction, which printed and stamped the Prussian idea upon every town from Poznan to Metz.

In a word, compulsory education of any shade or color was conscription:

It is a great iron engine for hammering something, generally the same thing, into great masses of merely passive humanity. Anyone who is moved, as we are, to set the man against the machine, will have certain suspicion of it at the start.[16]

G.K.'s Weekly considered C.P. Trevelyan's Education Bill, which proposed to raise the school leaving age from 14 to 15, to be essentially a device for the relief of unemployment, intended to keep working-class children out of the labor market for an extra year. Its editors were also upset over a clause in the Bill which promised relief to impoverished parents only if they could prove their need for aid. In practice, working-class parents were to be forced to endure the "impudent interrogation of petty officials" and surrender the right of family privacy before their "overseers" would consent to administer the law.[17] The Distributist League organized numerous protest meetings and public debates in order to defeat Trevelyan's Education Bill, a contrivance, it argued, which in effect created a year of "forced instruction" (since one could not learn under coercion) and further perpetuated state power and proletarian dependence. Trevelyan's scheme was considered profligate and symptomatic of a political system in which expediency was the guiding principle. *G.K.'s Weekly* and the Distributist League claimed credit for helping to defeat the Education Bill, thus taking pride in having played at least a small part in slowing down the encroaching servile state.

In the area of domestic politics, *G.K.'s Weekly* assumed a rather moderate course in its early years (1925-1928), voicing an interest in improving the position of the working class through trade unionism and reforming economic and social life via parliamentary politics. The latter objective seems paradoxical given the anti-parliamentary tone of the Chesterbelloc's earlier political commentaries. Yet, while Henry Slesser sat on the Labour Party benches, acting as parliamentary correspondent for *G.K.'s Weekly*, Chesterton and the Distributists seemed willing to endorse the Labour Party. Slesser convinced G.K.C. that the Labour Party was worthy of support, because it was the only party in Parliament combating plutocracy and the amelioration of the poor by servile means. Both men also had high hopes that the Labourites might accept the Distributist guild idea, which they felt could ultimately restore a belief in private ownership.

G.K.'s Weekly continued to insist that the party system was a gigantic fraud, but its editors felt that Slesser's efforts in Parliament were worthy of Distributist support. In the issue of October 10, 1926, Chesterton wrote that he could agree with Slesser's analysis of the Labour Party (he believed its resistance to capitalism was essentially rooted in medieval Catholic principles, that the Party would naturally oppose legislation which impinged upon the dignity of the individual, and that the trade unionists could be persuaded to accept the guild idea), and expressed the belief that something constructive might be achieved through parliamentary action. After all, as Chesterton was later to explain, there was no reason why Distributists should surrender Parliament completely to the plutocrats.[18] Throughout 1926 and 1927, *G.K.'s Weekly* and the Distributist League generally supported Labour candidates in the various by-elections, mainly because they believed that the Labour Party was doing more than any other group to fight English capitalism and defend the rights of workingmen. As long as it seemed possible to win the trade unionists to the guild idea, Chesterton's followers were willing to work within the framework of parliamentary government. Consequently, from 1926 through 1929, *G.K.'s Weekly* backed Slesser's drive to move the Labour Party towards medieval principles; and, for its own part, mounted a journalistic campaign against the government's efforts to undermine the growing political strength of the trade union movement.

The most significant political battle for *G.K.'s Weekly* centered upon the fate of Britain's coal miners and the general strike of 1926. The so-called coal question was the greatest source of animosity between capital and labor in the inter-war years. Coal was Britain's largest industry and had long been the symbol of class antagonism. By the end of 1924, as a result of the recovery of more efficient mines in Germany and Poland, Britain's coal mines began to run at a considerable loss. The owners responded by lowering wages and lengthening working hours, both of which were opposed bitterly by the miners. In September of 1925, a Royal commission under the chairmanship of Sir Herbert Samuel was appointed to inquire into the problems of the coal industry. The Samuel report of March, 1926, came up with no immediate solution to the difficulties, though it recommended a cut in wages along with concessions from the owners. Negotiations continued. The owners refused to budge on the wage issues; the miners demanded a national minimum wage and a complete reorganization of the coal industry. The government did little, though it clearly sympathized with the owners. By the end of April 1926 the T.U.C. had started to formulate plans for a general strike in support of the miners. Last minute efforts to avoid a showdown failed. On May 2, the government broke off negotiations and by the next day Britain was plunged into the chaos of a general strike.

Throughout the period of negotiation, *G.K.'s Weekly* steadfastly supported the miners, although its editors did not agree with the Labour Party's bargaining position. The paper particularly disapproved of the inclusion of a minimum or living wage in the trade union's list of demands. On principle, Distributists felt that arguments over wages only served to reaffirm the permanent division of property between employer and employee. The whole question of wage bargaining was based on the idea that labor was to be treated as a commodity, and the acceptance of a minimum wage, in the eyes of Chesterton's followers, could only perpetuate working-class dependency. A minimum wage was part of the "bread and circuses" of the servile state; accepting it meant slavery. Distributists opposed the entire wage system, insisting instead that the workers should demand ownership of the means of production. On the other hand, Chesterton supported the mine owners' proposal to gear wages to the prosperity of the mines. As far as he was concerned, the owners had made a significant concession on this issue, for they had, in effect, conceded that the miner was a partner in business and that what he might receive for services was part of the industry's profit. Chesterton advised the miners to insist upon a partnership provision, along with its logical corollaries: cooperation in control, co-equal power in management, and partnership in profits.[19] However,

G.K.'s Weekly refused to support the government's proposals for "mixed control" of the mining industry, a system by which the owners and government officials were to run the mines. Since the prewar strikes and the omnibus war, Distributists had learned that government officials could not be trusted, as they always tended to throw their weight on the side of the combine. Paradoxically, Chesterton claimed that he was also prepared to support the nationalization of the coal industry, for the mines were "abnormal and anomalous things" that could be privately owned only through monopoly and privilege. Moreover, the mines were impersonal objects to which one could not attach any sort of sentimentality:

We could sympathise warmly with such people if they really were attached to a mine like a peasant to a meadow; if we could picture them bending quaint bows against the quaintier birds and hunting pterodactyls and trilobites through those groves of gloom, like Robinhood in the heart of Greenwood. . . . There have been landlords and land-owners of all kinds who have fallen on their knees and kissed their ancestral soil. But there is something almost painful in the thought of the Duke of Northumberland embracing large lumps of coal and perhaps carrying away the traces of affection too well requited. There have been landlords even in poor and remote places who have really been local patriots and loved their place and people. But when it comes to the bottom of a black coalpit, the most amiable landlord is often an absentee landlord. And this kind of ownership . . . cannot involve the sort of instinct and identification which can ennoble property, and even ennoble inequality. . . .[20]

When the mine workers decided to strike, Chesterton's paper gave them its unqualified support. In the tradition of the *Eye* and *New Witness*, the editors argued that any workman had a right to strike at any time and for any reason. They recognized the horrible working conditions under which the miners lived and fully agreed with the demands for shorter hours. Instead of criticizing Baldwin for doing nothing to prevent the strike (a line taken by many pro-Labor papers), *G.K.'s Weekly* blamed the Federation of British Industries for engineering what it called a cruel conspiracy against the poor.

G.K.'s Weekly's strong defense of the miners' action—a special version of the paper typed up by the editors appeared during the general strike—brought considerable criticism from the Catholic community, and for weeks its editors were deluged with letters from readers who considered the strike to be a revolution. The hierarchy of both the Anglican and Roman Catholic Churches unequivocably condemned the action of the T.U.C.[21] This kind of official Church response had always irritated Distributists. As usual, the hierarchy was loath to commit itself to politics for fear of invoking criticism from the governing establishment. In clear defiance of this stand, Chesterton and his followers urged the public to take up the sword against political and economic injustice by supporting the general strike. The official position of *G.K.'s Weekly* was that the workers were forced into action because of a conspiracy by the government and the mine owners to smash trade unionism. Because of this, the journal defended the decision to strike as being the only reasonable defense against plutocracy.[22]

The T.U.C. called off the general strike on May 12, though the miners stayed out of work for another six months. By December, 1926, the miners gave in and slowly drifted back to the pits, forfeiting both higher wages and shorter hours. The strike had a disastrous impact on the workers and the trade union movement. The miners lost some 60 million pounds in wages, nearly half a million men throughout British industry lost work during the strike because of coal shortages, and the trade unions, financially exhausted, suffered a precipitous decline in membership. Throughout the long and bitter negotiations, the government had clearly given way to the belligerent mine owners. In order to insure their final victory over organized labor, the Conservatives in Parliament passed the Trades Disputes and Trade Union Bill. This piece of vindictive legislation made sympathetic strikes illegal, placed severe limitations on trade union political funds, and forbade civil servants to join associations affiliated with the T.U.C.

As a legal expert, Slesser was given charge of leading the opposition's attack on certain questions of law in the Bill. Most of Slesser's colleagues were primarily concerned with how the legislation would affect the welfare of the union movement. However, in the end, Slesser's Distributist views prevailed: he was determined that the fight should center on the deeper principle of individual rights and not be obscured by an overinsistence on trade unionism as such. Both in Parliament and in various public debates, Slesser argued that the Bill was an unqualified attack by plutocracy aimed at placing the workers in a condition of slavery. Slesser, *G.K.'s Weekly*, and the Distributist League, which held numerous meetings in Essex Hall protesting the legislation, believed that the Bill was perpetrated by the conspiring Federation of British Industries with the sole purpose of destroying the trade union movement.

After the Trades Disputes and Trade Union Bill was passed into law in 1927, all evidence suggests that Chesterton and the Distributists began to turn against the Labour Party and the trade union movement. This shift in attitude was the direct result of what Distributists considered to be labor's growing willingness to collaborate with industrial capitalism and the governing establishment. In November of 1927, Sir Alfred Mond, Chairman of Imperial Chemical Industries and, in the Chesterbelloc's opinion, the archetypical monopoly capitalist, formally proposed that the major employers and the T.U.C. General Council undertake a series of discussions for the promotion of industrial cooperation. Ben Turner, Chairman of the T.U.C. General Council, accepted Mond's invitation and throughout 1928-1929, Britain's major industrialists and trade union officials participated in what came to be called the "Mond-Turner" talks. In July, 1928, the group published an interim report proposing various measures for dealing with unemployment, increasing industrial efficiency, and improving worker-employer relations. The report suggested that the owners should fully recognize the trade unions as the sole bargaining agencies for workers, and it recommended that plans be made for the establishment of joint consultative machinery by the T.U.C., the Federation of British Industries, and the National Confederation of Employers' Organizations. Mond and those industrialists who inspired the talks, hoping to seize the initiative following labor's defeat in the general strike, intended to salve the bruises of the trade union movement and enlist its cooperation with capitalism by making various concessions to union welfare demands. As an incentive for collaboration, the owners offered full recognition and encouragement of trade union membership, and proposed to help reduce joblessness by making changes in the unemployment insurance system. The Mond-Turner proposals were anathema to Distributists, for they considered this closer understanding and cooperation between employers and employed to be the chief buttress of the servile state. Labor's willingness to participate in the talks was a sad indication that the trade unionists had given up their fight for ownership of the means of production. The guild idea had been expunged from the trade union movement by the insidious promise of security.

As a means of countering the popularity of the Mond-Turner proposals, *G.K.'s Weekly* took the offensive, demanding that the trade unionists push for ultimate control and ownership of industrial production by first settling the coal dispute in their favor. For this purpose, Chesterton, Slesser, and Penty, in numerous articles throughout 1928 and 1929, proposed that the government acquire the coal mines and lease them to a federation of miners' guilds. They recommended that the guilds be allowed government credit for the rent of the mines and for the eventual purchase of plant machinery. A special committee elected by all the employees of the mining industry would carry on the business of the old directors and plan appropriate measures for the complete reorganization of the industry. Permanent management of the pits and the sale of produce (coal and electricity) were to rest solely with the miners' guilds. Each guild would own the plant, sell the coal, and pay its members on the basis of sales.[23]

The Distributists were completely unsuccessful in their efforts to induce either the trade unions or the government to settle the mining problem on guild principles. By the early part of 1929, after Slesser's retirement from Parliament, *G.K.'s Weekly* agreed with the Communists that the Labour Party had sold out to monopoly. Indeed, both the trade union and Labour Party leadership had embraced "Mondism," and this meant that it was no longer possible for Distributists to support parliamentary government. In the early part of 1930, the editors of *G.K.'s Weekly* announced that MacDonald's cabinet and the entire Labour Party had succumbed to the sorcery of the party system. Most of those chosen to serve in MacDonald's government came from Labour's right wing, which had supported the Mond-Turner talks; even more outrageous, the old Fabian enemy, Sydney Webb, was selected to head the Colonial Office. In its first few months in office, the new Labour government failed to approach the coal mine problem along Distributist lines and made only half-hearted attempts to repeal the odious Trade Disputes Act of 1927. On February 22, 1930, *G.K.'s Weekly* bitterly denounced such feckless conduct. The Labour Party politicians, it argued, had been converted to "respectability"; they had become a "real party" by entering the full political system with the understanding that all the rules laid down by parliamentary precedent would be scrupulously observed. Labour had now earned its badge of respectability; its leaders had graciously become "good parliamentarians" but in violation of the old socialist revolutionary tradition:

In the days of William Morris they had talked of destroying the Houses of Parliament by blowing them up or, more picturesquely, of shelling them from the river. . . . But now their own aim is to preserve Parliament, to make it permanent, to make it safe.

G.K.'s Weekly explained that it had given up on parliamentary politics. The new course of action was to be revolution from without. Any change would have to be imposed upon the parliamentarians.[24]

In August 1930, the Distributist League reevaluated its former position of giving support to the trade union movement, and decided to modify its stand on this issue: trade unions henceforth were considered "the last bulwark of the workers against capitalistic oppression," but the League could not extend official backing to the movement for it was believed that trade union objectives had no point of contact with Distributist aims.[25] Maurice Reckitt, always a voice of moderation within the Distributist circle, was chagrined at the prospect of the League's withdrawal of support from the trade union movement. He argued that the trade union movement had been the one authentic achievement of nineteenth-century democracy, and despite its shortcomings remained the single effective force to overcome plutocracy and the bureaucratic tendencies of the servile state. Reckitt believed that the unions might be able to encourage true guild activity along Distributist lines once the financial monopoly of capitalism was broken. In the meantime, Distributists of all persuasions were urged to support the trade union movement.[26] Despite Reckitt's pleas, the League announced in October

1930 that Distributists would not support trade unionism until its leadership definitely renounced "pink Socialism in favor of worker-ownership-control."[27] After the League explained its attitude about the labor movement, neither it nor *G.K.'s Weekly* ever again demonstrated noticeable favor towards trade unionism. Belloc, after this point, saw trade unionism as just another organ of the capitalists to control British workers.[28]

Once it became clear that the Labour Party could not be won over to the guild ideal, *G.K.'s Weekly* and the Distributist League began to expound the principles of monarchism. Belloc's anti-parliamentary sentiments had always remained strong in the Distributist movement. In a meeting at the Devereux in June of 1927, H.E. Humphries, author of the League's textbook on Distributism, had delivered a major speech on the desirability of a popular monarchy with personal power to appoint and dismiss the ministry. Basing his arguments on Belloc's writings, Humphries pointed out that monarchism would be the ideal form of government in a truly Distributist state. Humphries was convinced that all forms of central democratic representation tended to become corrupt; for this reason, he favored some type of "enlightened" or "elected" form of responsible and hereditary monarchy in which various local bodies would do much of the executive work.[29] However, this particular proposal was not given backing in *G.K.'s Weekly* or in the various League branches.

It was only after the Mond-Turner proposals and after the disappointments of the second Labour government that Distributists began to pick up on Belloc's anti-parliamentary arguments. In an article in *G.K.'s Weekly* in August 1929, H.S.D. Went, one of the founders of the Distributist League, raised the "servile state-party system" theme and explained that the traditional structure of Britain's government had decayed beyond repair. He described Parliament as a contemptible body of plutocrats, and explained that democracy was impossible in England since the democratic spirit had been expunged from its political tradition. Went insisted that the only hope for the survival of English greatness lay in a restoration of the monarchy to full political power.[30] In the same month, Belloc, for the first time in *G.K.'s Weekly*, expounded the fundamentals of the anti-parliamentary position which had been worked out years before in his *House of Commons and Monarchy.*

In the General Election of 1931, the Distributists declined to support any particular party. Belloc wrote that the election would bring about the complete breakup of both the party and cabinet systems and called for a revival of monarchical government with a consultative body representing the "real interests" of the nation.[31] At the end of 1932, as if to highlight the League's folly of trying to convert the Labour Party to Distributist principles, Belloc explained that he had actually given up on Parliament ever since the failure of the Marconi crusade:

I have since that date refused to take any further part in any attempt to cleanse what I think is beyond cleansing. Public life now stinks with the stench of a mortal disease; it can no longer be cured.[32]

By August 1935, Chesterton wrote that, as things now stood, he personally was willing to look into fascism, whereas parliamentarianism was not worth looking into at all.[33]

Distributists thus trod the respectable path of parliamentary politics for only a few short years. A willingness to cooperate with the political establishment seems to have dissipated completely by 1930. This disappointment with the trade union movement and mainstream politics became all the more acute with the onset of worldwide economic depression. The social dislocations of the depression years produced an epoch of unprecedented political philosophizing. To the Distributists, it seemed as though the capitalist system, and everything associated with it, were on the verge of complete destruction. Yet they were not alone in this feeling. The horrors of war and the major economic collapse which followed convinced many Western intellectuals that the old icons of liberalism and nationalism had failed and that new gods would have to be found in order to pull Europe back on the rails of sanity. This topsy-turvy world of the inter-war years, a period of shattered values and hollow men, certainly contributed to the general popularity of fascist and communist ideologies. But Distributism, unlike fascism, was not a child of World War I and the spiritual crisis of the 1920s and 1930s. To a remarkable extent, the Chesterbelloc had anticipated the death of liberal values, and they warned of the chaos that would ensue in its wake. Despite these timely warnings, the Distributist circle was soon to be drawn into the vortex of rightist authoritarian political theorizing which swept postwar Europe. This more despairing side of the Distributist movement will concern us in a later chapter. We shall now examine how the Chesterbelloc proposed to bring about the social and political reforms necessary for the Distributist state.

CHAPTER VII

Developing the Distributist Program

Even more important for *G.K.'s Weekly* than the practice of politics was the popularization of Distributist social and economic principles. It was for this purpose that both the paper and the Distributist League were founded. Since the particular details of the Distributist state had been outlined only vaguely in the earlier writings of the Chesterbelloc, *G.K.'s Weekly* and the League took up the task of completing their definition. Chesterton hoped that his journal could serve as a frank and open debating forum for the discussion both of what Distributism should be and how it might be put into practice.

Distributists did not agree completely on what issues should take priority in their general attack on modern industrialism, nor were they always in agreement as to the exact methods needed to implement the social and economic ideas of the Chesterbelloc. One major group, headed by the leaders of the Birmingham branch (Harold Robbins and G.C. Heseltine), felt that Distributists should spearhead a full-scale return to an agricultural village-based economy. Eric Gill was mainly concerned with restructuring Britain's monetary system as the first step towards Distributist reform. McNabb and Penty led the anti-machine forces, arguing that civilization could be saved by Distributism only if man totally abandoned machinery. Chesterton, for his part, acted as the referee for these competing groups, publicly encouraging their debates in the pages of *G.K.'s Weekly*.

On the most general terms, all Distributists agreed that the Chesterbelloc ideal included more than a mere redistribution of wealth and private ownership. In the words of Herbert Shove, Distributism was the golden road back to something greater than property: it was a return to "the philosophy of balance." Distributists intended to create a new world in which men could find the proper balance between the needs of the heart and the mind. It was "intellectual freedom" that would matter most, and in order to express their intellect men would require private property.[1] G.C. Heseltine (secretary of the Birmingham branch, author of numerous books on agriculture, and himself a successful smallholder in Yorkshire), described Distributism for the *Catholic World* as simply a makeshift title for a comprehensive social philosophy which its advocates would define in terms of the problems of the hour. The chief function of the movement, Heseltine optimistically added, was to serve as "a seed-bed" for the future leaders of civilization.[2] It was also generally agreed that Distributism was a doctrine aimed at the utter destruction of capitalism. Harold Robbins insisted that the movement intended to destroy the millionaire, mass production, and, to some extent, industrialism.[3]

The officials of the Birmingham branch, along with Vincent McNabb, published numerous essays and books on the importance of revitalizing the agricultural sector of Britain's economy.[4] In particular, these Distributists championed the restoration of smallholdings. Heseltine, for example, insisted that food could be produced more economically on small, privately owned plots of land.[5] McNabb also supported the principle of smallholdings, but adopted the more controversial position of arguing that the major problems of agricultural production could be mitigated by avoiding the use of machinery completely. While admitting that machines led to greater output, he insisted that high-yield mechanized agriculture required large, complex transportation systems and raised the costs of distribution. Thus, he felt that agriculture was economically most efficient when the area of production was identical with the area of consumption.[6]

McNabb believed that farming had been totally ruined in England because the rural areas had been turned into a virtual agricultural factory. According to this argument, Britain was moving through a self-perpetuating cycle of money-grubbing and moral decay because of her reliance on machine mass production. McNabb, who believed in village self-sufficiency, steadfastly opposed the mechanization of agriculture because he felt that machines would force the farmer to produce for money and the market economy and not for consumption. He believed that this would develop into a vicious cycle, since the market factor served as an incentive for the introduction of more machinery and bigger farms, which would have the effect of displacing families and dispersing them to the cities. In order to subsist in the capitalists' world, the land-worker had to obtain money by selling his produce in a market. The more he produced, the farther he would be required to send his produce. Such circumstances, argued McNabb, robbed the farmer of his liberty of action: it delivered him over to the machinations of the market, the transportation network that served it, and the financier who provided the credit to buy and work the land until the harvest could be sold and paid for.[7]

Nearly all the Distributists tended to be anti-urban, because they felt that the city was too far removed from the lifeblood of the soil. It was believed that city life could enslave the worker to the routine of capitalism by making him too dependent on "modern conveniences" and the security of a regular wage. Yet, unlike McNabb, most of the Distributists interested in agriculture did not agitate for the elimination of machine production; instead they devoted most of their efforts to the more practical task of trying to convince the government to provide more assistance to the small independent farmer. In accordance with their essential beliefs that land was the source of real wealth, and that for the exercise of freedom man should own the soil on which he worked, they also asserted that the majority of men should at all times till the land: the Distributist state rested on peasant proprietorship.

Most Leaguers did support McNabb's proposals for decentralizing the agricultural sector of Britain's economy. Heseltine, for example, recommended an agricultural system of individually owned "mixed farms," where workers in certain specified areas would be supplied with all the fertilizers, machinery, and transport necessary for meeting the consumption needs of a local market.

Yet, even while formulating the broad outlines of this new state, most Distributists did not insist that all men would have to practice farming or hand craftsmanship. H.E. Humphries, author of the League's first textbook, *Liberty and Property* (1928), wrote that Distributists were not fanatics:

If a man wants to do things by machinery, or work in a factory, he will do so. Some people like hand-made goods, others are indifferent. . . . Those who do not want the responsibility of property and like to rely on a master, will work for a wage on the farm or in the workshop. Our conception of a civilized state is one in which men will want responsibility, and the exercise of their own wills in the control of their own business. . . . The essential is liberty, and when there is the variety . . . liberty is as completely established as is possible in economic affairs.[8]

Variation in the methods of economic organization and production and the coexistence of a large number of independent companies within each industry were considered important for preserving economic independence within the Distributist state. According to Humphries, it was the idea and practice of ownership that was important, not the form it might take.

Eric Gill's Distributist essays dealt chiefly with the problems arising from the use of money in modern society and the necessity of restoring ownership to the working classes. He was persuaded that the ills of unemployment and all economic problems (indeed, even moral and sexual problems) could be solved if Britain's leaders abolished usury and the "trade in money." It was his conviction that currency should exist only as a means for exchanging goods and as a measurement of production. In Gill's analysis, the government's chief monetary responsibility should be the regulation of money supply so that purchasing power would better correspond to the strength of industrial and agricultural production. He felt that the currency system as it presently existed was a convenient tool of bankers and moneylenders in whose interests the power of the monarchy had been destroyed. This particular approach to the currency problem became the stock in trade of most Distributists and was further elaborated by Belloc in his various essays on the international monetary conspiracy.

Gill's other great economic concern was the relationship of the working man to property. Unlike many of the Catholic clergy, who asserted that private ownership of property was fundamentally a moral issue, Gill emphasized that men needed a sense of ownership to inspire responsible workmanship and quality in production. It was in this respect that the denial of private property became a breach of morals: a decline in the quality of work was in itself immoral. Gill was greatly troubled that the Catholic clergy had ignored these kinds of issues relating to the necessity of private property. Corrupted by five centuries of commercial rule and the consequent development of materialism, the clergy failed to recognize that the foundations of modern industrial civilization rested upon basically evil and unchristian assumptions. In the modern philistine environment the idea of human work had become a concept with no association to anything but money. The common arts, the means by which the basic necessities of life were provided, had become submerged in the mechanical system of international moneylenders. Gill consequently chastised the clergy, and even the Church hierarchy, for refusing to condemn the structure of modern industrialism and its currency system. For Gill, the obscenity of industrialism was that it destroyed the very thing which could give work its ultimate *raison d'être*: namely the creation of something good to serve man's spiritual, intellectual, and physical needs. Industrialism ineluctably had reduced the necessities of man's sustenance (food, clothing and shelter) to a mere material significance. It also had degraded work and reversed what Gill considered to be the priorities of Christian civilization. Leisure which, like sleep, was meant to refresh the laborer so work could be renewed with greater vigor, had become the end for which work was done in modern civilization. A life of pleasure had become the object of the secular industrial state.[9]

Gill was not a particularly controversial figure within Distributist circles, though his strong personality and outspoken opinions on economic and social issues furrowed the brows of the Catholic clergy. Generally speaking, his views on money, work, and property were a major contribution to Distributist theory, and Gill himself always remained one of the movement's most influential writers. But just like most other Distributists, Gill was far too rebellious for many Catholics and was often criticized for extremism.

The most disputatious of the Chesterbelloc following, the men responsible for most of the arguments over the proper definition of Distributism and its methods of reform, were A.J. Penty and Maurice Reckitt. As early as 1925, just after Chesterton's paper began publication, they touched off a major debate over the proper formula for bringing about a Distributist society. Reckitt refused to support the contention that machinery and industrialism could not serve man and hence had to be scrapped. His chief objection to industrialism was its large-scale organization which, tending to monopoly, rendered small-scale ownership an impossibility. Instead, accepting the benefits and necessity of machine production, Reckitt asserted that a return to normal social relationships could best be served through a more equitable distribution of consumer purchasing power. Rather than beginning with what Distributists saw as their chief objective, namely the redistribution of property, Reckitt proposed distributing income or shares in industry to individuals and families.[10]

Penty quickly took issue with this position, since he felt it would be impossible to convince people to part with their wealth voluntarily. In Penty's view, industrialism was an unyielding, incurable disease, and if Distributism were to become a reality, there would have to be a change in the spirit of men, which naturally required the abandonment of industrialism. He rejected Reckitt's proposal, because it aimed "to stabilize society in its present upside down condition."[11] Penty called himself part of the "Fundamentalist" school of Distributism, which had concluded that there could be no solution to societal ills apart from a return to the simple conditions of life. The "Empiricists," he explained, were those like Reckitt (old collectivists who read the *Servile State* and became guild socialists), who turned to "Distributivism" but were about to spoil the idea by interpreting it in terms of a reshuffle of industrialism rather than as a return to fundamentals.[12]

Reckitt, for his part, was mainly interested in synthesizing Distributism with a new economic theory called "social credit." This unusual fiscal philosophy was developed by Major C.H. Douglas, a friend of Orage, who first popularized his theories in the pages of *The New Age*. Douglas believed that the science of economics should concern itself chiefly with commodity distribution and that the problems of economic recession could be solved if people were given an adequate supply of money to spend. The "social credit" theory was based on the premise that there was never enough money in circulation to purchase available goods.[13] Douglas felt that the government could eliminate the currency bottleneck by simply printing more money. Prices could be fixed by law, each citizen would be presented with a "national dividend," and the overall expansion in purchasing power would permanently eliminate the perennial evil of "poverty amidst plenty."

Reckitt was convinced that the Chesterbelloc alternative could be put into practice only through the principles of Douglas' social credit ideas. Thus he repeatedly called upon the League to draw up a practical plan for the implementation of Distributism via the mechanisms of social credit. Reckitt fundamentally disagreed with the League's official policy of acting solely as a propagandist organization (a "seed-plot" for the germination of values, principles, and ideas), and insisted that the movement had to get something concrete accomplished. In Reckitt's view, the economic order was already collapsing, a clear indication of this being the state's inability to distribute the goods it produced. Like most Distributists, he believed the postwar depression to be the result of financial manipulation. Consequently, he urged Distributists to attack the money monopoly by demanding a redistribution of income. This approach was necessary as a precondition for a "system of distributed tangible assets, in land and small workshops and other forms of concrete property."[14] For this purpose he proposed the establishment of labor or credit banks, which would be the repository of all wages and salaries of those working in industry. Each worker would have a voting share in the bank, and, in turn, the banks would enjoy a constant flow of currency from those who produced goods. This credit scheme, in which every worker was entitled to a dividend for each contribution to the labor bank, would ultimately allow the workers to assume the means of production by buying out the capitalist and, consequently, bring about true democracy by eliminating the monopoly of finance.[15.]

Distributists were continually criticized for their petulance, indecisiveness, and failure to develop a systematic plan for social, economic, and political reform. These criticisms were unfair in many respects. First of all, it must be emphasized that *G.K.'s Weekly* and the Distributist League, from the moment of inception, were primarily intended as propagandist organs, whose objective was to influence public opinion. They did not fail in this endeavor, for the influence of Distributist ideas was considerable. Secondly, over the years Chesterton, Belloc, and the Distributist League did develop what one could label a Distributist program, with stated aims, principles, and practical suggestions for implementing certain necessary reforms. Yet, in no one piece of writing was a systematic account of Distributism ever given, nor was the Chesterbelloc ever sufficiently clear in explaining their attitude towards practical politics. Belloc's final proposals for the practical implementation of Distributism appeared in his book *The Restoration of Property* (1936). This was not a complete statement, however, and to be appreciated fully it must be read as a sequel to *The Servile State* (1912). Likewise, Belloc's political views were expressed in various books over the years, the most succinct statements appearing in the *House of Commons and Monarchy* (1922). Chesterton's political and social views were never stated as clearly as those of Belloc. Generally speaking, his evasive—perhaps even elusive—feelings on these subjects seem to have been taken from Belloc. His support of Mussolini is a fairly good example of Belloc's influence.

Still, it is necessary to attempt a definition of what these men meant by Distributism. However, arriving at a textbook definition is rendered doubly difficult by the fact that while most Distributists argued bitterly over theory and practice, Chesterton himself made it a policy to maintain a disinterested position above the storm and stress of League debates on these issues. Chesterton's position vis à-vis the League was one of moderator, judge, and peacemaker. Moreover, Chesterton was prone to using paradox, confusing fairy tales, and symbolism as literary devices. For this reason it has sometimes been difficult to understand his real intentions.[16] Nearly every feuding faction within the Distributist movement was able to cite Chesterton's writings in support of its position. Nevertheless, a definite image of Chesterton's Distributist ideas did emerge during the *G.K.'s Weekly* years. A close reading of his journal articles from 1925 through 1936, and his criticism of Reckitt and Penty, certainly reveal what Chesterton did not accept as Distributist doctrine.[17] Distributism was not to be merely "three acres and a cow."

Although the Reckitt-Penty debates caused some turmoil in Distributist circles, they did have the virtue of forcing Chesterton to clarify his own ideas on the proper methods of bringing about a Distributist society. Both Chesterton and the League found it necessary to repudiate Penty's anti-machine approach to Distributism.[18] Penty later modified some of his extremist views and after Chesterton's death wrote an official Distributist manifesto, but throughout the 1920s he continually alienated most Distributists by upholding controversial notions about social and economic reform. In particular, he asserted that the private ownership of property need never be an absolute requirement in the Distributist state. The ownership of property, he insisted, could be justified only on the basis of how much social service its owner supplied to the community. In addition, Penty did not think it possible to redistribute property while wealth was in the hands of a financial and industrial plutocracy. Thus he proposed the abandonment of both the finance system and machinery and called upon Distributists to work towards replacing the fluctuating currency system with a standard or fixed price scheme controlled by guilds. With respect to property, Penty suggested that there should be no private ownership as such, but that land be held by the state and managed by local agricultural guilds. This would give the cultivator protection from the capitalist and would confer absolute security of tenure, while regulating ownership to serve the social needs of the community.[19]

Penty's views brought forth an adamant response from both the League and *G.K.'s Weekly*. Chesterton was particularly hostile to his position on property. Did Penty mean that the state should deter people from getting too fond of property by keeping them from having any property to be fond of?

It seems to me a little like preventing them drinking too much beer by preventing them from having beer to drink. . . . The whole point of liberty and property is that the citizen, when he says daily, 'Lead us not into temptation,' does not address that remark to the policeman.[20]

G.C. Heseltine objected to Penty's scheme of communal land-holding, because it would lead inevitably to the development of complicated bureaucracies and breed political discontent.[21] And, of course, most Distributists were convinced that peasant proprietor-ship was a mandatory requirement for social and political stability. Moreover, the League never fully believed that a system of fixed prices, in the absence of diffused proprietorship, could ever be a panacea for economic independence. Even as a tool for bringing about the redistribution of wealth, fixed prices required a type of coercion and bureaucratic control that most Distributists could not accept. Many considered obligatory guild membership, fixed prices, and even quality control infringements of liberty and were willing to countenance them only if public welfare could be preserved by no other means.[22]

In response Penty wrote that he could not abide by the League's trust in laissez-faire principles, for economic liberty produced mo-nopoly and industrial slavery. He disputed Chesterton's assertion that change could be achieved through moral suasion and called upon Distributists to utilize real economic and political weapons in their fight against industrialism.

In July 1927 Chesterton clarified the Distributist position vis-à-vis the Penty controversy. He explained that Distributists were not against the use of machinery as such, but would fight machinery if it were used as a device to concentrate the holding of property and wealth. Chesterton believed that it was better to have smaller ma-chinery serving smaller property, but admitted that there were numerous instances in which the use of large-scale machinery was necessary for industrial production. In such circumstances, Distri-butists would have to insist that the machinery be owned not merely corporately, but so that the shares in it would constitute "some sort of property for each, as well as public property for all." On this point Chesterton seemed to be reasserting his belief in worker ownership of the means of production. G.K.C. did not completely reject the practicality of Penty's ideas on fixed prices; instead he insisted that Distributists could not believe in fixed prices as a substitute for the redistribution of property. A real Distributist, it was explained, need only be against "the destruction of property, personality, creative thrift and honourable independence."[23]

In sum, Belloc and Chesterton, unlike Penty, were not primitive medievalists. Penty pined for a static society in which all forms of competition and commercialism would have disappeared. Although Belloc was anti-capitalist, he was not against the principle of competition but against capitalism's tendency towards monopoly, which, in itself, would eliminate free enterprise. Chesterton and he sought to mitigate the excesses of industrial capitalism so as to restore the small man to a more secure position in the marketplace of free competition.

Chesterton and the League also rejected Reckitt's social credit proposals. Even Belloc, who seldom took much interest in the official Distributist movement and the League, came out against the Douglas credit theory on the grounds that it would require a massive bureaucracy and too much state intervention in economic affairs. Chesterton, for his part, refused to accept social credit because it would not revolutionize industrial society. While Reckitt had emphasized that the Douglas method had the distinct advantage of not disturbing the framework of Britain's legal and social system, Chesterton hoped to see that system completely destroyed. Distributists did not want society to evolve unconsciously into something new:

It may be that Englishmen have lost their liberty unconsciously; we do not want them to regain it unconsciously. Still less do we want them to regain it so hazily that they have not the vigilance to guard it; that they may be bamboozled into the acceptance of half of it; or of half of a plausible substitute for it. There may not be a revolution in the State, but I fancy there must be some sort of revolution in the soul, before the average modern Englishman loses the soul of the proletarian and gains the soul of the proprietor. And this revolution in the things of the soul seems to me to come most sharply and vividly through the things of the body . . . things and not theories; things and not abstractions or numbers or documents or debits or credits.[24]

The real danger was that social credit would make life too easy, and men might never realize that a fundamental change of heart and a total rejection of modern culture were needed to revitalize Western civilization.

Chesterton's own feelings about Distributist theory and the measures required to transform it into reality were discussed in scattered articles throughout the early months of *G.K.'s Weekly* and subsequently incorporated in a book entitled *The Outline of Sanity* (1926). Its publication was meant to serve as a guideline for League discussions as well as to clarify basic Distributist principles. It was also intended to quell the voices of pundits who had chastised Chesterton for neglecting a plan of action for building a Distributist society. In very clear language, *The Outline of Sanity* proposed two distinct stages for the implementation of social reform. First of all, the drift of property and wealth towards monopoly and the corresponding destruction of small ownership had to be halted. The individual consumer could play a role in this effort by mounting a boycott against big shops, chain stores, trusts, and monopolies. It was important that the people be made to realize that the monopolist momentum was not irreversible. Chesterton believed that the individual citizen could do something to modify the tendency towards the servile state; once the plutocratic pressure was removed, or even eased, the appetite for private ownership would revive. The state could also assume an active role in this first stage of confrontation by outlawing the plutocratic business techniques (such as price wars and below-cost selling) that destroyed small businesses. The government might also provide free legal services to the small property owner so that he could better defend his holding in a court of law. In short, Chesterton was confident that the individual Englishman could halt the deterioration of modern society, provided he were informed about the evils of monopoly and given a fighting chance by the state.

The second and more positive stage of Chesterton's reform called for the development of a model Distributist community, comparable to Gill's "cell of good living," which could serve as a moral and practical inspiration for the construction of a more normal society. He suggested a balanced industrial-agricultural society with a solid peasant base as the working model. It was to be a family-oriented society of diffused property in which every man could direct the affairs of his own life, construct his own environment, eat what he liked, and wear what he pleased. The ownership of small-scale property would provide excitement to life, help inculcate responsibility through personal choice and introduce the challenge of being creative within limits. Once again, the government was asked to give Distributists a helping hand. Chesterton proposed that the state initiate special differential taxation so as to discourage the sale of small property to big proprietors and facilitate the purchase of land by the propertyless, destroy primogeniture, protect and subsidize needed experiments in small property holdings by tariffs if necessary, and sponsor educational programs designed to encourage handicrafts and farming. Lastly, workers were urged to organize special guild organizations which ultimately would buy out the capitalists and exercise cooperative control of all industry.

In October 1927 Chesterton introduced more specific reform measures and suggested that Distributism might even be brought about through the existing machinery of government. This was Chesterton at his most optimistic, for at this juncture he had hopes that the necessary changes could be effected almost entirely by one financial act. The first part of Chesterton's proposed legislation called for a special "Tax on Turnover" which would serve to weaken the operation of trusts, combines, and all forms of big business. According to this plan, Britain's dying agricultural sector would be revived by breaking up large landed estates; the government could draw up a tax on undeveloped land, making it unprofitable for those who hoarded real estate for tax write-offs and speculation. Parliament would be purged of plutocrats by a section of the act making it mandatory for all M.P.'s to disclose the source of party funds used in their campaigns. These funds could be subjected to crippling direct taxes, the revenues from which would be used to finance land banks for would-be farmers. The sale of titles could be made financially prohibitive through a high sales tax, and the banks were to be reformed or even abolished by stabilizing currency rates. This same all-encompassing financial act would also help reduce the national debt by requiring that all profits over a 6 percent dividend be turned over to the Exchequer.

Chesterton's second proposal was that the government should replace the present overextended marketing set-up with local or regional systems. In place of huge marketing centers, such as Covent

Garden, London, each major city could be divided into several distribution centers. Every area would possess its own central market, supplied by nearby farms and tapped by small shops in the immediate vicinity. These regional distribution centers, managed jointly by suppliers and retailers, could eliminate the profiteering middleman.

Chesterton's proposal for far-reaching government legislation smacked of Fabianism, but he sincerely believed that the burdens of its enforcement could be eased if the acts were worded in a way that would be intelligible to the average citizen. A special Distributist Chancellor of the Exchequer, not being "a servant of the F.B.I., or the financiers, or the oil magnates, or any other system of wire-pulling or back-stair politics . . . could word his act in clear, simple language, having nothing to conceal, nothing to 'give away,' and no axe to grind."[25]

Although Chesterton's suggestions were intended to revolution-ize British society completely, his approach was distinctly gradual-ist. Voluntary accession to Distributism was essential for the lasting success of Chesterton's ideals. Men could not be coerced onto the countryside or into trade guilds because that would destroy the personal freedom that Distributists fought to protect. Similarly, a draconian confiscation of wealth and property would have the effect of undermining the love of ownership that Distributists were trying to revive. Unlike socialism or communism, Distributism was not a thing that could be "done" to people; it was an approach to life that could only be fulfilled through the approval and active participa-tion of people. To Chesterton, Distributist reform really meant moral change:

It must be done in the spirit of religion, of a revolution and of . . . a renunciation. They must want to do it just as they would want to drive invaders out of a country or to stop the plague.[26]

Distributism by fiat would destroy its ultimate purpose, which was to encourage a new society of independent, responsible freeholders. Such a state could only be achieved by free choice. Since the people would not attack the evil of monopoly capitalism until they had learned to hate it, Chesterton felt it essential that his followers initiate moral reform by showing modern civilization to be hateful. Thus the most practical line of action for Distributists was to educate the public about the moral evils of modern society.

Belloc's proposals for bringing about Distributism were contained, in their most complete form, in *An Essay on the Distribution of Property* (1936) and *The Crisis of Our Civilization* (1937). These books were both more detailed and more pessimistic about reform than *The Outline of Sanity*, for by 1936 Belloc had almost given up hope of ever turning the tide against capitalism, socialism, and big government. He disavowed any attempt to provide general schema for the restoration of freedom and property, because contemporary society had deteriorated beyond the point of salvage. The ultimate renewal of small ownership could never be achieved through any single reform scheme or administrative action by the state, but only through a change in mood: "It is too late to reinforce it by design . . . our effort must everywhere be particular, local, and in its origins, small."[27]

Chesterton agreed that Distributism could never be achieved through laws or the instruments of government; its success depended upon the will of the individual citizen. This explains why both Chesterton and Belloc remained vague about the political and economic steps needed to bring about Distributism. In a very practical sense, Distributism could only be accepted as a meaningful alternative if people were first made aware of the insidious diseases of capitalism and collectivism. The implementation of Distributism first required a revolution in values and ideas: political change would come after the requisite moral transformation.

Belloc's later writings on Distributism complemented Chesterton's social theories and can be taken as a further and perhaps final extension of what the Chesterbelloc meant by Distributism and the Distributist state. Less idealistic than Chesterton, Belloc claimed that the Distributists would only attempt to change the general tone of society and restore small property as a common feature of the state, not as a universal rule. The new social and economic arrangement would neither be perfect nor egalitarian, since that was impossible in a society which championed personal freedom. There would be some rich people, some comparatively poor and propertyless. Yet everyone would have a chance to have a share in the means of production, and the prevalence of private property and economic freedom would be the distinguishing mark of the society.

Belloc recognized that monopoly had become so pervasive that well-divided property had almost disappeared from English society. For this reason, he felt that it would be necessary to invoke the power of the state to aid the small man in regaining his freedom. In *An Essay on the Restoration of Property* (1936), Belloc proposed an elaborate plan for the reestablishment of a small independent peasantry and classes of craftsmen and merchants, the three socioeconomic groupings he felt necessary for the creation of a free society. An essential feature of his scheme was a system of differential taxation to be applied against chain stores, multiple shops, large-scale retail sales, and corporation advertising. The revenues from these taxes would be used to provide financial aid to small businesses. Belloc also suggested that the state might charter and legally protect cooperative credit institutions for small farmers, craftsmen, and merchants. Large-scale factory production necessary for certain commodities was to remain a part of the economic structure, but the small craftsman and entrepreneur would become a permanent fixture of the system, serving as a model for others to emulate:

His presence would be an object lesson in freedom and establishment, and . . . a hint to his neighbors to change their own condition . . . from one of wage slavery to one of independence.[28]

This same plan would also be used to help the small farmer. Progressive taxes were to be leveled against the sale of property so as to discourage large accumulations of land and augment the proliferation of small purchases.

It was also argued that the guild modeled along medieval lines could be the best safeguard for the small unit against monopoly. These would be self-governing, legally chartered units, each with an internal managerial hierarchy exercising authority over price-setting and controlling social order. Belloc explained that each guild was to serve as a protective agency for the private ownership of property, and, most importantly, the guilds would strive for the ultimate control over the means of production.

Belloc underscored the necessity of state intervention, because he was persuaded that a well-balanced system of property holding could not spring up by itself against the economic tendencies of the day. It had to be artificially induced, and, once restored, the system required constant sustenance lest it lapse back into capitalism. Just as unchecked parliamentary politics turned to plutocracy, so private property inevitably tended to capitalism in a free enterprise economy. Belloc claimed that he was chiefly concerned that the powers of the state be used to protect the middle classes (the "fly-wheel" of society, as he called them) against excessive property taxation. High taxation, which he claimed had been caused by usurious interest rates on war loans and social services, had effectively blocked the accumulation of small property, thus strangling the middle class and strengthening the sinews of monopoly and plutocracy. In *The Crisis of Civilization* (1937), Belloc seemed to suggest that it would require dictatorial power to save what he called "the middle class standard."[29]

More specifically, Belloc contended that the proper reform of English society necessitated the recovery of the general spirit of Catholicism. Since institutions were formed by the moral spirit which animated society, they were maintained only so long as men adhered to the spiritual impulse from whence the institutions arose. Believing that economic freedom in the past had grown out of the Catholic faith, Belloc maintained that Distributism could not remedy social ills until the world was converted to Catholicism. The guilds, the cooperative system, and the whole network of safeguards for property had been the fruit of a culture which had evolved out of Catholic doctrine:

We cannot build up a society synthetically, for it is an organic thing; we must see to it first that the vital principle is there from which the characters of the organism will develop.[30]

But Belloc did not insist that reform required a conversion to the Catholic Church. "Catholic culture," as he employed the term, was not meant to imply universality of belief, nor was it used to define a condition in which even the majority of citizens were Catholic. According to Belloc's definition, a nation or a civilization became

Catholic when its governing, economic, and social institutions were motivated by the Catholic spirit.

Unlike their Fabian adversaries, Chesterton and Belloc felt that Distributists could not indulge in the practice of charting out elaborate plans for a future ideal state. For this reason they steadfastly refused to outline a Wellsian-type plan for the perfect Distributist society. The particulars of that future would rest with the citizens who might actually be engaged in the construction of the new state. Like Belloc, Chesterton was an outspoken anti-utopian and did everything within reason to discourage his followers from partaking in the kind of systems-building that characterized their Fabian opponents. Not only did he warn of the totalitarian miseries that could be produced by the scientific machine state, as revealed in the London of 1984 (*The Napoleon of Notting Hill*), but he also demonstrated that utopian societies designed along medieval lines could be equally tyrannous. In many of his major novels (*The Napoleon of Notting Hill, The Ball and the Cross,* and *The Return of Don Quixote*), efforts to construct the perfect medieval state end in complete failure. Adam Wayne's own version of the ideal medieval state on Notting Hill became a stifling despotism, and to everyone's satisfaction the evil thing was destroyed by rebellious men demanding their freedom. In *The Ball and the Cross* (1910) the medieval theocracy created by the story's master villain, Professor Lucifer, developed into a nightmare with no freedom or diversity. What appeared to be a society of prearranged laws ended up being a dictatorship where discipline—living according to hard and fast laws—became more important than justice. Lucifer's garden asylum was a society of elites which legislated all thoughts and even beauty (a presage of Huxley's *Brave New World*), yet the reader quickly recognizes that this regulated life is unreal, because it does not tolerate imperfections. In order to achieve success, Lucifer had to run his society as a machine, oppressing individual freedom, imagination, and romance.

Chesterton generally distrusted large-scale social and political movements, since they tended towards corruption or, at best, promoted group dynamics at the expense of the individual. In *The Return of Don Quixote* (1927), one of Chesterton's most unequivocal denunciations of medievalism, the reader ultimately discovers that the League of the Lion, which sought to establish a medieval state, was simply a creature of the capitalists who manipulated both the movement and the state for their own selfish interests. The true hero of the story emerges in the person of a union official who, in opposition to the medieval league, pushes for a corporative-type arrangement which would give the workers ownership and control of the means of production.

The message seems clear: Chesterton, in the anarchist tradition, was suspicious of politics—particularly political movements—distrusted power, and detested all forms of social planning. He had an essentially organic vision of society. Man's customs and values were seen to have been shaped by the peculiar force of circumstances, and like the branches of a tree, they were the product of slow growth through the seasons of time. But nowhere was it stated in certain terms how man would develop. Since there were no laws of history, how could the intellectual make specific predictions about the future state? Hence G.K.C.'s reluctance to fill in the details of his outline of sanity—the Distributist state. Yet the basic Distributist axioms were always kept in the forefront of the League's crusade for sanity. They called for a change in spirit and outright rebellion against oppression. Such, at least, was the *modus operandi* and the key to success for Chesterton's fictional heroes. What was to emerge from the ashes of the totalitarian state would be decided by those who took the responsibility for making the revolution. As Distributists they at least would have developed a working philosophy of life which could serve as the foundation for making the proper choices as to how the new society might function.

Belloc's anti-utopian political views were more sharply articulated than Chesterton's. Long before G.K.C., Belloc had abandoned the belief that judicious reform was possible in a community controlled by a Parliament of plutocrats. He felt that economic changes for the benefit of the small man would only occur if political power were decentralized and rearranged in guild units organized according to natural economic classes and productive functions. In all likelihood the ultimate necessity of exercising sovereignty over the autonomous guild networks would require dictatorial power. Because monarchy had been a traditional part of England's governing process, Belloc believed that a monarch, aided by what he called the

"Councils of Real Interests" (representatives of the various independent guilds), could best provide the responsible authoritarian leadership necessary for the large modern state. Yet, unlike Maurras and the *Action Française*, Belloc never believed firmly in the political efficacy of the European royalty. Belloc only preached monarchism because he thought it might be the most convenient tool available for fulfilling the authoritarian role which degenerate modern society so desperately needed. What he really wanted was a dynasty of heroic strong men who could force society above the narrow pursuit of petty hedonism:

I have no doubt that monarchy is what is needed now in every European nation, and by the French most of all because they are the most vigorous; but I do not think that the setting up of an existing dynasty like that of Philip of Orleans would be of the least effect, and I very much doubt in this country whether the present reigning family could ever take on the function. What will save our society when it comes will be some new line of dynasties sprung from energetic individual men who shall seize power.[31]

Chesterton and Belloc were never completely clear about the details of Distributist political reform or about political structure within the future Distributist state, although they were willing to provide general suggestions for the implementation of their ideals. In part, their reluctance to set up more specific political outlines was due to the profound disillusionment with Parliament that each man had experienced in the years before the Great War. But most importantly, like anarchists, the Chesterbelloc never believed that Distributism could ever come about through political maneuvering. Politics was simply superstructure, a mere reflection of the moral underpinning of society. Their major task was directed towards modifying the values of British society, and they believed that this required a propagandist assault against the mistaken notions of prevailing public opinion, not political systems-building.

Nevertheless, throughout the 1920s and 1930s there was a steady stream of practical suggestions from numerous writers in *G.K.'s Weekly* as to how both the government and the League could help bring about the fundamental economic changes necessary for Distributism. Members of some of the more active League branches preached from street corners and in public parks so as to bring the Distributist message directly to the people. *G.K.'s Weekly* asked individual Distributists to avoid factory-made items by supporting handicraft industries. Directories of small privately owned businesses were drawn up by the League as guides for Distributist shoppers, who were urged to buy locally at small shops "in such a way as to make the shopkeeper more of a craftsman and less of a middleman, and the shop more of a workshop and less of an emporium."[32,33] In order to weaken the powers of finance and banking, Distributists were told to avoid the use of money. Special workshops on home craftsmanship and garden farming were organized by League branches in Glasgow, Liverpool, and Birmingham. The object was to teach Distributists the art of self-sufficiency in order to escape reliance on the money economy.

In November of 1931 the League began publication of a monthly newsletter entitled *The Distributist*. This two-penny paper was designed for circulation within the League and was to replace "The Distributist League" section in the *Weekly*, which was no longer able to provide enough space for items relating to branch activities. *The Distributist* was edited by C. O'Brien Donaghey, and the various League branches took turns publishing it. Leaguers hoped that their newsletter would provide the needed link between the major branches and isolated Distributists. For this purpose, the editor encouraged the open discussion of League policy and outlined, for permanent reference, important work being undertaken by the members.

The most significant and practicable Distributist reform proposal was an unemployment manifesto called "The Birmingham Scheme," which was drafted by the League's Birmingham branch in June 1928. This particular plan was updated periodically and more than 17,000 copies had been published by 1933. The Birmingham scheme was designed to eliminate the economic waste of the dole and to relieve industrial unemployment by reviving Britain's decaying agricultural economy. The Birmingham Distributists proposed that the state solve the food import problem and eliminate unemployment by relocating workers on the soil as farmers. The scheme called for the government to capitalize on money allocated to the dole by investing approximately 2,060 pounds (a figure somewhat above the actuarial figure of 1,733 pounds per family presently spent on relief) for the settlement of families on 25-acre holdings equipped for farming. It was carefully calculated (based on actual average farming costs in the Midland counties) that the 2,060 pounds could pay for the cost of purchasing a freehold (which would be mortgaged to the holder in 30 yearly repayments), the tools, livestock, and seeds needed to make a start in farming, and 15 months preliminary subsistence. The Distributists were certain that men would prefer farming to the dole and that even factory workers might opt for a chance to return to the soil if the government could only make it practical by creating both the means for purchasing freeholds and the necessary agricultural training programs.

The plan's main objective was the establishment of the Distributist ideal, a free peasantry which could sustain itself on the land and yet supply produce to the industrial sector by marketing its surplus. Additional proposals were included in the scheme for the cooperative selling of surplus produce and the local sharing of agricultural tools and machinery. All this could be accomplished, so the Distributists argued, by a minimum outlay above the cost of funding the dole. It would effectively assuage the ills of unemployment and the high cost of importing foodstuffs, as well as balance an aging, overblown industrial economy. The plan was well received in Catholic circles: Michael Derrick, writing in *Blackfriars*, saw it as strikingly similar to President Roosevelt's plan to encourage economically distressed families in rural areas to escape unemployment by becoming self-sufficient.[34]

In April 1930, the Distributist League placed a resolution before the Prime Minister urging the appointment of a Royal Commission to study the feasibility of implementing their proposals. Unfortunately, the government did not give any serious consideration to the Birmingham scheme. The Agricultural Marketing and Land Utilization Bills, introduced in 1930 and 1931 respectively, were far removed from Distributist principles. The Agricultural Marketing Act, designed by the Minister of Agriculture, Dr. Christopher Addison, and passed into law in 1931, provided for special control boards with powers to grade, sell, and set prices on farm products. Distributists attacked Addison's Bill as a draconian infringement on both marketing and farming practices, since the boards had the legal power to impose their solutions on dissenting minorities.

Addison's Land Utilization Bill, which sought to establish a Land Corporation for the encouragement of large-scale farming, was equally abhorrent to Chesterton's followers. Distributists were encouraged to see that the government was taking an interest in agriculture, but they were wholly opposed to plans for the proliferation of anything but smallhold farming. Entrepreneurial farming was opposed by Distributists on strictly moral principles. Yet, in a practical sense, they believed that large-scale agriculture would reduce production (since it was thought that smallhold intensive farming could yield more food per acre) as well as eliminate the need to return greater numbers of people to the agricultural profession. Thus large-scale farming would have the effect of perpetuating the unemployment crisis.

The Land Utilization Bill was emasculated beyond recognition by the House of Lords. Distributists were generally pleased with its fate; the section concerning large-scale experimental farming was knocked out and what was left of the Bill dealt primarily with the extension of smallholdings and agricultural training for the unemployed. But its modified provisions fell far short of what the Distributists had called for in the Birmingham scheme. Furthermore, the Act did not remain in operation very long, being suspended in 1931 on grounds of financial stringency.

In the final analysis, it cannot be said that the Distributists were in need of a program or that they lacked the resolve to carry their ideas into practice. *G.K.'s Weekly* and the League appear to have succeeded in their efforts to complete the definition of Distributism. This being the main objective, the next task was to persuade people to consider the Chesterbelloc alternative. If Chesterton and the League failed in the second mission, it was partly because the government would not listen to them.

CHAPTER VIII

The Influence of the Distributist Idea

Most writers have ignored the Distributist side of the Chesterbelloc.[1] This is unfortunate, for their social and political theories influenced a wide and significant section of the English-speaking world, from well-respected intellectuals and journalists to small shopkeepers and farmers. Distributism's most visible impact in Britain was on the back-to-the-land movements, all of which publicly voiced a desire to return to the kind of "ordinary human living" advocated by Chesterton and Belloc. The various Catholic land movements grew directly out of Distributism, and even the secular movements in England and America had clear ideological connections with its program.

The two largest and best-known of the Catholic back-to-the-land movements, the Catholic Land Federation and Marydown, were developed primarily as a means for solving the severe unemployment problem in Catholic communities. The leaders of the Catholic movements also believed that a return to the land would have the further effect of strengthening patriotism, religion, the freedom of the individual, and family life. Vincent Baker, author of a major land movement book, *The New Maryland* (1935), wrote that practical and working Catholic land colonies could both expose England to the "Truth of Catholicism" and stem the persistent drain of young people from the Church, which in Catholic parlance was called "leakage." By making the atmosphere "Catholic," Baker explained, the land movements could effectively fight unemployment and the influence of communism, and perhaps even convince England to return to its "ancient allegiance" within one or two generations.[2]

Baker's aspirations aptly reflected the atmosphere in which the land associations were launched. Plans for a Catholic back-to-the-land movement were first drawn up in Glasgow on April 26, 1929. The organization took the name "The Scottish Catholic Land Association," and on May 27, 1931, at Broadfield Farm, Symington, Lancashire, it established a training center for young men who wished to learn farming and settle on the land. The concept spread quickly, and by 1934 there were five additional associations in operation, all of which were blessed and officially encouraged by the Vatican.[3] These organizations, sharing the same general views and objectives, set up their own training programs, and each had a local bishop, or bishops, providing official patonage. The six Catholic land associations were initially united by a standing joint committee, which coordinated decision-making and kept the various groups in contact with each other. In 1934 they joined together in a loosely knit association called the Catholic Land Federation, under the chairmanship of Reverend Monseignor Dey, with Belloc's son-in-law, Reginald Jebb, as secretary. Two journals were inaugurated to serve as newsletters and propaganda organs for the movement. *Land for the People*, with the Reverend John McQuillan, D.D., as its editor, was the official publication of the Scottish Association, while the *Cross and the Plough*, edited by Harold Robbins, was the designated mouthpiece of the English and Welsh Catholic Land Association.

The essential objective of the Catholic Land Federation was to set up small "mixed" farms with their allied secondary trades (handicraft industries), so as to create completely self-sufficient Catholic rural communities which would serve as the springboard for the emergence of an independent peasantry.[4] Leaders of these movements insisted that the settlements were to be based on the principles of the Encyclicals *De Rerum Novarum* and *Quadragesimo Anno*, and special emphasis was placed on the necessity of reviving ownership in private property. In order to instruct the Catholic urban proletariat on the techniques of farming, special educational centers were developed, with three-year courses in practical and theoretical farming. This was meant to prepare Catholic families for the transformation to rural living. Spiritual exercise was also an important part of the trainee's program. Each day began with a Mass, and regular lectures on such topics as theology, ethics, and agricultural science were provided by the farm staff and special guest speakers.

The other major land movement under Catholic auspices was the Marydown Farming Association. This was the creation of T.W.C. Curd, editor of *Towards*. Some of its most active supporters were long-time Distributists, such as G.C. Heseltine, W.J. Blyton, and Bryan Keating, all of whom sat on the provisional committee. Marydown, which Curd described as an extension of the work being done by the Catholic Land Association, was conceived as an experiment to save the Catholic ideal of the home. Its overall philosophy of settlement was the same as the other Catholic land movements, though Marydown differed in organization. Curd's association was based in Elstead, Surrey, on a 200-acre cooperative settlement worked by Catholic families already experienced in farming. Unlike the other six associations, which provided training programs for the uninitiated and were financed by voluntary contributions, Marydown attracted professional farmers and was organized as a holding company. The settlement got its start through a generous land grant by Colonel G. Fitzgerald and subsequently supported itself by issuing interest-bearing stock (20,000 shares were circulated at 1 pound each) and by the sale of surplus produce. Heseltine wrote that the Catholic public responded enthusiastically to the new enterprise: there was a long waiting list of buyers just ten weeks after the company was registered, as Catholics from all over the world applied for membership.[5]

In addition to the land settlement schemes, Catholics also set up special agricultural training facilities for young people who lived in urban centers. The main objective of these programs was to stanch delinquency and "leakage" from the Church by training the idle young for employment on Catholic farms. Special hostels were established, along lines developed by the Y.M.C.A., where boys went through a rigorous "disciplining and reconditioning" program. After three months of moral and technical instruction, the young recruits were sent to Catholic farms where they were given additional training, room and board, and paid a small wage for agricultural work. A typical training program was the South of England Land Association's Old Brown's Farm in Chartridge, near Chesham, Bucks. Opened in March 1932 the farm consisted of some 150 acres. The association's program was open to single men drawn from all walks of life but united in one common aim: "the building of a free Catholic peasantry." The trainees were given a three-year course in both practical and theoretical farming. After having completed this stage of training, the men were to set up their own small family farms in self-sufficient communities consisting of land-workers and craftsmen. These training programs were generally successful, and a few won long-term financial support and encouragement from the Ministry of Labour until the outbreak of World War II.

All the Catholic back-to-the-land movements were initially successful. Both Marydown and Dey's association had long waiting lists of family men who wanted to be admitted to their programs. The movements were also given considerable encouragement by the Distributist League, *G.K.'s Weekly*, and much of the Catholic community. Even John Maynard Keynes, who considered it a move in the right direction for mitigating unemployment, urged the government to provide some type of financial support to the land experiments.[6] Father McNabb was its most outspoken and enthusiastic backer, however, calling the land movements the most essential form of a "Catholic Action": it was a work on behalf of the home and family—that "tiny, divinely-instituted, cooperative society"—and "any work on behalf of *that* is a divine work."[7] Chesterton, F.N. Blundell, Heseltine, W.J. Blyton, and H.J. Massingham consistently lent their journalistic support, while *The Month*, the *Dublin Review*, *Blackfriars*, and *The Tablet* were among the major journals which gave space and editorial support to the back-to-the-land experiments.

Generally speaking, Distributist aims were similar to those of the Catholic Land Associations and Marydown, except, as W.R. Titterton pointed out, that the League never felt it necessary for all members of agricultural colonies to be of the same faith. The League included many non-Catholics on its membership rolls, whereas both the Catholic Land Federation and Marydown were open to

Catholics only. Distributists, recognizing a need for market farming, also objected to the Catholic back-to-the-land movement's overemphasis on subsistence agriculture and its renunciation of machinery.

Meanwhile, the number of Englishmen desiring to take up smallhold farming had been steadily swelling throughout the inter-war years. In July 1930, for example, the Minister of Agriculture claimed that since 1926 there had been more than 14,000 applicants for smallholdings, and, of this number, the government had fulfilled only 3,242 requests. Yet these figures included only those people who actually attempted to procure land and, as such, was no indication of the potential demand for smallhold farming. In April 1934 the Ministry of Agriculture appointed a team of special investigators to examine the economic problems of four depressed areas: Cumberland, Durham, South Wales, and Scotland. Their report appeared in a white paper released in November of that year. All the commissioners made reference to a pervasive desire amongst people to get back to the land and recommended more government funds for the proper expansion of agriculture.

Chesterton and the Distributists were probably right in their belief that there was a high demand for smallholding in Britain, and that a lack of government initiative and capital discouraged people from even considering this occupation as an alternative to industrial employment. Sufficient data demonstrating the viability of smallhold agriculture also seemed to exist. A special study on East Anglian farming, undertaken by Cambridge University in 1934, revealed that the large-scale mechanized farms, which employed little labor, were having serious financial problems, whereas the smallhold farmers, using two or three times as much labor, had been reasonably successful. A.W.M. Kitchner, writing in the *Economic Journal* of December 1934, reported that the Cambridge study indicated that, compared to large-scale farming, the small farm had a greater resistance to low prices, produced twice the value of produce per acre and provided work for twice as many men per acre. All of this yielded an 80 per cent increase in what was called "social output." Moreover, from 1908 through 1926, when the government had subsidized smallholdings, 73 per cent of the 26,000 men who secured holdings had become successful farmers.[8] Yet the government did not provide any substantive support to the Catholic back-to-the-land movements, and the various associations, after getting off to an encouraging start, lapsed into failure.

Many non-Catholic land movements in Britain were also inspired by Distributist ideas. This can be seen particularly in the career of Montague Fordham, the founder of the Land Club Union, which later became the Rural Reconstruction Association. Once described as "the most genuine of the Distributists,"[9] Fordham developed links with Chesterbelloc ideas through contacts with social credit, Father McNabb, and A.J. Penty. Fordham had long-established ties to agriculture. He was raised as a youth in the countryside and after World War I served as an adviser to the Society of Friends' mission to revive agriculture in East Prussia. *The Rebuilding of Rural England* (1924), the bible of the Rural Reconstruction Association and a book of wide-ranging influence on governmental agricultural policy, contained the essence of Fordham's ideas about land reform. Basically, Fordham hoped to combine Penty's guild ideas with social credit as a basis for the reconstruction of agricultural life in Britain. He proposed to rehabilitate the economic base of rural England by using state capital (given interest-free to all workers) to bring the land into full cultivation and by returning as many workers as possible to the soil. All of this was to be carried out by a national agricultural guild. This guild would also have the power to negotiate and guarantee a national system of just prices. Like McNabb and Penty, Fordham believed that consumer prices could be reduced considerably through sound guild management and by a more efficient system of agricultural distribution, which, by passing the middlemen, could deliver goods directly from producer to consumer.

The basic conduit through which all questions concerning distribution, credit, and prices would be arranged, was what Fordham called the "land council." This body was to mitigate the dangers of bureaucracy inherent in the national guild. Fordham wanted the land council to be a democratic, representative organization consisting of producers and consumers on the parish level, a unit of organization small enough to appreciate local needs. The council would serve as a board of control (with total responsibility for welfare, education, and the development of social life) and own the parish land. Those who worked the soil would be, in effect, tenants of the parish council. Fordham hoped that the property-owning councils would be small enough to give all its members the spirit of independence and simple personal dignity that was a hallmark of the medieval guilds. It was intended that these parish organizations would elect a federation of salaried delegates to serve on the national guild—a chamber of agriculture—which could deal directly with the state. The large guild, representing all the county federations, would have links as weak as possible with its affiliated councils so as to insure local initiative and freedom. Fordham believed that this guild arrangement could prevent the large accumulation of capital in the hands of a few wealthy individuals or corporations and thereby eliminate the major source of poverty and servitude.

Fordham's proposals for reviving agriculture were generally well-received by Distributist circles, and even the *Cross and the Plough* admitted that the Rural Reconstruction Association's manifesto could stand as Catholic Land Association propaganda. The editor of that journal voiced a few minor criticisms of Fordham's program—notably his overemphasis on prices and controls at the expense of the actual ownership of property. The Rural Reconstruction Association also claimed credit for inspiring several of the government's marketing schemes for agriculture—schemes opposed by the Catholic Land Association, however, out of its belief that they brought more power to government bureaucracy and curbed the independence of small farmers by encouraging the commercialization of agriculture.[10]

Most other land reform programs influenced by Distributist ideas were not as successful as that of the Rural Reconstruction Association. One such program was advanced by the Empire Development and Settlement Research Committee under the chairmanship of Henry Page Croft, M.P. This organization lobbied the government to provide funds for the British Empire Settlement Association, which hoped to train men in Britain for self-sufficient farming and then settle them in Canada and Australia.

Somewhat more successful, however, was the National Home-crofts Association established by J.W. Scott, a professor at University College of South Wales and Monmouthshire, Cardiff. Like the Distributists, who were interested in the economics of small groups, Scott believed that the revival of self-sufficient, mixed farming communities was one way to combat urban unemployment. With the aid of the *Spectator*, Scott was able to buy a tract of land near Cheltenham in 1926. Ten families were settled there in houses built by the National Homecrofts Association, a public utility society registered at Cardiff. Each family was given one-third acre of land for rearing poultry, animals, vegetables, and fruit. The second phase of Scott's experiment was to bring unemployed men into the scheme to be trained in farming and handicrafts so as to supplement their dole. By 1934 the Cheltenham farm had developed its own miniature market, where each crofter sold his surplus and purchased goods with a special "domestic currency" consisting of paper units earned by doing work on the commune. Scott's Homecroft Association hoped to break the vicious cycle in which industry destroyed its own market by creating a productive commune that could produce more buyers. This would be accomplished, argued Scott, not by unemployment largesse or faked "purchasing power" (referring to social credit) but by giving the worker an opportunity to become self-providing.[11]

The Homecroft experiment was expensive. The necessary funds were voluntarily subscribed, but little was given by the better-known charities. *G.K.'s Weekly*, however, gave the scheme a great deal of publicity from 1936 through 1937. Much of the preparatory work (building the houses, clearing the land, etc.) was done voluntarily by Scott's students during vacations. Scott hoped to develop two additional schemes involving 500 men each with 15 to 25 acres per farm. However, this required considerable sums of money which were never forthcoming.

A highly successful experiment in self-sufficiency along Distributist lines and very similar to those started by Scott, was Dartington Hall, Devonshire, founded by Leonard and Dorothy Elmhirst in 1925. The original purpose of Dartington Hall was to reestablish the ethos of the medieval manor. The Elmhirsts wanted to renew the countryside by creating worthwhile conditions of work and pay, thereby halting the drift of people to the cities. Dartington Hall became a well-established commercial undertaking with an excellent boarding school for the liberal arts, a training program in forestry, an extensive farm, and highly-skilled handicraft industries.[12]

Other agricultural-handicraft experiments along Distributist lines were Peter Scott's Brynmawr, South Wales, and the Land Settlement Association of John Hoyland. Like Gill and Penty, Peter Scott recognized the need for workers to control their productive environment and set out to build a cooperative commune in Brynmawr, at that time a derelict township in South Wales. The construction of a new community was begun in 1929, centering around a bootmaking and furniture firm. Scott was able to win substantial aid from both government and private sources, because his scheme could provide work and job skills for unemployed miners. As Brynmawr expanded, several affiliated experiments emphasizing self-reliant farming and handicraft production were begun at UpHolland (near Wigan); Parbold Hall, Billinge, Pemberton; and Ashfield House, Standish. John Hoyland was inspired by Brynmawr. Feeling that the time was ripe to "proletarianize Christianity," Hoyland founded the Land Settlement Association. The purpose of this body was to settle cooperative groups of 30 men on five-acre farms.[13]

A general back-to-the-land movement aiming to establish an independent peasantry, contrary to what its backers contended, could never have been a cure-all for Britain's unemployment problems. Nor could it have appealed to a large enough section of the nation's urban population, the bulk of which had no inclination whatever to take up agricultural employment. Although the land movements started out with considerable popular support, as employment increased by the middle of the 1930s, interest in returning to the land diminished rapidly. By late 1935, the editors of *The Tablet*, an influential Catholic journal which had vigorously supported the back-to-the-land ventures, announced that a thorough investigation of British agriculture had convinced them that a great multiplication of smallholdings would have no appreciable effect on unemployment and, when recklessly employed, could even bring on more serious troubles.[14] The final remark seems to have referred to difficulties arising from the conduct of certain eccentrics involved in the Catholic land movement. Gill's friend, Donald Attwater, who was closely involved with the various land associations, explained that a plethora of land colonies manned by bearded religious cranks—demonstrating utter contempt for Protestants, city life, radios, and machinery, and who reaped with a hook—had fallen under the influence of certain freakish Distributists and, as such, did much to discredit the land movement in the public eye. Attwater felt that the land associations should have been less dogmatic, have opened their membership to all groups regardless of religion, and have avoided the narrow land colonizing which only served to cut Catholicism off from the agricultural traditions of those already in the countryside.[15]

It was indeed true that the backward-looking temper of certain individuals associated with the land experiments caused considerable problems for the movement as a whole. These same zealots brought incalculable hardships to the Distributist League as well. A long-time Leaguer, J.Desmond Glesson, told Maisie Ward that there was a hard-core of unstable types who drifted quite naturally into the Distributist movement. These particular elements, Glesson explained, were primarily responsible for setting up the ill-prepared and crankish land colonies that foundered in failure, all of which reflected badly on the Distributist League:

There was a certain kind of person who drifted to Distributist meetings; possibly because he had outstayed his welcome elsewhere. Knowing little enough of the matter, he was instantly anxious that something should be done. He was very impatient of any talk, and since there was a good deal of talk at the Devereux, he was very impatient with Distributists. 'Talk' to him was a mere form of condemnation. But there was something else about this type which was even more interesting. He had always just left a job; he never seemed to be in a job. And if you talked to him you would discover that this was the way he had drifted along all his life: he was always getting work and always losing it.

Continuing in the same vein, Glesson wrote that:

It was this type which was always ready to set out on some new agricultural adventure and when fully embarked, to show the same loose qualities that he had shown in the earlier phases of his life. What happened was that on two or three occasions a band, not necessarily of Distributists, but rather of people who had been attending Distributist meetings went off to form Land Settlements in different parts of the country. And when they set out, the only sure thing about them was that they would shortly be back in town. They were not the sort to dig themselves in; it was not land work so much that distressed them as work. They had not the knowledge for the tough task they had undertaken and they lacked application even had they the knowledge. . . . Worse still, some of the settlers were religious folk and instead of starting-in on the work of the settlement, they must needs create a diversion by attempting to set up chapels and what-not and generally show a much greater interest in devotion than in digging. Needless to say none of these settlements settled anything, but the quality of this type of settler.[16]

One of the Catholic Land Federation's leading publicists, Harold Robbins, editor of the *Cross and the Plough*, brought much un-needed public attention to the somewhat controversial ideology of the land programs. Robbins, like McNabb and Penty, publicly championed a kind of medieval utopianism and was an unqualified machine hater. The *Cross and the Plough* insisted upon the need for completely self-sufficient and exclusively Catholic land colonies, and opposed the introduction of any mechanization whatsoever in agriculture on the ground that they would reduce the need for manpower in primary production, thereby weakening the rural family: " . . . machines were in fact introduced to enable capitalists to make more and easier money."[17]

Another radical Distributist, Father H.E.G. Rope (a regular contributor to the *Cross and the Plough*), citing the *Protocols of the Learned Elders of Zion*, wrote that machinery and modern industrialism were part of a "Judeo-Masonic plot" to throw Christians into the ranks of the proletariat by forcing them off the land.[18,19] The radical fringe Distributists were frequently taken to task for their rigid medievalism by other Catholic publicists. Undaunted, they fought back with ever increasing vigor, always insisting that they were following closely the principles of St. Thomas Aquinas and the Doctors of the Church, who had advocated a strictly agricultural society. Particularly sensitive to criticism, the beleaguered radicals would sometimes lash out by casting such deprecatory epithets as Thomistic "deviationists" and "sociological Molinists" at their co-religionist adversaries.[20]

While the ill-repute of table-thumping cranks crippled the land associations, it was their inability to procure governmental and Church financial support that ultimately caused their demise.[21] The most serious blow came in November 1935 when the Archbishop of Birmingham informed Harold Robbins that the Catholic hierarchy had decided not to provide official sanction to the Catholic Land Association. The Church felt that it could ill afford to raise money for the land experiments, which it did not think could remedy unemployment, when funds were badly needed for the construction of new schools, churches, and housing.

Representatives of the Catholic Land Federation also petitioned Cabinet ministers for governmental financial aid, but funding was never forthcoming. Agricultural trainees were unable to draw unemployment insurance because the government had decided that farm work was uninsurable and that land settlement, the ultimate objective of the Catholic associations, would serve to remove the laborer from potential industrial employment. The North of England Catholic Land Association, an amalgamation of the Manchester and Liverpool associations, was the only Catholic back-to-the-land unit able to continue existence after 1937. In that year, after much tedious petitioning and hard work, an agreement was finally concluded to enable trainees to draw funds through the Unemployment Assistance Board. The land association was also able to win financial support from the Land Settlement Association (a body created by the government to encourage resettlement of the unemployed in farming), but only after making sizeable policy and program revisions. A special training center was established according to L.S.A. guidelines, and the North of England Catholic Land Association continued to operate until 1942.

While Distributism provided the initial stimulus and much of the ideological energy for the various land movements, these experiments proved to be ephemeral. Of longer-lasting importance was the influence of Chesterbellocian ideas on the general political temper of Catholic journalism. In particular, Belloc's religious polemics served to break down the defensive mentality of British Catholics. Following Belloc's lead, Catholic writers became increasingly more vocal and willing to assume controversial positions on the major political issues of the day. This point was aptly expressed by G.M. Turnell: "The fact that Catholicism was suddenly championed by two writers (Chesterton and Belloc) whose names were known all over England and whose works were on every stall freed the uneducated and half-educated Catholic from his 'inferiority complex'. . . ."[22] The unique Chesterbelloc polemical style and various aspects of their socio-political theories can be recognized clearly in the works of such well-known Catholic writers as Christopher Dawson, Douglas Woodruff, J.B. Morton, Ronald Knox, and Edward Quinn. In addition, Chesterton and Belloc, along with the Distributist League, introduced Catholic social and economic principles to certain elements of the British public which hitherto had been completely unacquainted with Catholic teachings.

Blackfriars remained the most stouthearted proponent of Distributism, and many of the Chesterbelloc circle (Gill, McNabb, Pepler, *et al.*) wrote for the journal on a fairly regular basis. Writing in *Blackfriars*, Michael Derrick saw Distributism as "applied Thomism" and the only definite and constructive Catholic social policy in England.[23] *The Tablet*, *The Month*, and the *Dublin Review* also appeared to approach social and political issues from an essentially Distributist position. In October 1943, for example, *The Tablet* proclaimed that "Government by elected chambers can only be a healthy and good form of Government when it rests not on proletariats, but on responsible electorates consisting of independent and property owning individuals." An Anglican publication, *The Church Times*, devoted its lead article on January 4, 1929, to a critical analysis of the three major political parties and concluded that Distributism as preached by "Chester-Belloc" offered the only real solution to Britain's economic problems. On March 21, 1930, the same publication further clarified its political position:

We entirely agree with Mr. Chesterton's Distributist League, that security and stability of the democratic State depend on the ownership and control of property. 'Back to the Land' is a practical policy, calculated . . . to reduce the gravity of the coal problem, the cotton problem, and the problem of unemployment.[24]

Of special interest was the influence of Distributist ideas on the League of the Kingdom of God (L.K.G.), an organization formed in 1923 by various dissatisfied elements within the Church Socialist League. Most of the members of the L.K.G. were Anglo-Catholics. Opposed to the Church Socialist League's drift towards collectivism, they were highly suspicious of plutocracy and recognized the necessity of applying Catholic theology to social and political reform. Although the L.K.G. never aligned itself to any political party, it tried to pressure the Anglican Church into assuming a more active role in the social and political issues of the day.

The leading figures in the L.K.G. (P.E.T. Widdrington, Slesser, Penty, and Reckitt) published a collection of essays in 1922 entitled *Return of Christendom*, intended to lay a foundation for the construction of a Catholic sociology by utilizing Distributist and social credit theories. Its authors formed the nucleus of what was called the "Christendom" group, which became the moving force behind the L.K.G. They shared a common attitude on the necessity to infuse Catholicism with contemporary social ideas. One well-known member of the group, N.E. Egerton Swann, claimed that the three most important ideas behind Christendom's efforts to construct a Catholic sociology were distributed property, the just price, and a guild system for industry.[25]

Beginning in 1926, the L.K.G. published a quarterly paper on League views in a special section of *The Commonwealth*, the official organ of the Christian Social Movement. As its influence and membership expanded, the League began publishing its own journal, *Christendom*. Initially under the editorship of Reckitt, Ruth Kenyon, W.A. Dermant, and Widdrington, *Christendom* appeared as a monthly in 1931 and was published on a regular basis until the end of 1950.

The L.K.G.'s greatest importance lay in its influence on the Anglo-Catholic Summer Schools in Sociology. The School first met at Oxford in 1925 and was organized by the Anglo-Catholic Congress Committee jointly with the Fellowship of Catholic Priests and the L.K.G. However, from the beginning, the Christendom group managed to dominate the Summer Schools. The high point of Distributist influence in Christendom circles occurred in 1927. In that year the Anglo-Catholic Summer School, under the sway of L.K.G. intellectuals, allied itself with the Distributist League. Consequently, the syllabus and study circle discussions of the 1927 Summer School drew heavily upon the ideas of Chesterton and Belloc. The Christendom group and their journal also gave much support to land settlement schemes, especially those forwarded by Fordham's association, and they were instrumental in getting the Fourteenth Annual Summer School (1938) to concentrate its efforts on rural problems. The School essentially followed Fordham's thinking on rural reconstruction, but it rejected the idea of creating a peasant proprietorship on the continental model as impractical. Still, on general questions concerning collectivism and private property, the Christendom group always supported the Distributist approach.[26]

The influence of Distributist thinking can even be discerned in the ideas of Major Douglas and the social credit movement. Although Chesterton and Belloc disassociated themselves from Douglas' theory, a good many men, including not only Reckitt (who kept a foot in both camps) but also such writers as Orage, Philip Mairet, Christopher Hollis, Montague Fordham, Geoffrey Davies, Eric Gill, and Father F. H. Drinkwater, shifted in and out of both Distributist and social credit circles. Both movements displayed a contempt for finance, parliamentary politics, bureaucracy of all sorts, and industrialism, and both made rather exaggerated claims about Jews and international conspiracies. Much of this can be seen in Orage's the *New English Weekly*, which was established in 1932 to popularize social credit theory. Belloc helped Orage get this venture started and frequently wrote for the paper. Like the papers of Chesterton and Belloc, the *New English Weekly* attacked internationalism, was prepared to link communism with international finance, and also championed Mussolini for a time. Orage's paper could also be abrasively anti-Semitic. Social crediters and Distributists frequently sat on the same side of the fence concerning social and political issues, and they also tended to recognize the importance of similar things, namely guilds, arts and crafts, the Middle Ages, and Catholic social philosophy.[27]

The Chesterbelloc social philosophy also had influence on an international scale. In her biography of Chesterton, Maisie Ward has listed numerous movements in the United States, Canada, Australia, New Zealand, South Africa, and even Ceylon that were directly inspired by Distributism. In the United States, Chesterbelloc principles were best represented by the Pulitzer prizewinner, Herbert Agar, a regular contributor to *Commonweal* (a proponent of Distributist social ideas) and editor of *Free America*, a journal which claimed to be a mouthpiece for American Distributism. Catholic Social movements and several secular agricultural organizations in Australia and Canada also claimed to have direct connections with Distributist philosophy.

The history of *The American Review* (1933-1937), which was formerly known as *The Bookman*, deserves special mention as a product of Chesterbellocian influence. Many of the contributors to this American publication were British Distributists (Penty, Harold Robbins, Gregory Macdonald, Chesterton, Belloc, Douglas Jerrold, *et al.*). The journal was founded in April of 1933 for the purpose of popularizing the ideas of the so-called Southern Agrarians (a group who claimed to be American Distributists) and those of Irving Babbitt and Paul Elmer More. Its editors announced that they would draw primarily on the philosophy of Chesterton and Belloc, and, to a lesser extent, on the writings of T.S. Eliot, Charles Maurras, Leon Daudet, Wyndham Lewis, and Christopher Dawson. As a journal of politics, literature, and economics responding to "the widespread feeling that the forces and principles which have produced the modern chaos are incapable of producing any solution" without returning to "fundamental and tested principles," *The American Review* was to be a forum for the "Radicals of the Right" or "Revolutionary Conservatives."[28] The paper's strong links to basic Distributist philosophy were very clear at the end of its first full year of publication. The editor, Seward Collins, announced its central doctrine to be:

. . . the necessity of restoring small and widely held property (to restore liberty to our society) . . . the urgency of setting the power of the people through its government above the power of the plutocratic regime which has brought us to chaos and to the threat of the orderly but servile refuge of collectivism.[29]

In the same issue Mr. Collins informed the readers that his politics were essentially "fascist," which he defined as a force that seeks to revive "monarchy, property, the guilds, the security of the family and the peasantry, and the ancient ways of European life."[30] Throughout its years of publication, *The American Review* defended Mussolini and praised the European experiments in corporatism, which it considered essentially Distributist in principle.

By the 1930s the Distributist circle had come to include several younger writers in Britain who were active as spokesmen for conservative social philosophy, among them Douglas Jerrold, Arnold Lunn, and Christopher Hollis. These three, along with Gregory Macdonald, also upheld essentially Bellocian views on matters of international relations. As with the early Distributist circle, Jerrold, Lunn, and Hollis shared a common distaste for Protestantism, liberalism, collectivism, monopoly capitalism, and the Enlightenment philosophical tradition. Echoing the views of Ruskin, whom he thought essentially Catholic in belief, Arnold Lunn, himself a Roman Catholic convert, castigated Renaissance humanism as misjudging man's character and for its hostility to the more sublime forces of the supernatural. The Renaissance was a rebirth of "pagan pride," explained Lunn, the pride of the humanist in conflict with the humility of the Christian:

Something very beautiful passed out of the world at the Renaissance, the beauty which was not the monopoly of a class or of a clique, but which found expression in the common things of common men, in the peasant's hut no less than in the palace, in the carving of a table for the poor man's house no less than in the carving of a statue for the rich man's hall.[31]

These writers were also convinced of the intrinsic sinfulness of man and saw the necessity of authoritarian moral and political standards in a modern world of ethical chaos. As a student at Oxford, for example, Christopher Hollis felt the need for some kind of religion, not as a means for assuring everlasting beatitude, but as a vehicle for establishing a disciplined pattern for secular life. Hollis explained that it was only natural for him to pass from *The Servile State* to Belloc's *Europe and the Faith* and "thus to challenge the prevailing Platonic agnosticism of the Dons."[32] The following was Douglas Jerrold's impressions of his student years at preWar Oxford:

The odd thing, looking back, was the complete lack of any interest in practical fundamentals. . . . The system of finance capitalism was never challenged by the Socialists, who merely wanted to get control of what they regarded as an efficient machine. War was regarded as a political possibility due to human reason, and to nothing else in the world. And by human reason was meant nothing more abstruse than the absence of a sufficiency of middle class Liberal politicians to ensure a perpetual progress. It is not the absence of wisdom but the absence of wholehearted speculative folly which surprises me. The absence not of moral virtue, but of original sin.[33]

An additional dimension to the ideas of this later circle of writers was their almost pathological hatred of the Soviet Union and communism. Belloc had demonstrated similar feelings after the 1920s. The Soviet Union rapidly displaced the hated Prussia as the chief source of Belloc's disquietude in matters relating to international affairs.

Other factors which served to hold Lunn, Jerrold, and Hollis together as a group were their militant Catholicism, a pugnacious approach to journalism, and a complete acceptance of the Chester-belloc socio-political critique. Writing in *The Month* (September 1932), Stanley B. James (another convert to Catholicism) praised Lunn's vigorous mode of controversy and declared him to be the "heir to the redoubtable Chester-belloc."[34] Though the Dons at Oxford were upset by Belloc's historical theories and warned their students to avoid his writings, Hollis claimed that he nevertheless "fell victim to the theories of 'Chesterbelloc,' to Belloc's thesis of the Catholic Church as Europe's creative force and of the coming of the Servile State, to Chesterton's proclamation of 'God's scorn for all men governing,' to his rhetorical verse and the vision of the Distributist society in which all men of small property bade defiance to the overweening claims alike of capitalists and Government officials."[35]

Of the three men, Douglas Jerrold was both the most radical and the most vocal proponent of Chesterbellocian social and political ideas. Fundamental to his politics was the Bellocian assumption that capitalism had destroyed monarchial absolutism in the Revolution of 1688 and that plutocrats had subsequently restructured the governing institutions of Britain to serve their own special interests. The Glorious Revolution, which Jerrold described as the victory of property over authority, had also unleashed the spiritual affliction which was responsible for the ennui of contemporary society and the Englishman's profound sense of psychological helplessness. In Jerrold's mind, the one thing that typified the listless inter-war mood—"its pathetic frivolous courage, its complete irrationality, its devastating divorce from every tradition of our race"—was the passing of the traditional caricature of "John Bull" for Stube's "Little Man," immortalized in the pages of the *Daily Express*. "John Bull is dead," Jerrold declared, and the popular press was correct in substituting for him, not the muscular, independent farmer or artisan, "but a poor, little, grinning Cockney clerk, fitting representative of a propertyless suburbanized army of taxpayers, caught in the wheel of a hopelessly disorganized world which he refuses either to accept or reject."[36] Much of this Jerrold had absorbed from Belloc, whose attack on the "Party System," he contended, had an impact within a certain sphere of English politics equivalent to the furor administered by Luther when he nailed the "Ninety-Five Theses" to the door of Wittenberg Cathedral. As Jerrold saw it, the psychological repercussion of Belloc's revelations was that:

Men no longer blamed their political opponents for the evil of the times: they began to blame the politicians. In so doing they were blaming themselves and thus acquiring a healthy doubt, by now intuitive throughout the Western world, of their own natural wisdom and virtue, which their fathers and grandfathers had been taught to regard as axiomatic.[37]

Belloc taught Jerrold and his friends the importance of money in public life and the necessity of probing beneath the surface of politics into that murky realm of plutocrats and wire-pullers from which parliamentary government was supposed to have sprung.

In 1931, Belloc, Alan Herbert, T.S. Eliot, Roy Campbell, and Wyndham Lewis prevailed upon Jerrold to undertake the editorship of *The English Review*. As editor from 1931 to 1936, he attempted to redefine Tory conservatism along essentially Distributist lines. Jerrold explained to the readers that his "New Conservatism" was opposed to the sham politics of Baldwin's Party (which, like Labour, was drifting perilously towards the abyss of communism), did not stand for high profits, big business, low wages, and the protection of vested interests and class privileges, but for the defense of individual liberty, the need for a redistribution of property and the protection of the small against the large property owner. Despairing of any meaningful reform through Parliament, Jerrold concluded by 1933 that Britain's problems must ultimately be cured through the construction of what he called the "Authoritarian" or "Ethical State." This was a revolutionary conservative expedient in which the parliamentary system was to be replaced by an Anglo-Saxon version of self-government in the various agricultural, craft, and service professions, all of which would be united through a strong central government under a chief executive (hopefully a monarch) who would act for the nation as a whole. This scheme was to be based upon a corporate-type governmental system with functional, not regional, representation. The "Ethical State" was to provide the workingman with true equality and political status and yet insure industry its liberty with "the added dignity of autonomous responsibility."[38] Jerrold claimed that such a program drew upon the tradition of Chesterton and Belloc. He believed that this particular scheme could provide the necessary means for reconciling the two most fundamental passions of the English people: "The passion for Liberty and passion for Order—the desire for Status and the desire for Freedom."[39]

Persistently at odds with the fecklessness of the majority of the Conservative Party, Jerrold and several of his right-wing colleagues, notably Sir Charles Petrie, Leo Amery, and Sir Robert Horne, organized a Tory splinter group known as the Independent Conservatives and ran Lord Lloyd on a corporatist platform against Stanley Baldwin in the General Election of 1935. This move was undertaken primarily because Jerrold and his friends were afraid that Baldwin was moving the Conservative Party towards socialism during a time when, as they saw it, the communists were making fearful headway in their efforts to take over the world. Jerrold wrote that he had even anticipated a bloody fight to the end with the godless communists, a struggle which would necessarily have destroyed parliamentary government for a dictatorship either of the right or left.

*   *   *

There was an obvious rightist bent to the ideas of the Chesterbelloc, which tended to give a rather reactionary quality to the Distributist movement. Indeed, their emphasis on the efficacy of the authoritarian corporatist state as well as their strong condemnation of liberalism and parliamentary government, disposed the Distributist circle to an acceptance of fascism. In particular, Douglas Jerrold and A.J. Penty were generally known as fascist fellow travellers, and various members of the League, believing Sir Oswald Mosley's program to be essentially Distributist, joined the British Union of Fascists.[40]

Several Catholic writers have chastised the Distributist movement for its unrealistic medievalism and extremist politics. But even more serious, it appears, was the feeling that Distributism drew gifted Catholic writers into phantasmal social projects, thereby weakening the more practical reforming efforts of the Social Catholic movement. J.M. Cleary, in an officially sanctioned study of the Catholic Social Guild published in 1960, considered Distributism to have been "a blind alley into which went many young and fervent Catholics of the thirties."[41] This seems to be the general opinion of those who have written on the Social Catholic movement.[42] In addition, many Chestertonian scholars have also considered G.K.'s interest in Distributism to have been an utter waste of talent.

The Catholic Social Guild (C.S.G.), the most important agency of the Social Catholic movement, was an especially persistent critic of Distributism, disagreeing with Belloc's concept of the servile state as well as with the Distributist attack on capitalism and the modern industrial system. The large majority of the C.S.G.'s membership was middle and upper middle class. The guild was founded in 1909, its chief objective being to draw Catholic workingmen away from the socialist movement. Under the influence of Henry Somerville, a man of rather narrow intellectual breadth who approached politics in a vaguely liberal fashion, the guild in the 1930s shied away from any radical or even mildly unconventional ideas on social reform. Somerville himself was a frank defender of big business and the capitalist system.

From the outset, the C.S.G. seemed to develop along ideological paths different from Distributism. The founders of the organization, Monsignor Parkinson, Virginia Crawford, and Leslie Toke, were all admirers of the Webbs and the Fabian Society. As opposed to the Anglo-Catholic Summer Schools, the Catholic Social Guild Summer Schools at Oxford, which began in 1920, gave no serious attention to Distributist philosophy. Unlike the Chesterbelloc papers, *The Christian Democrat*, the official journal of the C.S.G., looked askance at Mussolini and was not particularly enthusiastic about the policies of Dollfuss, Salazar, and Franco. Henry Somerville, as founder and editor of *The Christian Democrat*, was a forceful advocate of the Widows Pension Bill, the National Insurance Act, and most other state-supported welfare schemes, all of which, he insisted, were based on the teachings of Pope Leo XIII. Somerville also denounced the general strike of 1926, which the Distributists, of course, had applauded.[43] Indeed, Somerville was convinced that the strike *per se* should never be used as a tool to help the workers.

The inevitable battle between the C.S.G. and the Distributists became public in May of 1927, when Somerville wrote a critical review of Chesterton's *Outline of Sanity*, in which he rebuked the Distributists for their obsession with private ownership and the bogey of the servile state. Basically, Somerville felt that *De Rerum Novarum*'s emphasis on private ownership applied only to agricultural problems and property in land. Thus, unlike Chesterton and Belloc, he heartily supported minimum wage action and most Labour-sponsored social welfare legislation as the only realistic means with which to win decent living conditions for British working-class families. The Distributists, on the other hand, opposed this type of reform in the belief that it would make the worker dependent on the state, creating, in turn, a completely irresponsible "servile" citizen. In a direct criticism of the C.S.G., Chesterton wrote that the Pope's insistence upon the importance of the working class becoming owners was stated in *De Rerum Novarum* as a general principle, the assumption being that a man generally would deal better with all forms of property when it was his own. For this reason, the Distributists vowed to smash the capitalist system in order that the workers could become owners of the means of production.

At issue between the Distributists and the C.S.G.—and the entire Catholic Social movement, for that matter—was the latter's willingness to accept the permanence of capitalism and the modern industrial system. Most of those involved in the Catholic Social movement were prepared to work within the prevailing capitalist financial and industrial structures. The Distributists, however, were self-proclaimed revolutionaries ready to destroy both capitalism and everything connected with it, including parliamentary government. The gap between Distributism and the Somerville wing of the C.S.G. could not be bridged. After having studied Belloc's and Chesterton's ideas for nearly twenty years, Somerville concluded that Distributism was a species of Bolshevism, a reversion to savagery, and scandalous to Catholicism. As editor of the *Christian Democrat,* he told his readers that the Distributists were basically a lunatic literary set that did nothing constructive but play with words and coin clever phrases. Yet he clearly saw an insidious side to Distributism beyond its affinity with Bolshevism: it was taken far too seriously by Catholics, and non-Catholics had come to recognize it as a Catholic product.[44]

At least one Catholic historian has suggested that Distributism was chiefly responsible for the Catholic Social movement's lack of success in the inter-war years.[45] Because Distributism aimed at the construction of a totally new economic system, which was frequently recognized by the public as romantic and unrealistic, it drew a good deal of adverse criticism to all Catholic social thinking. J.M. Cleary contended that "lunatic fringe" Distributist land colonies directly damaged the C.S.G. agricultural programs and limited their book sales by creating bad publicity for all Catholic land experiments.[46] Echoing Somerville, nearly all the C.S.G. officials complained that Distributism drew popular support and talented writers away from their organizations. In 1924, for example, Monsignor Parkinson complained to Father O'Hea that "the intellectuals have practically disappeared from our meetings."[47]

These are all justifiable criticisms, especially when one considers that most of the best known Catholic intellectuals were involved with Distributism in one form or another. Yet it is also true that the ideas and personalities of Chesterton and Belloc were primarily responsible for the Catholic revival in twentieth-century England. Without the Chesterbelloc there would have been fewer forceful writers to assist the Social Catholic movement in the first place. As it was, with the exception of the Distributist circle, most English Catholics were essentially apolitical. Indeed, Somerville did his best to keep politics out of the pages of the *Christian Democrat* and the C.S.G. The few who did become involved in mainstream politics did not adopt particular Catholic positions on social and political issues. Catholic M.P.'s were either indistinguishable from the non-Catholic members of their party or did not remain long at Westminster. The fate of Belloc attests to that.

The general political and social complacency of British Catholics was a major target of the Chesterbelloc. Regardless of the embarrassment they brought to the Catholic community (Wilfred Sheed wrote that a Catholic student at Cambridge usually tried to hide Belloc's historical theories under the rug), there can be little doubt that Chesterton, Belloc, and the Distributist circle shattered the intellectual inferiority complex of British Catholics.[48] The Chesterbelloc did not bring Distributism into the flesh, but Catholicism in Britain certainly gained a new confidence in its mission to return the modern world to "Christian sanity."

CHAPTER IX

Foreign Affairs and Fascism

Chesterton's and Belloc's views on international affairs and fascism illustrate, once again, the yawning gap between them and mainstream British political thinking and also point up the difficulty of placing their careers into any distinct ideological category. Unfortunately, the diverse responses of *G.K.'s Weekly* and the *Weekly Review* to the international crises of the 1930s, moving uncompromisingly to the political right, produced internal tensions within Distributist circles, and, ultimately, brought an end to the Distributist movement itself.

In the area of foreign affairs, Chesterton's newspaper claimed to defend what it considered to be the "consistent and continuous tradition of Christendom" (i.e., Catholicism) against the combined forces of capitalism, totalitarianism, and Bolshevism.[1] This generally meant that *G.K.'s Weekly* was sympathetic to Italy, Poland, and France—though it abhorred French parliamentary politics—and opposed the policies of Germany, the United States, and the Soviet Union. As Belloc explained it, the "older civilizations" should march against the three perils of Russian Communism, the "defeated angry and never-satisfied Prussia," and American economic domination.[2]

Yet, unlike its successor, the *Weekly Review, G.K.'s Weekly* asserted that the powers of monopoly capitalism, spearheaded by Jewish Wall Street financiers, were a far greater threat than international Bolshevism. Chesterton called communism the peril against which

172

the various schools of fascists hoped to alarm the people, but un-bridled capitalism, in his opinion, was the real enemy:

It is not the Bolshevist but the Boss, the publicity man, the salesman and the commercial advertiser who have, like a rush and riot of barbarians, thrown down and trampled underfoot the ancient Roman statue of Vere-cundia.[3]

American imperialism, the barbarism of American money invading Europe, was deemed the most immediate threat to Christian civilization, because it worked secretly and was not easily recognized by its unfortunate victims. To Chesterton, the expansion of American corporate enterprise was a danger far greater than a marching army, for it was an insidious power difficult to fight:

I feel about the destruction of old Regent Street under a blaze of Broadway sky-signs very much what I felt about the destruction of old Adelphi Terrace under a blaze of German bombs. The only difference is that I knew that my countrymen were fighting with splendid and watchful valour against the bombs that destroyed the one street; and there is not the slightest suggestion anywhere that they are even attempting to prevent the destruction of the other.[4]

In a dialectic somewhat reminiscent of Marx, though with a substantially different twist, Chesterton explained that communism was a reaction against capitalism—"an unnatural child that hates its mother"—but since the mother (capitalism) was equally unnatural, now in possession of its fully matured strength, and hence imperialistic, it more likely would be able to kill the child. Hence the chief danger was not communism, which Chesterton felt was nothing more than an opposition party in Western Europe, but capitalist imperialism, which was invading the older and better ways of life with the base energy of corporate business. However, *G.K.'s Weekly* emphasized that Bolshevism was a practical threat in Eastern Europe, where only Catholic Poland, thrust like a sword between the "Byzantine tradition of Muscovy" and the materialism of Prussia, stood alone against the Soviet dictatorship; and here the ignorant capitalists were augmenting the latent danger by ignoring the defense needs of the Warsaw government.[5]

Most of the essays on international affairs in *G.K.'s Weekly* were written by Belloc and, somewhat later, by Gregory Macdonald. Indeed, the foreign policy line taken by the journal seems to have been determined by Belloc who, unlike Chesterton, had always taken an interest in diplomacy and was generally considered something of an authority on continental politics. Chesterton frequently wrote on international affairs as well, but his basic approach to the subject, although more temperate, seems to have been molded by Belloc's opinions. Contrary to general belief, G.K. was not always an enthusiastic supporter of Mussolini and Italian Fascism. Except for Chesterton's pro-Mussolini chapter in *The Resurrection of Rome* (1930), most of the accolades for Italian experiments in corporatism and authoritarian government came from Belloc, and what one might call the more radical Distributists—Douglas Jerrold, A.J. Penty, Herbert Shove, and others. In matters concerning international affairs and fascism, Chesterton was a voice of moderation and common sense. After G.K.'s death, the Distributist circle and his journal, which was now published as the *Weekly Review*, became more sanguine about dictatorship and fascism as useful expedients against the hazards of international Bolshevism.

At the base of Belloc's peculiar views on diplomacy in the interwar years was a firm conviction that a secret clique of Jews, whom he called the "Money Power," was preparing to take over the world. Belloc contended that these men had benefited through the Great War by issuing usurious loans to the Allies, and that their religious and financial ideas had largely dictated the terms of the Versailles Peace Treaty. According to this analysis, a defeated Germany had been saved from ruin because the American Jews feared to lose a good trading market. In addition, the various arrangements for reparation, including the Dawes and Young plans, were engineered to keep the European economies tied to America, with an optimum flow of capital directed back to investors on Wall Street. It was explained that these same financiers, being anti-Catholic, insured that Italy would be unjustly deprived of her war claims. Although the Italians had lost as many men as Britain, Belloc pointed out that they were not allowed the fruits of victory (not one solitary colony nor mile of territory on the Adriatic), except for a small strip of land in the north to insure an obvious frontier along the Alps.[6] To these conspiring forces, Belloc also added the French freemasons and anti-clericals who, he claimed, were partially responsible for preventing the construction of Catholic states along the Danube and Rhine Rivers. Instead, the French anti-clerical parliamentarians (freemasons and Jews), the powers of international banking, and an Anglo-American cultural sympathy based upon a common hatred of the Roman Church had combined to prevent Bavaria from becoming part of Austria and had resurrected the anti-Catholic Prussia along the Rhine. Of the new states created after the Armistice, only Czechoslovakia was given favorable treatment by the Allies, and that was because the Prague government was "violently and cruelly anti-Catholic."[7]

Although it had been impossible to prevent the resurgence of Poland, Belloc believed that the powers of finance were bent on weakening that state, both because it represented Catholicism in Eastern Europe, and because the Polish tradition of cultural independence would not have been favorable to the growth of capitalist industrialism. In the mind of the Chesterbelloc, these fears explained the Allies' refusal to support Poland's election to the Council of the League of Nations as well as Western approval of the Locarno Pact, both of which served to postpone a settlement of the Polish western boundary problem to the advantage of Germany.

Belloc repeatedly warned his readers throughout the 1920s and 1930s that the peace settlement was nothing more than an armed truce which could deteriorate into global war because of German economic and Italian political discontent. The Chesterbelloc alliance had little time for the League of Nations, since they felt it was devised to perpetuate an unjust peace settlement which had completely ignored the peculiarities of national traditions. Gregory Macdonald saw the League as a vehicle for spreading the ideas of "internationalism," which he considered to be the source of Europe's difficulties, since it meant collectivism and bureaucracy.[8] Moreover, the League was judged a paper tiger, vitiated from the start by its strictly secular parentage, and capable only of imposing an illusory international peace through the breezy ideals of disarmament. Douglas Jerrold criticized the League's policy of nonintervention as a cowardly expedient which favored the strong and injured the weak. All the Distributists appreciated the necessity of armed force and opposed disarmament and pacifism as unrealistic in the face of evil and contrary to the ideals of Christian brotherhood. The Chesterbelloc had always recognized the need to fight for freedom—after all, they regarded the Great War as a battle for liberty against tyranny—and for all practical purposes they felt that tyranny still prevailed. Chesterton, who saw pacifism as "peace at all costs," believed that the disarmament campaign had nothing to do with international amity but was simply a means to cut down defense expenditures, so that more money could be funneled to Wall Street to liquidate the war debt to America.

In their view, Europe was a powder keg ready to explode at a moment's notice, requiring constant vigilance, so as to check the menace which had once before nearly destroyed Christian civilization. They were not certain when the tempest would come, but when it did, it would be futile to talk of peace, for there could be, in the words of Chesterton, "no peace between Right and Wrong, and no compromise with original sin."[9] Yet there was hope. If the "corrupt masonic French parliamentarianism" were swept away in an outburst of popular rage, a military pact might then be drawn up between a rejuvenated Catholic France and Mussolini's Italy. Flanked by a "strong and sane" Italian dictator, who had already waged a successful war on secret societies and destroyed the disease of liberalism, France could uphold the ideals of a Catholic culture and impose respect on those states which opposed the faith.[10] For this reason, *G.K.'s Weekly* hoped that Britain would ally with Italy on matters of European concern. In addition, it favored the Royalist movement in France: "One of the most steady, sober and scientific movements of modern Europe." Although the paper could not agree with *Action Française* on all issues, it clearly admired its brainpower and political energy. Moreover, *G.K.'s Weekly* agreed with the movement's basic objectives. Maurras, its leader, was seen to have produced "a great mountain of serious social construction" designed to liberate France from a corrupt parliamentary system born in the lodges of freemasonry.[11]

Yet Belloc felt that such a sequence of events would have been difficult to engineer, since the international banking monopoly—"the principal political power of our time, having its headquarters in New York, with London as a branch office"—had already decided at Versailles to strengthen "the Reich" by milking the economies of France and Italy.[12] According to his analysis, the Jewish financiers were building up Germany, in whose industry they had made large investments, by shifting the burden of paying war reparations to the more agricultural nations, where they had few financial stakes. America had arranged it so that Germany's industrial network would be tapped only to the extent needed to repay indemnities to England, France, and Italy (so they could return war loans to America), but any rate of payment really injurious to German industry was to be avoided at all costs.

In his column "Current Affairs," Belloc consistently criticized Britain's diplomatic ties with the United States, on the grounds that an alliance would bring Whitehall closer into the grip of Wall Street. In a strictly military sense, it was also felt that an Anglo-American alliance in Europe would mean American naval superiority at sea, an abnegation of England's traditional balance-of-power objectives. Belloc's distaste for the growing military and diplomatic ties with Washington was clearly shared by Chesterton, who once remarked that he had hoped that the Crown would have taken the side of "civilization" in matters concerning foreign policy. Lamentably, Britain clung to American skirts, because she was "the *pied à terre* of the wandering international financier": "We have dipped the Union Jack in surrender to the Stars and Stripes, out of respect for the sort of Jew who cannot get into any club in New York."[13]

In *G.K.'s Weekly*, Chesterton both praised and condemned Mussolini and Italian Fascism. His most detailed response to the Italian experience appeared in *The Resurrection of Rome* (1930), in which Mussolini received critical acclaim for his social and political accomplishments. Chesterton and Belloc appreciated Italian Fascism, not because Mussolini ran the trains on time, nor for the reason that Fascism had provided a stimulus to Italy's fledgling economy, but because of their conviction that Mussolini had successfully rebelled against the perverted postwar economic and political settlement. In his characteristically caustic but colorful style, Belloc declared:

After the war, Europe, instead of continuing the rule of soldiers as it should have done, returned to its vomit; and the miserable parliamentary figures of the old degraded day put on again costume and grease-paint, filed back upon the stage, and began to play their old antics as though nothing had happened.[14]

But Italy had done better. Chesterton welcomed Mussolini for two reasons: the Fascists had rightly destroyed a sick parliamentary government, in which the rich employed the false ideals of liberalism to exploit the poor; and Mussolini was reviving the tradition of Rome as the citadel of Christian civilization against German barbarism. After a visit to Italy in 1929, in which he had managed an interview with *Il Duce*, Chesterton explained his impressions:

. . . the very faces of the crowd carrying the eagles or the fasces are not the shifty obliterated faces of a modern mob, but those faces of the old Roman busts which we have tried in vain to trace or remember when we saw them in beggars in Naples or waiters in Soho. So far as a man may give the sense of his experience in a single phrase: he has seen the return of the Romans.[15]

Without condoning Mussolini's forceful methods, he felt that the Fascists were moved to employ rough tactics because of the secrecy of their opponents, with the result that Mussolini did openly what liberal and democratic governments did secretly with the power of money. Nor did Chesterton feel that the Fascists had found a solution to the problems of modern government; he simply asserted that the modern liberal, who criticized Mussolini for all the wrong reasons, had not yet even discovered the problem. The problem, as G.K. recognized it, was the inability of liberalism to reform itself. At the beginning, republicanism had meant the "public thing," and those who espoused it sincerely wished their rule to be as popular as possible. Jefferson and the leaders of the French Revolution were men of the forum and marketplace, ruling among the people under an open sky. But then entered the secret society—a product of money and selfish interest groups—and with the serpent came the fall. While those of good will thought they were building a brotherhood of all men, power secretly passed to a coterie of conspirators with money to be used for private, rather than public interests. Mussolini was seen to have reacted against this republican rottenness in the name of ancient republican virtues: "He had reverted to the original ideal that public life should be public; and emphasized it in the most dramatic manner by stamping on the Secret Societies as on a tangle of vipers."[16] This was simply the acceptance of what Robespierre had called the civic necessity of virtue, and Chesterton firmly believed that Thomas Jefferson and the early republicans would have understood Mussolini completely.

While Italian Fascism did not embody Chesterton's ideal of justice, nor of Distributism, he felt it represented authority being employed in the interest of the nation and not of big employers. Mussolini had reestablished government as a force distinct from the interests of the governed. His was a despotism cleansed of capitalists, an authority acting "independently of Trade Magnates and Trade Unions and capable of giving orders to both."[17]

Chesterton objected to many facets of Fascism and disagreed especially with those conservatives who championed Mussolini's authoritarianism and tough stand on communism. He had nothing but contempt for reactionaries who cried for strong government without recognizing that they might feel its firm hand. Chesterton feared that Fascist authoritarianism could easily be turned into a public tyranny and that its hatred of pacifism could develop into an endorsement of militarism and territorial expansion. As early as 1926, he had warned that Britain should stand firm against the excesses of Fascism and that someday it might be necessary to fight that force in the Mediterranean.[18] But his most serious criticism was an intellectual one, and it applied to the ideas of both Mussolini and his French counterpart, Charles Maurras. Chesterton objected to their neglect of the common man and of what today one might call "the silent majority." A democrat at heart, he always distrusted movements which claimed superiority and special rights:

Merely counting heads may be, and generally is, a silly business. But if we substitute valuing heads for counting heads, it is rather likely to end in cracking heads. The representatives of both vigorous and virtuous minorities will value each other's heads by butting each other like rams.[19]

Fascism may have been a natural and practical response to the abuses of liberal democracy, but, as a political alternative, it lacked a fixed moral principle. Therein lay Chesterton's chief intellectual objection to the politics of Mussolini and Maurras. There had to be some set truth which could distinguish the sane from the mad minority; and until fascism, as practiced in Italy and championed in France, could come up with a clear-cut morality, Chesterton refused to have any truck with it.

Chesterton's friends were far more sanguine about Italian Fascism. In commemorating the tenth anniversary of the march on Rome, J. Desmond Gleeson, in *G.K.'s Weekly*, hailed Mussolini's success as a possible turning point in modern history. Italy had found a true hero who was creating order out of chaos, a new national life out of decay.[20] Belloc saw Mussolini reviving the "Latin bloc" (France, Italy, and Poland) as a new dynamic Catholic force in international diplomacy. Most Distributists praised Mussolini, because he had repudiated the sham politics of parliamentarianism and had given Italy the courage to assume a bolder position in European affairs. But the *Weekly*'s United States counterpart, *The American Review*, went considerably further, endorsing both the Fascist and Nazi revolutions as revivals of what it called the monarchial-corporatist principle.

Belloc's admiration for Mussolini was longer lasting and much less critical than Chesterton's. After meeting the Italian dictator in 1924, Belloc wrote that Mussolini was a well-read, unambitious man with sound political judgment. He was a patriot with a special driving power, which sprang from a hatred of parliamentarianism and the corruption of international finance. After Italy had demonstrated her aggressive intentions in Abyssinia in 1935, Belloc still considered *Il Duce* an "excellent" leader who had strengthened his nation to a remarkable degree.[21] Indeed, Belloc appears never to have criticized Italy's expansionistic foreign policy. Yet, like Chesterton, his visceral love for democracy made him suspicious of Mussolini's contempt for majorities.[22] Belloc believed that Mussolini was justified in reacting against the abuse of majority rule as epitomized in the travesty of parliamentary government, but he feared that Mussolini's complete disdain for the will of majorities ultimately would lead him into difficulties. Unfortunately, Belloc never bothered to elaborate on this issue, even after Mussolini entered World War II.

Douglas Jerrold praised Italian Fascism as the source of a Catholic spiritual renaissance. Mussolini's new Italy represented the long-deferred flowering of the "Puritan spirit" in the Catholic South: "It was . . . the most significant event in world history since the Puritan movement in Northern Europe four centuries before." Jerrold explained that both the Northern and Italian reforms had resulted in a "rebinding of man to God, a spiritualization of politics and the practical application of political methods to the service of religious ideals."[23] But unlike other puritanical reformers (such as Mohammed, Calvin, and Cromwell), Mussolini had not made the mistake of constructing an uncompromising theocracy. Because of the Fascist concordat with the Vatican, the human personality could be fully realized, for the state was given exclusive power in temporal affairs, while the Church retained supreme authority in matters concerning faith and morals.

Much like Seward Collins, Jerrold also recognized Italian Fascism as a type of corporatism aiming at self-government through functional guilds. As such, it was simply another means for reaching the same end pursued by parliamentary democracy: the control of national policy by the people in the interest of the community as a whole. Jerrold was concerned to see that Englishmen properly understand Fascism as simply a different path to freedom, an approach to sovereignty that was more in keeping with the Italian political tradition. The Italian experiment in liberalism had been a failure, because it was a doctrine imported from England, and those who championed it were aliens in tradition as well as race. These people had succeeded in providing Italy with political unity, but they had failed to meet her spiritual needs.

Jerrold asked Englishmen to appreciate the nonpolitical nature of Fascist corporatism, which was incapable of tolerating political liberty as recognized in the Anglo-Saxon tradition. The Fascist theory organized men for corporate action and self-government according to their functions in society, not as citizens of a political state. Thus, initiatives for change could emanate only from corporate units, of which every Italian was to be a member. Yet these nonpolitical corporations could not be created with undue haste, and because urgent problems could not await the construction of such new and experimental governmental machinery, Mussolini was obliged to assume extraordinary powers to take Italy through the postwar economic and political crisis. Jerrold desired that Englishmen give Fascism a chance to achieve its true purpose, which he believed to be the construction of the nonpolitical state organized on the functional principle through self-regulating democratic guilds. This daringly new experiment was still in a state of infancy, needing the protection of a patriotic dictator. One must appreciate, wrote Jerrold, that Fascism stands today about where the parliamentary system stood in the days of Elizabeth.

From the outset, A.J. Penty also recognized Fascism as an efficient means with which to implement the guild idea. D'Annunzio's adventure in Fiume, which Belloc had also supported with enthusiasm, was welcomed as the first full-fledged attempt to put into practice the corporate ideals as outlined in Pope Leo XIII's *De Rerum Novarum*. Penty felt that Mussolini's syndicalist movement was derived from the same principles and that his talk of corporatism was just another name for the regulative guild. Mussolini's Fascism seemed quite similar to Penty's own version of Distributism. Industry was controlled in Italy by a number of self-governing national guilds, large-scale enterprises were closely regulated by a central authority operating in the public interest, wages were fixed, dividends were limited to 6 per cent, and the State's governing body—Mussolini's Chamber of Deputies—operated on the functional, not territorial, principle, consisting of delegates representing the various guilds. Penty also admired the Fascist concern for reviving a prosperous peasantry and its stress on national economic self-sufficiency. Mussolini's programs, aimed at a return to the good times of the past, were inspired by a hatred of modernism: "Fascism . . . exists to defend tradition and human values while it seeks a wider distribution of property; it is Distributist rather than Collectivist."[24]

Although Penty could understand Mussolini's need to employ dictatorial methods (he had no other option given the threat of Bolshevism), he could not give Italian Fascism his full approval, because it championed the power of state over the rights of the individual. The Italian dictator had not only called his government "totalitarian" but had indeed coined the term "totalitarian state," by which he meant that the Fascist government was to exercise jurisdiction over every aspect of social life.[25] Penty recognized that such an idea could only grow at the expense of the needs of human nature which were satisfied in the principles of the legitimate corporatist state.

It can thus be said that the Distributist circle generally approved of Mussolini's politics.[26] In fact, of all the British journals, *G.K.'s Weekly* was one of Fascist Italy's greatest defenders. Yet almost to a man, Distributists opposed fascist authoritarianism for Britain on the grounds that it was alien to the nation's long tradition of aristocratic tolerance and geniality. Belloc and Chesterton recognized that Fascism, as an ideology which had sprung from the soil of Italy in response to peculiar needs, had nothing to offer the British. Fascism would fail in the United Kingdom, just as the alien ideology of liberalism had failed in Italy. Most other Distributists believed that Britons would have found it difficult to adapt to the rigors of Latin discipline and maintained that the British could more effectively revive their ancient democratic ideals through the principle of voluntary association. Harold Robbins, who claimed to follow closely the social philosophy of Chesterton and Maritain, considered the Fascist corporate state a contradiction in terms. It attempted to impose corporations, whereas true corporatism had to be fostered organically in small groups.[27]

The various fascist organizations in Britain took an active interest in trying to win Distributists to their cause. Representatives from Mosley's British Union of Fascists (B.U.F.), the Imperial Fascist League, and several other fascist organizations spoke at numerous League meetings and contributed countless letters to "The Cockpit" in an effort to acquaint Distributists with fascist principles, which they claimed were essentially Distributist in nature. Many parts of the fascist program were close to the hearts of Distributists. Even Harold Robbins noted that Chapter IV of Mosley's book, *The Greater Britain* (1934), was strikingly similar to the preamble of the Birmingham scheme. Mosley railed against the expansion of chain-stores that were choking the small independent shopkeepers and promised to destroy large business conglomerates in the interest of everyman. In *The Greater Britain*, he called for the elimination of Parliament and the "party game," proposed a program of democratic government on the local level and the absorption of working-class and professional associations into a hierarchical corporatist state.

The British Union of Fascists also claimed to be the only political party in Britain calling for a redistribution of property. Mosley's willingness to open the ranks of his organization to young men and new ideas certainly pleased Belloc (who believed that the next revolution had to be made by youth), while Douglas Jerrold warmly approved of the B.U.F.'s call for functional representation in gov· ernment. The fascist critique of parliamentary politics and their assaults on international finance and monopoly capitalism clearly impressed the Distributists. Indeed, at one time the editors of *G.K.'s Weekly* were disposed to suggest that the Mosleyites might come to see themselves as Distributists.[28]

The Distributists shared a common set of dislikes with the British Union of Fascists, and they admired the political idealism of Mosley's followers. But all this was not sufficient to bring them into the fascist fold. Not only was fascism considered unfit for the British temperament, but even more importantly, the Chesterbelloc alliance could not accept the fascist's permanent rejection of all forms of democracy and his emphasis on sovereignty residing in the state. Such an approach to political theory ran counter to the classical and Christian tradition; it was essentially Machiavellian, failing to recognize the existence of a natural law above both man and the state, which asserted the sovereignty of God. The implications of fascist principles were even worse than the servile state: the fascist ideological trajectory led straight to totalitarianism and the complete destruction of the human personality, whose true end was union with God, not the state.

The Distributist circle's rather sympathetic but qualified appreciation of Italian Fascism did not extend to Hitler's Nazi revolution. Except for a few thoughtless statements by Seward Collins, virtually all the followers of the Chesterbelloc had nothing but contempt for Nazism. Indeed, Chesterton was one of the first outside Germany to condemn Hitler's persecution of the Jews, and even Belloc, the irrepressible anti-Dreyfusard, denounced the Nazi Jewish pogroms as thoroughly immoral from the beginning.[28,29]

The Chesterbelloc hated Hitlerism because they thought it was Prussianism in its last and most virulent stage of madness. Prussia, "the pachyderm, the prehistoric monster of the old grey slime," was now working its barbarism through the mind of a Nordic crank.[30] In this they were wrong. Hitler was never the puppet of the Junker drillmasters, as Belloc claimed he was, and most Distributists, operating from that mistaken premise, neglected to recognize that many Nazis not only came from Catholic Bavaria, but were Catholics themselves (as was Hitler). Nevertheless, the Chesterbelloc's early warning about the nature of Hitler's expansionist foreign policy was prophetic. Chesterton not only foretold the Nazi-Soviet Pact (he emphasized that it was inevitable, since both Germany and the Soviet Union were anti-Christian and opposed to Western civilization), but also predicted that Hitler would spark a world war by taking over Poland. Similarly, G.K. properly recognized the practical implications of the Nazi Aryan myth.

Chesterton had discovered very early that Hitler's funny crooked cross represented something quite different from Mussolini's bundle of fasces. The latter stood for the glory of an empire which once had really existed, whereas the swastika represented something the world had never known, for the historic reality of Arminius, explained Chesterton, was nothing more than a German fairy tale.[30] Moreover, the Nazi was above all a racist and that set him apart from a Fascist, who, in Chesterton's eyes, was essentially an overzealous patriot. And Hitler's worship of race was deemed far worse than Fascism's excessive devotion to the nation; patriots respected boundaries, whereas the idea of race was "anthropology gone mad," the practical side of which meant an everlasting search for one's own countrymen in other people's countries. Hitler's racism was a sort of religion of the narcissistic, which made the individual German the sacred image he worshipped. Moreover, Nazism, with its aristocracy of blood, was a creed which tended to make each German his own god:

In this very vital and practical sense the heathen Saxon is himself Wotan, is himself Thor. But a large ploughman from Kerry, or a large policeman from New York, does not think that he himself is a little dark rose; nor does a heavy old Norman peasant in wooden clogs suppose that his face and figure resemble Saint Michael poised on a mountain above the sea.[32]

Perhaps Chesterton best expressed the real danger of Nazism and its most vital difference from Italian Fascism when he prophesied that

Hitler would inevitably attempt to preserve the purity of his Aryan race in a continent where all other races were judged impure.

A major break in Distributist ranks occurred with the Italian invasion of Abyssinia. *G.K.'s Weekly* had never been a particularly strong critic of Mussolini's foreign policy—such criticism would have been painful given the journal's Latin bias—but there developed a storm of protest from several leading Distributists when the paper neglected to deliver a forceful condemnation of Italy's conduct in Abyssinia. Chesterton was deeply disturbed over the controversy, and he died before the matter had been properly settled, though in a sense it never was. The Abyssinian affair and Chesterton's death proved to be a watershed in the history of Distributism, for after 1936 the paper and the movement shifted further to the right and in the process many of Chesterton's ideals were thoughtlessly cast by the wayside. In a sense, the Distributist circle lost its sanity after Chesterton's passing.

There appear to have been three different Distributist responses to the Abyssinian affair. Many loudly denounced the invasion as an unprovoked act of aggression, while others tended to excuse Mussolini on the grounds that he had been forced by capitalism to undertake a more dynamic foreign policy. Chesterton took a middle approach to the issue, condemning Mussolini but not with enough vehemence to satisfy the more moderate Distributists. Belloc, Jerrold, Gregory Macdonald, and the more radical Distributists, a group which Donald Attwater derisively called the "Latinophiles," refused to condemn the Italian action.[33] Some of these men felt as did Douglas Jerrold, who explained that Mussolini was conducting essentially a civilizing mission to bring a better and more Christian way of life to African barbarians.[34] An interesting variation on this theme was provided by Marshall McLuhan. In a reply to Distributists who had complained of the *Weekly*'s tame response to Mussolini, McLuhan argued that the future of European unity required Italy's consolidation (which the Abyssinian campaign represented), and that those who presumably understood Belloc's books would see that such vigorous missionary activity was necessary for the reconstruction of Christian Europe. McLuhan concluded his remarks by saying that Abyssinia was to be opened up like a cow by a butcher:

"It is literally a struggle between the sword and the pen—the banker's pen."[35]

McLuhan's remark about bankers underlined the major reason why the Latinophiles excused Mussolini's Abyssinian adventure. Belloc, Gregory Macdonald, and others believed that the "international moneylenders" were attempting to undermine French and Italian financial independence by forcing those countries off the gold standard. They explained this as part of the elaborate conspiracy of the "Money Power," that collection of faceless Wall Street bankers who had already managed to rig the reparations settlement so as to drain the finances of Britain, Italy, and France. These conspirators aimed to monopolize the world's wealth, and an important step in this direction was to make the major European economies completely dependent upon American finance. Sometimes this could be accomplished by issuing special loans calculated to draw the recipient closer into the clutches of Wall Street. Such had been the case with Britain, which had been extended credit in the sterling crisis of 1931 and forced off the gold standard because of pressures from American moneylenders. Now the attack was being prepared against those states which had managed to maintain their financial independence.

Gregory Macdonald and C. Featherstone Hammond, the author of a series of articles in the *Weekly* concerning the machinations of the "international credit system," saw the entire Abyssinian war as the outcome of Mussolini's attempts to break through this financial siege by obtaining raw materials outside the sterling market and the capitalist oil monopoly. Consequently, these Distributists opposed the imposition of economic and financial sanctions on Italy, believing them simply a political extension of the Money Power's attack on the gold bloc nations. Macdonald explained that the various proposals for an international boycott of Italian goods was just another ploy to make Italy lose gold reserves by having to pay in gold for her own imports. Macdonald and Hammond proposed a wider solution to the Abyssinian problem which was calculated to counterattack the conspiracy of the international financiers. Instead of recommending sanctions against Italy, a measure which worked to the favor of Wall Street's money schemes, they suggested the calling of an international conference to settle the major European debt, currency, and trade problems. Macdonald hoped that such a conference would take up the immediate task of drawing up a scheme for the free distribution of raw materials, since it was Italy's need for resources that had prompted the Abyssinian crisis in the first place.[36]

With respect to the entire question of international diplomacy, this group of Distributists felt that Britain should "reverse her engines" and initiate a rapprochement with Italy in order to build a wider alliance with France and Poland against the United States, Germany, and the Soviet Union. Macdonald's commentaries, in particular, created the clear impression that Latin Fascism was a positive force to be used against Bolshevism. At one point he was prepared to carry his argument one step further: in a letter to "The Cockpit," June 11, 1936, Macdonald pointed out that both Hitler's and Mussolini's movements were regenerations of nationalism against the pressures of international finance. He went on to say: "I am convinced that Russia, with its explicit atheism, has been associated with the implicit atheism of Money. Also Hitler and Mussolini *may yet* be the peace-makers of Europe. . . ." In short, Gregory Macdonald even appeared to show sympathy for Hitler once it seemed that the Nazi dictator would combat communism. Since both Belloc and Macdonald did most of the writing on foreign affairs, it was only natural that their Latin bias would color the *Weekly*'s coverage of the Abyssinian issue. Moreover, the journal had never made a secret of its bias: "Now we think . . . that no other organ of opinion is so much in sympathy with the Latin tradition as ours. . . . We are pro-French. . . . We are pro-Italian."[37]

A sizable group of Distributists was horrified by the *Weekly*'s arguments (which had seemed sufficiently pro-Fascist to win accolades from Ezra Pound) and demanded a denunciation of Italy's blatantly imperialistic designs.[38] Remembering Chesterton's pro-Boer days, they beseeched their leader to come down hard on the side of liberty against imperialistic oppression. Reckitt was so disturbed with the line taken by Chesterton's paper in the Abyssinian affair that he privately wrote G.K. to say that he was prepared to resign from the *Weekly*'s board of directors. Chesterton issued an apology, explaining that he had been on vacation when the crisis broke and was about to deliver a far-reaching statement on the issue:

I should like to ask you to defer your decision at least until you have seen the next week's number of the paper, in which I expand further the argument I have used in the current number and bring it, I think, rather nearer to your natural and justifiable point of view. Between ourselves . . . I do think myself that there ought to have been a more definite condemnation of the attack on Abyssinia.

Chesterton was particularly worried about the wider reverberations of Mussolini's intemperate conduct. In the same letter to Reckitt he added:

Very shortly, the mortal danger, to me, is the rehabilitation of Capitalism, in spite of the slump, which will certainly take the form of a hypocritical patriotism and glorification of England, at the expense of Italy or anybody else. For the moment I only want you to understand that this is the mountainous peril that towers in my mind.[39]

Reckitt understood Chesterton's explanation and decided to stay on. But Distributist opinion was deeply divided on the issue, for many were beginning to recognize the aggressive nature of Italy's Fascism. Even Penty changed his mind about Mussolini after the attack on Abyssinia. Penty saw that Mussolini, not having the courage to interfere drastically with the evils of industrialism, had betrayed his principles by seeking a solution along the old capitalist lines of colonial expansion. Penty no longer had any doubt about the real intentions of Fascism. Before the invasion of Abyssinia, the Fascist worship of the state could be interpreted as a reaction against liberalism and laissez faire:

But now we know that Mussolini has all along meant what he said in the dictum that 'Fascism believes neither in the possibility nor in the utility of perpetual peace.'[40]

Chesterton condemned Mussolini's Abyssinian adventure and Italian Fascism—a "Force just as false as imperialism"—but told his readers that the invasion was no worse than the methods used by capitalists, who could afford to work behind the backs of their victims by substituting dollars for bullets: "All my sense of history and human proportion revolts against the colossal contemporary hypocrisy; the modern agreement that a huckster may steal a horse, and a field as well, while a soldier must not look over the hedge of a frontier."[41,42] He was also outraged at the hypocritical position of the Western press, which had failed to criticize Japan's takeover of Manchuria but felt justified in mounting a hate campaign against Italy for doing the same thing in Africa.[43]

Chesterton's statements on the Abyssinian question were not strong enough to quell the criticisms of those Distributists who saw the incident in terms of the old Boer War issues. For weeks "The Cockpit" steamed with letters from irate Distributists who were willing to place Mussolini in the same category as the hated Hitler. Conrad Bonacina, Deputy Chairman of the Distributist League, was but typical of scores of Chesterton's followers when he told G.K. that he could not stomach the *Weekly*'s analysis of the Abyssinian crisis, which depicted Mussolini as a victim of a capitalist conspiracy forced into imperialist action by the secret pressures of international finance:

G.K.'s Weekly has always denounced Prussianism in unsparing terms, and nothing will convince me that Prussianism suddenly loses its savour of iniquity, just because it finds a Latin practitioner.[44]

Yet several months later another Distributist writing in "The Cockpit" could suggest that, in spite of "incidental sins and mistakes," Italy in her present "creative mood" was the greatest bulwark against Bolshevism and possessed the only mentality capable of appreciating Distributism.[45] G.K.'s little army was breaking apart at the seams.

Chesterton clearly failed to consider the Abyssinian issue within the framework of the same general principles he had employed over thirty years earlier when he gained public fame as a defender of the liberty-loving Boers. He was slow to judge, and too much went unsaid. Very little was ever mentioned about the sovereignty and freedoms of those who were being cut down by the Italian military machine, and the few criticisms which issued forth from Chesterton's pen lacked the sense of outrage that had marked his pro-Boer polemics.

Many long-time friends and admirers were chagrined by Chesterton's failure to denounce Fascist imperialism with his old Boer War fervency. Mrs. Cecil Chesterton lamented the weak defense of the people in Abyssinia, and, like others, she concluded that G.K.'s intense commitment to Catholicism clouded his judgment.[46] Such was probably the case, though Chesterton was truly disturbed over Italy's Abyssinian adventure and the rift it had brought about in Distributist ranks. G.K. was also growing weary and much of his former fieriness was rapidly diminishing.

The much-loved Chesterton died in June 1936, and his journal, renamed the *Weekly Review* in March of 1938, subsequently assumed a palpably pro-fascist outlook. Its editors generally lauded Mussolini and ignored Hitler's excesses, highlighting instead what they considered to be the far worse danger of international Bolshevism. The journal also tended to champion authoritarian policies for Britain, an expedient wholly contrary to the ideals of Chesterton and the early Distributist circle. The quality of Chesterton's paper declined precipitously and many familiar contributors tended to disappear from the scene.

The *Weekly Review* earned a reputation for upholding the fascist position in diplomacy and, throughout the last half of the 1930s, its editors proposed that Britain form an alliance with Hitler and Mussolini against the Soviet Union. Belloc, who assumed the editorship of *G.K.'s Weekly* after Chesterton's death, wrote of an impending Armageddon between the combined forces of Christianity and a revolution engineered from Moscow. The enemy had been secretly eating away at the soul of Europe, but Belloc knew who they were:

This group of men is Cosmopolitan and largely Jewish, with the Jewish intensity of purpose—whether humanistic, and Messianic or devoted to power of vengeance—the Jewish ability to act in secret, the Jewish indifference to property and national ideals, the fierce Jewish sense of justice and, above all, the Jewish tenacity. There has been much exaggeration of the Jewish element in Bolshevism, but no exaggeration of that element, however crude, is so inept as to affect ignorance of it: for it colours the whole affair.[47]

In the middle of 1939, the *Weekly Review* made the fantastic assertion that these Jewish financiers were forcing Germany into a world war so that they might issue another usurious loan to finance the whole affair.[48] The journal toned down its fascist bias after Italy and Germany declared war on Britain, though its editors always insisted that British politicians had forced Mussolini into an alliance with Hitler. The *Weekly Review* supported the Allied war effort but consistently emphasized that the number one enemy was the Soviet Union, not Nazism.

Whereas Chesterton's paper had assumed a political line that roughly paralleled the neo-Thomist position of the Dominicans' *Blackfriars*, the *Weekly Review* developed a stand strikingly similar to Douglas Woodruff's monthly, *The Tablet*. Woodruff's paper was probably the most influential and well-written Catholic lay publication in Britain, but it was repeatedly criticized by Catholics for its philo-fascism. Douglas Jerrold, Arnold Lunn, and Christopher Hollis, the latter of whom served on *The Tablet*'s board of directors, were regular contributors to this journal. Like the Distributist paper, *The Tablet* championed an authoritarian version of the corporatist state for Britain, looked to the restoration of monarchy in the Bellocian sense, and steadfastly supported the rightist politics of Mussolini, Franco, and Salazar. *Blackfriars* continued to support the broader Distributist social ideals of the *Weekly Review*, but its editors lamented the paper's infatuation with fascism and were highly suspicious of its excessive anti-communism.

The Latin bias of the Chesterbelloc alliance came into full bloom with the Spanish Civil War. This became a testing ground for the new weaponry of the dictators and a prelude to the holocaust which Belloc had long predicted, but it also served as a grindstone for political ideology. The civil war in Spain forced British intellectuals to take a stand on politics. One was obliged to choose sides, for in the words of the poet, Stephen Spender, it now became possible to see the fascist/anti-fascist question as a real battle of ideas, and not simply the bully-like seizure of power by dictatorship from weak opponents.[49]

While Spender and writers on the left portrayed the episode as a valiant humanitarian struggle for democracy against fascism, to the conservative-minded, Franco appeared as a patriot protecting the traditions of Spain from Bolshevism. Britain and the democracies, fearing that the war might spread into an all-European struggle, hoped to contain the fighting by pursuing a policy of strict nonintervention. This position became exceedingly difficult to maintain after it became clear that Germany and Italy were openly aiding the Nationalists. Yet the British government, France, and the United States continued to withhold aid from the Spanish belligerents, a policy which redounded to the benefit of the Nationalists. Failing to get assistance from the League of Nations, the beleaguered Republicans sought and received help from the Soviet Union.

Along with the conservative secular press—such as the *Daily Mail*, J.L. Garvin's *The Observer*, the *Daily Sketch*, and Woodruff and Hollis in *The Tablet*—Distributists were the most ardent partisans of the Nationalist cause. The *Weekly Review* dispatched Captain Raymond Johnes to Spain as its special war correspondent. Johnes made regular reports on the progress of the Nationalist armies and was alleged to have praised Franco as "the greatest knight of Christendom since the sixteenth century."[50] Belloc made a personal visit to the Nationalist front lines in 1939, while Arnold Lunn, in the employ of the historian, Arthur Bryant, wrote a pro-Franco book for the Conservative Book Club. *The Spanish Rehearsal*, published by Lunn in October 1937, after a special fact-finding mission to Spain, was designed to awaken the English public to the dangers of a communist takeover in Western Europe via the Spanish Republic. Douglas Jerrold, perhaps England's most notable defender of Nationalist Spain, managed to play a role in the revolution itself, for it was Jerrold who personally arranged to have a private airplane fly Franco to his troops in Morocco from his unofficial exile in the Canary Islands. Franco was seen to be waging the "Last Crusade," beating down the infidel Bolshevik in the sacred land of the "Counter-Reformation." Jerrold had some rather flattering words for Franco: "He may or may not be the great man as the world judges, but he is certainly something a thousand times more important—a supremely good man, a hero possibly; possibly a saint."[51]

Most writers for the *Weekly Review* refused to recognize Franco as a fascist but argued instead that his Falangists were patriots attempting to construct a new Spain modeled on the lines of the "corporative republic" as established in Portugal.[52] Dr. Antonio de Oliveira Salazar, Portuguese dictator, was a Distributist hero, seen as the creator of the first true corporate state in which political organization was based on the natural social structures of Church and family. The Portuguese dictatorship was not considered fascist, because Salazar himself asserted that he was bound by the moral and judicial principles of Christ, which were beyond the claims of the state.

Distributists considered the Spanish Civil War primarily a religious conflict. The mere fact that the Republicans were attacking the Catholic Church was reason enough for Arnold Lunn to support Franco: "Religion rather than economics is the key to the Spanish struggle and religion will determine the issue when the same battle is fought out on English soil."[53] In general, the Chesterbelloc alliance recognized the struggle in Spain to be a holy war between "world finance; world Jewry . . . world masonry . . . world socialism" and Europe's basic cultural traditions.[54] Interpreted as part of a worldwide attack on Christianity, the Spanish Civil War seems to have convinced Belloc that the Soviet Union was a far greater threat than Prussia. Indeed, after 1936 Belloc began to describe Hitler as a manifestation of "revived monarchialism": Nazism, like Italian Fascism, was an authoritarian movement in defense of Europe's common culture against atheist Bolshevik revolution. Belloc explained that the new Reich and Italy had risen as the enemies of the international moneylenders and communism—the "twin brother of capitalism." The only real difference, according to Belloc's analysis, was that the German monarchical impulse functioned through the activities of a fantastic Teutonic clique and was barbaric, whereas the new Italian monarchy was homogeneous in its religion and far more cultural, for it lived in the memory of classical Rome.[55] Other Distributists argued that fascism was indeed evil but a far lesser danger than communism, because the latter, like capitalism, was easily camouflaged.

Thus *G.K.'s Weekly* called upon the British government to intervene in the Spanish Civil War on behalf of Franco, and by 1937, its editors proposed that Britain form an alliance with Hitler against the Soviet Union. The journal was disappointed that the British government did not heed these recommendations, but its editors were at least able to take solace in the Nationalists' final victory in the spring of 1939. Franco's triumphant march through Madrid was greeted as a turning point in history: "Spain has awakened from sleep and saved Europe."[56]

Chesterton's departure also had a significant effect on the general political dynamics of the Distributist movement. Distributist organizations and ideas did not disintegrate immediately after 1936. Following Chesterton's death, Belloc and his son-in-law, Reginald Jebb, along with H.S. Paynter and H.D.C. Pepler, were appointed directors of *G.K.'s Weekly*.[57] Reckitt and Richard O'Sullivan resigned from the board of directors, but the new management vowed to carry on the paper in the Chestertonian tradition. The directors also promised to bring the *Weekly* into a closer and well-defined working alliance with the Distributist League. In July of 1936, the League held a special meeting to sort out the immediate leadership problems. Belloc was elected President of the organization (though in the past he seldom had taken an interest in League affairs), while Mrs. Cecil Chesterton, Eric Gill, and T.S. Eliot were chosen as Vice-Presidents.

Chesterton's loyal friends sallied forth to fill the leadership gap, but this was not enough to keep the ranks intact for very long. Many older Distributists left the League and dropped the journal because of the movement's steady drift to the political right. "The Cockpit" and "Correspondence" sections of *G.K.'s Weekly* and the *Weekly Review* were frequently filled with angry letters from well-known Distributists justifiably chastising Belloc and the paper for their fascist sympathies. Mosley's movement was not criticized nearly as much as it had been when Chesterton was in charge, and several Distributist contributors openly supported the political program of the B.U.F. The most blatant appeal for fascism in Distributist circles came from J.L. Benvenisti, a long-time Leaguer and a regular writer for the *Weekly Review*. In 1937, he published a book entitled *The Absent-Minded Revolution*, in which he explained that the concept of the servile state had slowly given way to communism and that Britain was falling into the grips not of capitalist bureaucrats but of Moscow-inspired officials who were planning to liquidate the bourgeoisie. No longer having any hope that British society could be transformed through the force of philosophy, Benvenisti believed that Distributism would be achieved only through the dictatorial power and personality of a single man. He recommended a fascist dictatorship based on the models of Mussolini and Hitler.[58]

Equally disturbing was the *Weekly Review*'s willingness to restrict the civil rights of those with whom it disagreed. In its leader of July 16, 1938, the editors condemned the Home Office's refusal to prohibit the 25th Freethinker's Congress from assembling in London. The *Weekly Review* argued that "freethinker" in this case was merely a euphemism for aggressive anti-God propagandists and that the Congress was part of a worldwide movement engineered from Moscow. Hence there was no reason to allow its participants freedom of speech, since communists never provided their enemies with such liberties: "In any event counter argument does not remove the stain of sacrilege or prevent it from polluting innocent minds." By permitting the "Anti-God Congress," the British government was aligning itself with the communist elements abroad, antagonizing its opponents, and, most serious of all, providing an official seal of approval to the sin of blasphemy. In order to prevent the occurrence of such threatening events in the future, the *Weekly Review* came out in support of Captain A.H.M. Ramsay's Alien Restriction Bill, a proposal aimed to prevent the participation of aliens in any activity or organization which preached ideas contrary to the religious mores of Britain. Captain Ramsay, a Conservative M.P. for Peebles and President of the anti-Semitic "Right Club," was one of the nation's most outspoken supporters of Hitler and the Nazi movement.

E.H. Haywood, E.S.P. Haynes (an old friend of the Chestertons and Belloc), and several other well-known Distributist writers vigorously protested the paper's position as completely contrary to the ideals of Chesterton. Harold Robbins, as editor of the Distributist-inspired *Cross and the Plough*, also took issue with the *Weekly Review*'s position. On August 8, 1940, the *Review*'s editorial had urged that Britain abandon parliamentary government on a territorial basis in favor of representation and government by corporations. Recognizing such a proposal to be an essential feature of fascism, Robbins warned Distributists against straying after this false god. Corporativism, he argued, could not be a panacea for Britain's social ills. Robbins recognized that representation by guilds was an important item, but that it could only succor and buttress something prior to itself, namely the family, which in turn was reinforced and made effective by the possession of property. Robbins feared that the *Weekly Review* was reversing Distributist priorities and thereby threatening the freedom of the individual and the family.

Yet it became clear that Robbins, Haywood, and Haynes were voicing a minority opinion. Not only were the readers of the *Review* relishing the ideas of the B.U.F.—as can be evidenced by numerous pro-fascist letters to the editor—but the editors themselves tacitly embraced fascist ideology when they allowed A.K. Chesterton to advance his views in their paper. A.K. Chesterton, G.K.'s second cousin, was one of Britain's leading fascist intellectuals. He held a very important position in the hierarchy of the B.U.F. and had been editor of the organization's two chief propaganda journals, the *Blackshirt* and *Action*. He officially resigned from Mosley's association in March of 1938, mainly because he felt that the B.U.F.'s uncritical advocacy of Nazism was dishonest and compromising to British patriotism. Thereafter, he became a regular contributor to the *Weekly Review*, though he did not drop his extremist political convictions. Chesterton's articles propounded essentially fascist and anti-Semitic themes, both of which complemented the paper's monomaniacal campaign against communism. His essays championed the return to corporatism and the guilds, though, unlike the earlier Distributist guildsmen, he felt that the state was obliged to assume dictatorial political control.

A.K. Chesterton's authoritarian sentiments were echoed by other writers on the paper as well. For example, in reference to military conscription, a subject of great debate amongst Distributists, the *Review*'s correspondent, Mr. Vincent Wright, recommended a most unChestertonian expedient:

I submit that a period of compulsory national service is in itself a good thing which should survive the war . . . to be in operation when men have turned their swords into ploughshares and their spears into pruning hooks.[59]

Throughout the last years of its existence, the political sections of the *Weekly Review* were totally preoccupied with what it called the worldwide communist conspiracy. The Beveridge proposals (which

laid down the basic structure of Britain's welfare state), the various
international conferences which were designed to establish a world
peace and monetary association, were all roundly condemned as
communist devices to take over the world. The *Weekly Review*
announced its ultimate renunciation of Chesterton's ideals when it
took up the cause of imperialism. The paper emphasized that
Britain could survive as a great nation only if it upheld its imperial
tradition. Britain and the Empire were to remove themselves from
the world financial and trading system so as to hold forth against
international Bolshevism.[60]

The Distributist League continued in existence for only a short
while after Chesterton's death. Without G.K. as the source of inspiration and peacemaker, the organization became hopelessly faction-
alized. There were still brief moments of enthusiasm. In November
of 1937, J.J. Twist of the Birmingham branch, with the assistance of
W.P. Witcutt and others, formed a Distributist political party. The
organization received the official backing of the *Weekly Review*, for
the editors believed that the communists had infiltrated the Labour
Party and that it was necessary to give those who disagreed with both
socialism and capitalism a third political choice. But this singular
outburst of action was short-lived. The party never amounted to
anything—by the end of 1937 it claimed 1,000 members and four
branches—and, with the outbreak of war in 1940, the Distributist
League was disbanded. A new organization was formed in March of
1947. Touted as the "second spring of Distributism," this particular
association outlasted the *Weekly Review* by a few years, but it never
became a movement of any size or importance.

The *Weekly Review* ceased publication in March of 1947. It
survived Chesterton's departure by a decade, though many of the old
guard were justified in believing that the Distributist tradition had
followed their leader to the grave. Belloc had worked hard to keep
the paper in operation, for he realized that it was one of the last truly
independent journals in Britain and the only platform from which
he could still freely expound his political and social views. With the
persistent efforts of able Chestertonians like Reginald Jebb, Hilary
Pepler, and Lewis Filewood, the *Weekly Review* struggled at its best
to maintain the battle against statism and monopoly capitalism,
and it continued to uphold the basic Distributist ideas concerning

private ownership and guild principles. Yet the journal had developed a one-dimensional approach to political issues that was wholly uncharacteristic of *G.K.'s Weekly.*[61]

A chronic shortage of operating capital proved to be the ultimate reason for the demise of the *Weekly Review*. Belloc could no longer afford to give his time to the venture in the absence of a regular salary, and the paper itself had great difficulty attracting good writers who would contribute articles without pay. Belloc best expressed the dilemma in 1939 in a letter to Lady Phipps:

There are hosts of second-rate cranks who will write their fingers to the bone for nothing, but who first of all cannot write, and secondly see everything quite out of proportion, especially when they are on the right side. Many people who agree with us on one point or another are shocked by the rest of the points. The idea of supporting small property and independent farming and saving the country from being proletarian is vaguely regarded as Communism; and we get lots of complaints from people who say that they seem to discover a Catholic tone about the paper. We also get complaints from Catholics who want it to be a sort of sacristy organ; and we get complaints from people who hate the Italians and have an admiration as well as a horror of Berlin.[62]

The extremist politics of the *Weekly Review* made Belloc's fundraising drives especially difficult. The people approached for contributions tended to regard Belloc as personally responsible for the paper's crankishness, even though he had long removed himself from its editorship. And Belloc was not prepared to accept financial help from wealthy parties who were willing to lavish money on publishing schemes, for he generally disapproved of the methods by which those fortunes had been made.

The *Weekly Review* became a shrill and ineffective voice in the paling tradition of Chesterbellocian journalism. In the end, Chesterton's Christian ideals were snuffed out in a tangle of rightist polemics. Maurice Reckitt best summed up the end of Distributism when he wrote:

. . . when the author of the *Outline of Sanity* died, distributism, being left without sanity, died too. When England's greatest modern democrat laid down the flaming torch he had held aloft through so long a night, the movement grouped round him spluttered out as a damp squib mid the showy and mechanical fireworks of Fascism.[63]

Yet at the close of this drama the editors of the *Weekly Review* were convinced that they still might witness the dawning of the Distributist age. In December of 1946, Reginald Jebb pointed with pride to the Blackpool Conservative Conference's decision to embrace the principle of "property-owning democracy" as an official part of its political and social program. Sadly—for him at least—this was what Chesterton had called a "straw in the wind." Distributism was truly dead.

CHAPTER X

Summing Up

The memorable Chesterbelloc partnership was a natural arrangement which grew out of a mutual distaste for imperialism and the philosophical anarchy of the *fin de siècle*. Despite the initial meaning of Shaw's portmanteau, the Chesterbelloc came to signify in the popular mind a particular Catholic approach to the social and political problems of modern Britain. At the base of their views was a strong belief in democracy and the common man and an appreciation of the social importance of private ownership and family life. These two men of enormous literary talent mounted a vigorous journalistic crusade and political movement that sought to beckon a decadent nation back to the fixed standards of an essentially Christian way of life.

The socio-political ideas propounded by Chesterton and Belloc, which came to be called Distributism, merit scholarly attention for a variety of reasons. Most importantly, Distributism was not an incidental phase of Chesterton's and Belloc's literary careers. Rather, it was the all-consuming passion which formed the basis of their philosophical assault on the evils of capitalist-industrial society, and indeed on the whole process of modernization itself. Unlike many modern English writers, who gave only superficial attention to politics, Chesterton and Belloc considered the exposition of the Distributist critique their most important moral duty. Distributist ideas color virtually all of their writings, and are therefore essential to a proper appreciation of the literary careers of Chesterton and Belloc.

Distributism is also of interest as intellectual history, for it constituted a revolutionary response to the conformity of the modern industrial age, and had a momentous impact on an entire generation of Catholic writers, not to mention those on the political left, such as G.D.H. Cole, R.H. Tawney, and the guild socialists.[1] The Chesterbelloc's critique of collectivism tore gaping holes in Fabian philosophy and many people were drawn away from Fabianism because of it. In retrospect, Distributism seems to have been a generation or two in advance of the practical world. Indeed, one could argue that the Chesterbelloc's ideas have an even greater relevance to the problems of post-industrial than of industrial society. There is abundant evidence to suggest that contemporaries are now moving in many of the same directions prescribed by the Chesterbelloc. For example, a major study published in Britain by Earth Resources Research Limited for the Population Stabilisation and Friends of the Earth, and released in the summer of 1974, warned that people in Britain would go hungry before the end of the century unless immediate and drastic steps were taken to increase domestic food production, limit population, and devise agricultural systems that require less energy. The report stated that due to the direct connection between energy and food prices, growing pressures on world food production, and the increasingly marginal returns of greater energy application to agriculture in Britain and other developed countries, it would be necessary in the future to utilize small unit and labor intensive agriculture. Wide-ranging experiments in decentralized industrial production are presently being undertaken in Sweden, the U.S., and elsewhere, precisely because management has discovered that the assembly line process has seriously undermined labor morale and the quality of workmanship. Marshall McLuhan's sociological studies have been concerned with many of the same sorts of issues that preoccupied the Distributists—namely, the impact of industrialism and technology on the life styles of individuals—and McLuhan's writings about the detrimental cultural effects of runaway modernity reiterate a theme familiar to students of the Chesterbelloc: "Today the tyrant rules not by club or fist, but, disguised as a market researcher, he shepherds his flocks in the ways of utility and comfort.''[2] In *Take Today: The Executive as Dropout* (New York, 1972), which deals with the drastic changes brought about by the shift from industrialism to the electric world of programming, McLuhan attempts to demonstrate the cultural necessity for decentralizing work and human organization.

Donald Attwater in 1951 argued that Distributism was ahead of its time, but that such a basic concept would always remain in the minds of men. He believed that eventually it would be rediscovered because of the sheer boredom of the twentieth-century welfare state.[3] Whether or not he was aware of it, Len Murray, General Secretary of the Trades Union Congress, was certainly pointing in this direction when he told Terry Coleman of the *Manchester Guardian* (February, 1974) how important it was that British trade unionists were beginning to rediscover their true radical identity. In terms reminiscent of Distributist orthodoxy, Murray explained that the principles of those who founded their movement were both Christian and ancient:

The driving force of those people . . . was their sense of injustice, their sense of humiliation; it was being robbed of such dignity as they possessed previously, and it was a revolt. I think that is being reborn.

Murray felt that this sense of grievance had been reawakened during the miners' confrontation with the Heath government in the early months of 1974:

I think [the confrontation results from] a consciousness of injustice, and a consciousness of lack of dignity. The sort of jobs they're required to do, and the mechanistic nature of their life. . . . This is a rediscovery, of the archaic things, the basic things, the fundamental things. That sounds very funny . . . pontificatory, but I believe that a lot of very simple things are very true, and they need to be reasserted. So often the simple things get covered up by complexities.[4]

Finally, the present trend back to the basics of simple living and the new assaults on the dehumanizing technology of industrial capitalism demonstrated in the works of E.F. Schumacher, Paul Goodman, Ivan Illich, Jacques Ellul, and Michael Harrington, among others, and the increasing popularity of ecologically-minded, back-to-the-land periodicals such as Britain's *Resurgence* and the *Country Journal* in New England, attest to the current relevance of Distributist social and economic objectives.

In the beginning, the Chesterbelloc felt that social and political reform might be achieved through parliamentary politics. However, Belloc's personal encounter with what he called the "party system" convinced him that constructive change could come about only if the public were made to realize the insidious power of money, which, in his view, completely controlled parliamentary government. Hence, in 1911 he and Cecil Chesterton launched the *Eye-Witness*, a journalistic venture which aimed to convince the public that the nation's political system was riddled with corruption. The *Eye* and *New Witness* were not polite papers: they were intended to shock readers by laying bare the rottenness of British politics. The literary partnership of Hilaire Belloc and Cecil Chesterton, two controversialists with enormous capacities for hate, resulted in some rather rancorous journalism. Their potential for careless extremism was certainly manifested in the Marconi affair (an incident which served to alienate Belloc and both Chestertons from mainstream politics), and by the end of World War I the *New Witness* had earned a reputation for being not quite balanced on the subject of Prussians and Jews.

Belloc had an answer for what he felt was the deterioration of British politics and a bungled peace. According to his analysis, the old British aristocracy had been replaced by a clique of vulgar plutocrats who danced to the whims of financiers. To remedy this ill, he and Cecil Chesterton had called for some sweeping parliamentary changes and a restoration of monarchical prerogative. G.K. Chesterton fully absorbed the political views of his brother and Belloc and also shared their convictions about the importance of cleaning up corruption in British political life. G.K.'s true feelings about such matters were revealed when he insisted upon carrying on his brother's journalism after the latter's death in 1918. As editor of the *New Witness* and *G.K.'s Weekly*, he kept these reactionary political ideas in the public eye, while at the same time championing his own affirmative ideal of the Distributist state.

Distributism and indeed the Chesterbelloc's whole approach to life were firmly rooted in the tradition of the Roman Church. This factor in itself made it inevitable that their political movement would function outside the normal paths of British politics. The fact that Chesterton and Belloc perpetually emphasized their ties with Rome undoubtedly prejudiced their case with the public, for Britain was steeped in an almost unbroken anti-Catholic tradition. In addition, the strong Whig-Protestant bias in British intellectual circles forced the Chesterbelloc to indulge in unusually tendentious historical polemics. Belloc, in particular, appears to have exaggerated his ideas just to get a public hearing. This only served to highlight the Chesterbelloc's public image as unrespectable political extremists. The *New Witness*'s savage attacks on those associated with the Marconi scandal and the Northcliffe papers further isolated the two writers, so that after the First World War they were effectively prevented from expressing their views in the major English newspapers.

On the whole, the ideas of Chesterton and Belloc were not taken seriously by the political and religious establishment. There was good reason for this: if carried to its logical conclusion, Distributism would have led to revolution and anarchy. Like the Levellers of old, the Chesterbelloc fully intended to turn the world upside-down. Although Chesterton and Belloc had a negligible impact on mainstream politics, their perceptive judgment of industrial society and parliamentary government gained them an enthusiastic following amongst those who were upset at what they perceived as Britain's aimless drift into the twentieth century. Those who considered themselves part of the Distributist circle also approached politics and social issues from fundamentally Catholic assumptions. Opposed to the socialist complexion of the Labour movement as well as to the capitalist sympathies of the Tory Party, the Chesterbelloc alliance asserted that modern man needed the determinate standards of a hierarchical society, the security of private ownership, and a healthy family life in order to exercise the Christian ideal of freedom.

G.K.'s Weekly and the Distributist League were the major vehicles for bringing about the kinds of changes the Chesterbelloc felt necessary for Britain. Where Cecil Chesterton's papers undertook the burden of convincing the public that corruption existed, G.K.'s journal aimed to get the public to do something about it. In Chesterton's words: "Instead of horrifying men by facts they do not know [which had been the editorial objective of the *Eye* and *New Witness*], we have the desperate task of making them discontented with the facts they do know." Men had to have the scales removed from their eyes so they could appreciate "how utterly unreal is the real state of things." "The serious business will begin when they have at last seen the joke."[5] Throughout its early years of publication (1925-1929), *G.K.'s Weekly* expressed a willingness to work through the system (the parliamentary Labour Party and the trade union movement), since it seemed the most sensible way to extend Distributist principles. But after the Labour government's failure to modify the Trades Disputes Act of 1927 and after the trade unionists warmly supported the Mond-Turner proposals (which Distributists saw as a major step towards the implementation of the servile state), the Chesterbelloc alliance lost faith in both the Labour Party and the trade union movement. It now seemed painfully clear that the workers had been bought off by fringe benefits and higher wages. The trade unionists had given up their struggle for control and ownership of the means of production, an objective which Distributists deemed essential to a just society. Similarly, Distributists were convinced that the feckless Labour cabinet (which had included many men from the Party's right wing who supported the Mond-Turner talks) had renounced its true radical origins by embracing the party system. Since the Labour Party and the trade union movement remained deaf to the guild idea, *G.K.'s Weekly* and the League were obliged to reassert the reactionary proposal that Parliament be displaced by monarchical rule. It seemed that Britain's democratic system was beyond repair. The money power had thwarted reform by co-opting the new Labour government.

The overall efforts of *G.K.'s Weekly* and the League to popularize Distributist ideas were seriously compromised by internal ideological disputes. Ceaseless debate over the methods and objectives of Distributist reform in the pages of the *Weekly* created the impression that the movement was riddled with dissension. The so-called extremist group—although a distinct minority—opposed the use of machinery and proposed a purely agricultural economy for Britain, thereby giving a medievalist and hopelessly anachronistic image to Distributism. This clearly damaged the reputation of Chesterbellocian social thinking within both Catholic and secular reformist circles. However, the official Distributist line was a good deal more open-ended than this, calling for a "mixed economy" of industrial guild production and small farms. The movement was also severely criticized for its failure to draw up a reform program. Chesterton and Belloc did draft a series of clear and quite reasonable proposals for bringing about a redistribution of property. However, it was not felt necessary to draw up a blueprint for the Distributist state, for such projections were considered the prattle of Fabian utopians and other such visionaries who believed it possible to manipulate future societies. In general, Distributists opposed the whole notion of utopias. Nevertheless, the Distributists forwarded reform proposals designed to bring about specific social and economic changes. Many of these proposals deserved closer attention than they got; it was unfortunate, for example, that the government chose to ignore the Birmingham scheme, since a few of its suggestions might have ameliorated at least some of the economic and psychological ills of the depression years.

Chesterton and Belloc were mainly interested in educating the public about Distributist theory. *G.K.'s Weekly* and the League were intended only as propaganda organs: they were to show man the beauty and adventure of owning property. Ultimately, the success of Distributism depended upon individual men who would desire the liberty and self-reliance that private ownership could bring. Unlike socialism, capitalism, and fascism, Distributism could not be imposed on the majority by a narrow coterie of revolutionists or well-financed wirepullers. In the tradition of anarchism, Distributism could not be realized through laws or the sinews of bureaucracy: it had to be desired by common man and would endure only through the will to possess property. Thus the Chesterbelloc had to make people aware of the efficacy of Christian social and economic values as the basis for the intellectual revolution which was the prerequisite for the practical implementation of Distributism. This meant that the nation would have to return to essentially Catholic values; but given Britain's Protestant tradition and the secular and bureaucratic temper of postwar industrial society, such a requirement was probably impossible to fulfill.

In the final analysis, the Chesterbelloc did not fail completely in this Sisyphean endeavor, for their ideas were the inspiration of the Catholic back-to-the-land movements and the mainspring of the neo-Thomistic revival in Catholic intellectual circles. Equally important was their success in breaking down siege Catholicism in England. As Douglas Jerrold put it: "The Chesterbelloc brought Catholicism out of private and into public life."[6] Their aggressive polemical writings destroyed the Catholic intellectual's inferiority complex and offered him some well-thought-out social and political principles with which to challenge the ideological assumptions of the modern world.

The Chesterbelloc alliance was not an imitative movement. There was an obvious parallel with the French Right; indeed, Belloc greatly admired Maurras and Déroulède, and all three propounded similar anti-Semitic themes. But the resemblance was only skin-deep. Distributism developed independently of contemporary continental political thought, though it seemed to have some affinity with nineteenth-century continental romanticism and its cult of the middle ages. Belloc's peculiar conception of Catholicism as culture certainly appears to have been unique for his own generation.[7] His view of monarchy was not the same as that of Maurras, nor did he share the anti-republicanism of the elitist French Right. Finally, Chesterton's application of Thomist principles to contemporary society was made without reference to continental Catholic social philosophy.

The Distributist movement was also unique in the context of English political tradition. Drawing upon a mélange of attitudes and ideas (Chartism, Burkean organicism, French revolutionary thought, socialism, anarchism, populism, and liberalism), the social philosophy of Chesterton and Belloc was a peculiar hybrid of both radical and conservative ideas.[8] Although leaning to the right, many of their intellectual sympathies were with the left. Belloc began his political career as a Radical Liberal, Chesterton always called himself a Liberal in the radical tradition, and both men flirted with anarcho-syndicalism during the prewar years. Most Distributists conspicuously emphasized a loyalty to the social and anarchistic ideals of Ruskin and Morris, as well as to the egalitarian concepts of the early socialists. The Chesterbelloc ultimately rejected the labor movement because of its statism. But on the whole, Distribut-

ism seems to have had closer ties to the tradition of English conservatism; it looked to the past for social and political models, recognized
man as a fallen creature, and appreciated the practical necessity of
hierarchy, social deference, religion, and strong family ties. Much
like Carlyle, Arnold, and other nineteenth-century romantic conservatives, Chesterton and Belloc were always casting their nets for
heroes (Mussolini and Franco were seen to possess heroic qualities),
detested the narrow uniformity of industrial society, and placed
importance on the necessity of social variety, which, they argued,
could only be maintained through the possession of property. Most
importantly, the Chesterbelloc was never against the idea of class: as
opposed to the left, its attacks were not aimed at the social structure
but at those within the occupations who were thought to be perverting the social contract.

The Chesterbelloc alliance championed what it called the politics
of reaction, but Distributists refused to have anything to do with
British fascism (at least before Chesterton's death) or with Conservative reactionaries. Unlike the Tory Right, the Chesterbelloc had
strong links with Liberal radicalism and were staunch "little Eng-
landers" unalterably opposed to the British imperial tradition.
Moreover, some of the *Weekly*'s most bitter attacks were directed at
the major spokesmen for Tory conservatism—Rothermere, Chur-
chill, and Beaverbrook—mainly because of their designs to perpetuate the status quo. Nor was there much connection between the
Chesterbelloc and the writers of the reactionary right. Poets like
W.B. Yeats and Ezra Pound talked of the need for a hierarchical and
ordered society, but this was due to their vision of ordinary men as
feeble and despicable beasts. Chesterton and Belloc saw the need for
authority because of original sin, and they advocated religion, not
totalitarian ideology, as a solution to the problem. The Chesterbelloc wrote for everyman: Eliot, Yeats, and the so-called "reactionary
intellectuals" aimed their esoteric words at the elite and brooded
because they could not find an audience of sufficient intelligence to
understand them.[9] Chesterton's and Eliot's religious views were
remarkably similar, but unlike the Chesterbelloc, Eliot was no
democrat.[10] At one point Eliot expressed doubt as to whether ordinary citizens were ever informed enough to have the right to a
political opinion. Eliot's fellow reactionaries were even more ex-

plicit in their scorn for the common man. Wyndham Lewis considered the masses "a crowd of useless things" and called for a strong
ruler who would treat the people like dogs for their own good.[11] The
political systems advocated by Lewis, Pound, Eliot, Yeats, and D.H.
Lawrence, having nothing but contempt for Chesterton's ordinary,
"beer-drinking, creed-making, fighting, failing, sensual, respectable man," rested firmly on the theory of elites, and when they wrote
about social issues it was only for artistic reasons.[12] For some of these
intellectuals, literature—not man or God—became the end. Man
was deemed destined to create something more important than man:
"art." Thus was the individual subordinated to the cultural ideal.
Chesterbelloc and the reactionary intellectuals may have shared an
appreciation for the organic society, but the Distributist's sense of
priorities stemmed from a completely different legacy—that associated with the radicalism of William Cobbett and the vigorously
independent yeoman who owed allegiance to no one but God and
country.

The Distributist circle dissipated after Chesterton's death. G.K.
himself was partly responsible for this, since, in the end, he found it
too painful to criticize Italy, a Catholic power, for the sin of imperialism. The singular Bellocian view of Catholicism as culture
blinded the movement to the crimes of Italy. But if the Distributist
alliance was seriously weakened after 1936 because of the death of
Chesterton, who alone was capable of holding the factions together,
it was Belloc and the Latinophiles who delivered the final blow to
the unity of the group. The *Weekly Review*'s uncritical support of
Mussolini's foreign policy, its growing willingness to sanction
fascist measures for Britain's domestic ills (despite the fact that
Chesterton had persistently condemned the policies of the B.U.F.),
and its proposal for an alliance with the dictators against the Soviet
Union, had the cumulative effect of drumming the true Distributists
out of the movement.

In the end, the Distributists fell victim to that sin of exaggeration
which Chesterton had once called heresy. They stretched a portion
of Catholic truth out of its proper and well-balanced perspective.
The Latinophiles had been guilty of a special intellectual failing—
that heretical oversimplification of one complex of ideas (Bolshe-

vism, Jewish finance, and Catholicism as culture) at the expense of the intricate whole. Distributism lost its balance, and hence its own sanity.

Notes

INTRODUCTION

1. *See* Paul Goodman, *New Reformation: Notes of a Neolithic Conservative* (New York, 1970), p. 148.
2. *See* Paul Goodman, *People or Personnel: Decentralizing and the Mixed System* (New York, 1965), p. 12.
3. Goodman, *New Reformation*, p. 149. These general sentiments are revealed throughout anarchist literature. For more, *see* April Carter, *The Political Theory of Anarchism* (London, 1971), George Woodcock, *Anarchism* (Cleveland, 1962), and Paul Eltzbacher, *Anarchism* (New York, 1958).
4. This term was coined by Gregory Macdonald in his "The Other Face: Chesterton's Later Journalism," *Chesterton Review*, Spring/Summer, 1975.

CHAPTER I

1. André Maurois, *Prophets and Poets* (New York, 1935), p. 193.
2. "A Gap in English Education," *The Speaker*, May 4, 1901, p. 129 ff. *See also* Dudley Barker, *G.K. Chesterton* (London, 1973), p. 90.
3. G.K. Chesterton, *What's Wrong with the World* (New York, 1910), p. 105.
4. Maurice Evans, *G.K. Chesterton* (Cambridge, 1939), p. 49.
5. "Wells and the World State," *What I Saw in America* (New York, 1922), pp. 233-36.
6. "On the Open Conspiracy," in *Come to Think of It* (New York, 1931), p. 110.
7. James G. Nelson, *The Early Nineties: A View from the Bodley Head* (Cambridge, Mass., 1971), p. 299.
8. H. Grisewood (ed.), *Ideas and Beliefs of the Victorians* (London, 1949), p. 23.
9. G.B. Shaw, "Economic Basis of Socialism," in *Fabian Essays*, G.B. Shaw, ed. (London, 1889), p. 24.
10. Quotes taken from G.K. Chesterton, *The Victorian Age in Literature* (London, 1916), pp. 109-111 and the *Daily News*, June 26, 1909, as cited in A.L. Maycock, *The Man Who Was Orthodox* (London, 1963), p. 130.
11. G.K. Chesterton, "Milton and Merry England," in *A Gleaming Cohort* (London, 1926), p. 184.
12. G.K. Chesterton, *Heretics* (New York, 1905), p. 29.

13. *Ibid.*, p. 32.
14. *Ibid.*, p. 50.
15. G.K. Chesterton, *Orthodoxy* (London, 1908), p. 10.
16. James Marcus Ryan, "G.K. Chesterton as Literary Critic" (unpublished Ph.D. thesis, Department of English, Boston University, 1950), p. 30.
17. G.K. Chesterton, "At the Sign of the World's End: The End of the World's End," *New Witness*, May 4, 1923.
18. Chesterton, like several other well-known writers who converted to Catholicism in the inter-war years, was raised in the Anglican Church. For many converts, Anglicanism, with its legacy of latitudinarianism, lacked the fixed principles of authority and doctrinal discipline which they saw so splendidly exemplified in the tradition of the Roman Church. Chesterton joined the Church because it provided the rudder of dogma to an otherwise rudderless ship.
19. Orage's paper became one of the leading intellectual journals of the day, providing a neutral meeting ground and sounding board for writers of new and different points of view.
20. Wallace Martin, *The New Age under Orage* (New York, 1967), p. 231.
21. Evans, *G.K. Chesterton*, p. 3.
22. Maycock, *Man Who Was Orthodox*, p. 21.
23. G.K. Chesterton, *George Bernard Shaw* (New York, 1950), p. 85.
24. *Ibid.*, p. 67.
25. G.K. Chesterton, *All I Survey* (New York, 1933), p. 111.
26. G.K. Chesterton, "The Mystagogues," in *Miscellany of Men* (London, 1912), p. 180.

CHAPTER II

1. Hilaire Belloc, "The Liberal Tradition," in *Essays in Liberalism*, Hilaire Belloc *et al.* (London, 1897), p. 7.
2. Captain Dreyfus was a Jewish officer in the French Army who was unjustly accused of passing military secrets to the German General Staff. He was found guilty of treason by a military court in 1894 and deported to Devil's Island. In the meantime evidence accumulated showing his innocence. The Army refused to reconsider the case, unwilling to admit that it had made a mistake. Generally speaking, the conservative and rightist element in France (anti-Republicans, the Church, landed interests, anti-Semites, royalists, etc.) rallied to the Army's side, insisting that a retrial would be "unpatriotic" and only serve to weaken the nation's confidence in the military. In 1899, after years of tumultuous debate, Dreyfus was pardoned and, in 1906, fully exonerated.
3. Chesterton's late-blooming anti-Semitism can be attributed to Belloc, and it has had a deleterious effect on his reputation. W.H. Auden, a long-time admirer of G.K.'s novels and poetry, purposely stayed away from his nonfictional writings because of Chesterton's reputation as an anti-Semite. (W.H. Auden, *G.K.C.: Selections from His Non-Fictional Prose* [New York, 1970], p. 11.)

4. Belloc was probably right on this count. Douglas Woodruff claimed that when he was at Oxford, some thirty years after Belloc, the dons were still hostile to his memory. This was due, wrote Woodruff, not so much to Belloc's advocacy of the French Revolution but to his anti-Dreyfus line and his exaggerated political views. Interestingly enough, Belloc always insisted that he was anti-Dreyfus, not anti-Dreyfusard.

5. *See* Robert Speaight, "Belloc the Writer," *Spode House Review*, August 1972, pp. 11-19.

6. *See* Arnold Lunn, *And Yet So New* (New York, 1958), p. 65. For an opposite view, *see* Rev. Philip Hughes, "Mr. Belloc's Reviewer Replies," *Clergy Review*, April 1935, pp. 317-322.

7. Lunn, *Yet So New*, p. 79.

8. Hilaire Belloc, *Danton* (New York, 1928), p. 37.

9. Hilaire Belloc, *A Companion to Mr. Wells' 'Outline of History'* (San Francisco, 1927), p. 4.

10. Robert Speaight, "The European Mind: Hilaire Belloc's Thought and Writings," *Times Literary Supplement*, May 21, 1954, p. 321.

11. Hilaire Belloc, "On Jonathan Swift," in *Conversation with a Cat* (London, 1931), pp. 130-132.

12. Hilaire Belloc, *The Cruise of the Nona* (London, 1925), pp. 54-55.

13. For a discussion of the literary and political style of French rightist writers *see* Richard Griffiths, *The Reactionary Revolution: The Catholic Revival in French Literature, 1870-1914* (New York, 1965).

14. Frank J. Sheed, "Belloc the Apologist," *The Tablet*, July 25, 1953, p. 82.

15. *See* Belloc's *A Shorter History of England* (London, 1934).

16. Douglas Woodruff, "Hilaire Belloc: His Life and Work, An Outline of Activities and Achievements," *The Tablet*, July 25, 1953, p. 79.

17. There also may have been a personal or psychological dimension to Belloc's loathing of the rich. He once told Douglas Woodruff that his mother lost a considerable amount of money to an acquaintance who played the stock market. The loss forced Mrs. Belloc to sell the London property she inherited from her father and to retire to a small house at Slindon, Sussex. Belloc said that he was not told about this until much later, but that henceforth in the presence of rich people his mother and sister would say: "Down on all fours, down on all fours; these people are very rich!" This seems to have had an ineradicable impact on Belloc's sensitivities. He came to hate his family's obeisance to wealth and vowed to fight it for the rest of his life. *See* Douglas Woodruff, "The Radical and the Catholic," *The Spode House Review*, August 1972, p. 21.

18. Hilaire Belloc, *Danton*, p. 7.

19. *Ibid.*, p. 7.

20. Hilaire Belloc, *Napoleon* (London, 1932), pp. 16-21.

21. Speaight, "European Mind," p. 322. (Douglas Woodruff also wrote that Belloc had a great admiration for the writings and doctrines of Maurras. *See The Tablet* [July 25, 1953], p. 79.)

22. Marie Belloc Lowndes, *Where Love and Friendship Dwelt* (New York, 1943), p. 59.

23. Speaight, who lamented the influence of Maurras on Belloc, believed that had he come across Charles Péguy instead of Maurras in those impressionable years, he would have been a better guide to those who were shortly to fall under the sway of his brilliant pen. (Robert Speaight, "Personal Column," for *The Tablet*. Copy sent to Mr. T.C. Burns, November 20, 1969. "Speaight Papers," Special Collections, Mugar Library, Boston University, p. 3). This seems to have been true especially in the case of the two Chestertons.

24. This was a movement of concerned Catholics, lay and clerical, who endeavored to restore a Christian tone to English life. The effort was inspired by Pius X's encyclical *On Social Action* (1905), which first coined the phrase "Catholic Action." Pius X urged Catholic lay readers to attempt a reform of society according to Christian principles, but issued a warning against romantic revivalism, explaining that the Church had to adjust to the changing needs of modern society. In Britain this effort took on many forms, encompassing several different movements (Distributism and back-to-the-land included), all of which worked towards the amelioration of socio-economic conditions and the strengthening of the Catholic family.

25. Speaight, "Personal Column," p. 2.

26. Renée Haynes, *Hilaire Belloc* (London, 1953), p. 17. This book contains an excellent section on Belloc's religious views.

27. Many Distributists saw the *Partito Nazionale Fascista*, and other such groups in Austria and Spain, resurrecting Catholic culture.

28. John P. McCarthy, "Hilaire Belloc: Critic of the New Liberalism" (unpublished Ph.D. thesis, Department of History, Columbia University, 1969), p. 37.

29. A.L.S., A.N.S. to A.P. Watt and Son. Bleakhouse, Slindon, Arundel. July 18 and August 6, 1903. Belloc Correspondence, Henry W. and Albert A. Berg Collection, New York Public Library, Astor, Lenox and Tilden Foundations.

30. C. Creighton Mandell and Edward Shanks, *Hilaire Belloc: The Man and His Works* (London, 1916), introduction.

31. *See* Hilaire Belloc, *The Place of a Peasantry in Modern Civilization* (Manchester, 1910), pp. 279-80.

32. Maisie Ward, *G.K. Chesterton* (New York, 1943), p. 183.

33. Hesketh Pearson and Hugh Kingsmill, *Talking of Dick Whittington* (London, 1947), p. 212.

34. Nor was Belloc quick to forgive: "May all my enemies go to hell, Noel, Noel, Noel" was his Christmas message one year. (Wilfred Sheed, *The Morning After* [New York, 1972], p. 267.)

35. Edward J. Collins, "Distributism," *The Irish Monthly*, January 19, 1944, p. 7.

36. William B. Furlong feels that the relationship between G.K. and Belloc was basically fatuous. *See* his *GBS/GKC: Shaw and Chesterton, The Metaphysical Jesters* (University Park, Penn., 1970), p. 11.

37. *Blackfriars*, July 1936, p. 486.

CHAPTER III

1. G.K. Chesterton, *The Autobiography of G.K. Chesterton* (New York, 1936), p. 163.
2. G.K. Chesterton, *The Everlasting Man* (London, 1925), p. 158.
3. Hilaire Belloc, *The Alternative* (London, 1947), p. 41.
4. G.K. Chesterton, *What's Wrong with the World* (New York, 1910), pp. 341-342.
5. These arguments were used extensively by the back-to-the-land movements of the inter-war years. Many of these organizations, which endeavored to bring British families back to agriculture and handicraft production, were inspired by the Chesterbelloc social idea. Indeed, the largest Catholic back-to-the-land movements were almost all engineered by members of the Distributist League.
6. G.K. Chesterton, *The Outline of Sanity* (New York, 1927), pp. 29-30.
7. Belloc previously had been turned down as a candidate because of his religion by five different constituencies.
8. Robert Speaight, *The Life of Hilaire Belloc* (New York, 1967), p. 191.
9. Hilaire Belloc, "The Eye Witness," *Weekly Review*, October 29, 1939.
10. *Parliamentary Debates*, House of Commons, 4th series, CLII (February 22, 1906), p. 614. As cited in John P. McCarthy, "Hilaire Belloc: Critic of the New Liberalism" (unpublished Ph.D. thesis, Department of History, Columbia University, 1969), p. 76.
11. Roy Jenkins, *Asquith: Portrait of a Man and an Era* (New York, 1966), pp. 162-163.
12. *See The New Age*, December 7, December 21, 1907; August 8, 1908. This seems to have provided some of the grist for *Emmanuel Burden*.
13. McCarthy, "Hilaire Belloc," p. 100.
14. Hilaire Belloc, "On Licensing," *The English Review*, June, 1909, p. 600. As cited in McCarthy, "Hilaire Belloc," p. 102.
15. Hilaire Belloc, *The Times*, February 14, 1910.
16. Belloc did stand for a third term in the December 1910 election but then withdrew his candidacy under pressure from the Suffragettes. However, he had been abandoned by the Liberal Party machine after his first election to Parliament.
17. Starting on March 25, 1909, Cecil Chesterton began a series of articles in *The New Age* highlighting the falsehood of the Chesterbelloc's critique of socialism.
18. *See* "Notes," *The New Age*, February 29, 1908.
19. Cecil Chesterton, "How the Rich Rule Us," *The New Age*, July 28, 1910.
20. Cecil Chesterton, "Hilaire Belloc," *Living Age*, December 15, 1906. As cited in McCarthy, "Hilaire Belloc," p. 127.
21. Hilaire Belloc and Cecil Chesterton, *The Party System* (London, 1911), pp. 33-34.
22. *Ibid.*, p. 29.
23. Christopher Hollis, *The Mind of Chesterton* (Coral Gables, Florida, 1970), pp. 113-114.

24. Belloc and Chesterton, *Party System*, pp. 101-104.
25. *Parliamentary Debates*, House of Commons, 5th series, XI (October, 1909), p. 1958. As cited in McCarthy, "Hilaire Belloc," pp. 139-140.
26. Belloc and Chesterton, *Party System*, p. 158.
27. Hilaire Belloc, *The Servile State* (New York, 1946), p. 50.
28. *Ibid.*, p. 76.
29. Hilaire Belloc and J. Ramsay MacDonald, *Socialism and the Servile State* (London, 1911), pp. 5-11.
30. Pope Leo XIII, "The Condition of Labor," *Five Great Encyclicals* (New York, 1939), pp. 2-7; 15-17; 22-23.
31. Chesterton often emphasized violence and struggle in his fictional writings. Yet he was not a man of action himself and probably was never completely serious when arguing for battle in real life. Moreover, like most men of his day, entirely unexposed to the brutality of later generations, he certainly could not have conceived of the physical and moral damage which could result from social violence.
32. As quoted in Frank A. Lea, *The White Knight of Battersea: G.K. Chesterton* (London, 1946), p. 64.

CHAPTER IV

1. *See* "Will the Bill Do? *Eye-Witness*, June 22, 1911.
2. Hilaire Belloc, "Honest and Dishonest Insurance," *Eye-Witness*, June 6, 1912. *See also* "The Fraud of the Poll Tax," *Daily Herald*, November 24, 1913.
3. Junius, "Open Letter to a Trade Union Secretary," *Eye-Witness*, July 20, 1911.
4. G.K. Chesterton, *Irish Impressions* (New York, 1919), p. 84.
5. Cecil Chesterton, "Emancipation and the Wage System," *The New Age*, April 25, 1912.
6. *See* "Two Strikes: 1889-1911," August 17, 1911; "The Victory of the Rich," August 24, 1911; "The First Step," August 31, 1911 and "Tom Mann and Westminster," May 16, 1912. The *Eye-Witness* opposed the Labour Disputes Bill for essentially the same reasons that it denounced the Insurance Act: the state (under plutocratic control) was constructing a bureaucratic device that would regulate the working classes to servile status.
7. Edwin E. Slosson believed Chesterbelloc's socio-political ideas to have been close to the *Sillon* of Marc Sangnier, which was condemned by papal encyclical in 1912. Slosson saw both Chesterton and Belloc to be syndicalists, labeling Chesterton an "English Sillonist." *See* Edwin E. Slosson, *Six Major Prophets* (Boston, 1917), p. 158.
8. Mrs. Cecil Chesterton, *The Chestertons* (London, 1941), p. 92.
9. *Ibid.*, p. 114.
10. It must be said that Belloc was one of the first, if not the first, to draw public attention to the sale of honors.
11. Mrs. Cecil Chesterton, *The Chestertons*, pp. 119-120.

12. For a detailed discussion of Chesterton's battle against eugenics *see* Margaret Canovan, *G.K. Chesterton: Radical Populist*, (New York, 1977), pp. 66-72 and her "Chesterton's Attack on the Proto-Nazis: New Light on the Black Legend," *The Chesterton Review*, Spring/Summer, 1977, pp. 246-259.
13. "Comments of the Week," *New Witness*, October 4, 1918.
14. Brocard Sewell, *My Dear Time's Waste* (London, 1966), p. 25.
15. H.G. Wells, "An Open Letter to G.K. Chesterton," *New Witness*, August 10, 1916.
16. Junius, "An Open Letter to the Readers of the Eye-Witness," *Eye-Witness*, June 13, 1912.
17. Cecil Chesterton, "The Wrath of Mr. Wells," *New Witness*, July 27, 1916.
18. *Ibid.*
19. G.K. Chesterton, *The Autobiography of G.K. Chesterton* (New York, 1936), pp. 205-206.
20. It should be pointed out that Rufus Isaacs and Herbert Samuel were the first Jews, outside of Disraeli, to have served in a British cabinet.
21. Cecil Chesterton, "For the Defense," *Eye-Witness*, July 4, 1912.
22. Cecil's claim appears to have been false. He was never able to produce evidence of this, nor has anyone else. The charge of corruption regarding the granting of the contract was dropped immediately by the Select Committee, because there was no evidence to support it.
23. *See* Frances Donaldson, *The Marconi Scandal* (London, 1962), p. 185.
24. Eleanor Jebb, *Testimony to Hilaire Belloc* (London, 1956), p. 63.
25. G.K. Chesterton, "At the Sign of the World's End: An Open Letter to Lord Reading," *New Witness*, December 13, 1918.
26. As quoted in Dudley Barker, *G.K. Chesterton* (London, 1973), p. 218.
27. *Daily Herald*, April 15, 1914.
28. F. Hugh O'Donnell, "20 Years Later," *New Witness*, February 12, 1914.
29. Theodore Maynard, "A Literary Freelance in London," II, "The *New Witness* Group," *The Catholic World*, June, 1931, p. 282.
30. Letter to Maurice Baring (August 31, 1916), ed. Robert Speaight, *Letters from Hilaire Belloc* (London, 1958), p. 73.
31. Chestertonians are now willing to examine the charges of anti-Semitism more openly. This is the case with recent works by Ian Boyd and Margaret Canovan. For an excellent, detailed discussion of the origins and manifestations of Chesterton's racial views, and how some contemporary Chestertonians feel about them, *see* Owen Edwards, "Chesterton and Tribalism," and J.M. Purcell; Brocard Sewell; John Sullivan; Peter Hunt; and Gregory MacDonald, "Another Look at 'Chesterton's Tribalism': Some Responses to Owen Edwards," *The Chesterton Review*, Fall/Winter, 1979-80, pp. 33-96.
32. Hilaire Belloc, *The Jews* (Boston, 1922), pp. 4-5.
33. *Ibid.*, pp. 51-61.
34. Belloc's position on the Jews was almost identical to that of the French Right. Maurras' initial dislike of the Jews stemmed from his distress at the growing number of foreigners to be found in French public affairs. He concluded at an

early age that these "aliens" were incapable of understanding France's problems fully, because they had no roots in French tradition. Like the Chesterbelloc, Maurras also insisted that Jews were incapable of assimilation into national cultures and that they directly threatened national vitality by living within the community. Moreover, *Action Française* considered the Jews to be divorced from the soil. They possessed a vagabond wealth which knew no boundaries and could be packed about like a suitcase from one capital to the next.

35. G.K. Chesterton, *The New Jerusalem* (New York, 1921), pp. 276-277.
36. *Ibid.*, p. 289.
37. This was also the official position of the *New Witness* when Cecil was editor.
38. Christopher Hollis, *The Mind of Chesterton* (Coral Gables, Florida, 1970), p. 159.
39. In his book on Cecil Chesterton, Brocard Sewell says that Cecil and Gilbert Chesterton wrote anti-German propaganda for the British government. He claims that most of their essays were directed at foreign audiences, though certainly very few foreigners could be expected to read the *New Witness*.
40. *See* Eugen Weber, *Action Française* (Stanford, Calif. 1962), p. 97.
41. Cecil Chesterton, "Perverted Germany," *New Witness*, March 30, 1916.
42. Cecil Chesterton, *Perils of Peace*, p. 230.
43. Letter to E.S.P. Haynes (September 20, 1915), ed. Robert Speaight, *Letters from Hilaire Belloc*, p. 365.
44. Alfred Harmsworth (Viscount Northcliffe) can be said to have begun the age of the mass media in Britain. At the height of his power, at least half the publishing enterprises of Fleet Street (newspapers and magazines) were under his control.
45. "In the 'Evening Standard' Diary there was a perfect passion for mentioning the names of Chesterton and Belloc. I have cut down the space alloted to advertising them. Now their names seldom appear. Besides, their journalism is so dull, and their statements are utterly unreliable." (A.J.P. Taylor, *Beaverbrook* [New York, 1972], p. 229.)
46. *See* Sewell, *Time's Waste*, p. 28.
47. G.K. Chesterton, "At the Sign of the World's End: The *New Witness* and the New Situation," *New Witness*, December 20, 1918.
48. Generally, Belloc saw this rebellion as having unleashed the following events: (1) the rapid extension of physical science and with it the rise of quantitative thinking—i.e., materialism; (2) the rise of capitalism (in Belloc's definition "the possession of the means of production by the few, and the exploitation of the many"); (3) the corruption of the principle of authority to the point of confusion with mere force; (4) destructive skepticism, which began from the spirit of complete negation and led ultimately to a belief in nothing but force; (5) and finally, the universal extension of despair. This sort of historical criticism was quite typical during these years within the philosophical circles of the English Right. The emphasis on original sin, the Fall, and the growth of destructive pride and materialism (all of which were seen to have grown out of the Renaissance and Reformation) were constant themes in the essays of T.E.

Hulme, Romain de Maetzu, and other self-proclaimed reactionaries writing in Orage's *The New Age*.

49. Hilaire Belloc, *Europe and the Faith* (New York, 1920), p. 252.

50. T.E. Hulme had offered the same warning: religion was a basic human need "parallel to appetite and the instinct of sex."

51. This interpretation was not shared by the Catholic hierarchy. In fact, Belloc's position on this matter directly contradicted that taken by Pope Benedict XV. The Pope opposed the war from the beginning, assuming a position which he called "apostolic pacifism." The Vatican felt that the war should have been avoided at all costs, since conflict on such a scale would irreparably damage European civilization. Benedict XV even spoke out against conscription ("a monstrous tyranny") and did his utmost to bring the war to an end on a policy of "no annexations and no indemnities." Cecil Chesterton, on the other hand, eulogized conscription as a beneficent invention of the French Revolution and thought anyone who criticized it "an irresponsible crank." (Hollis, *The Mind of Chesterton*, p. 162.) Belloc and Cecil Chesterton also opposed terminating the war on a premature peace plan.

52. Belloc, *Europe and the Faith*, p. 261. Belloc's view of European civilization as fundamentally Catholic was certainly exaggerated. Yet many Catholics accepted his thesis. Even the non-Catholic philosopher, C.E.M. Joad, contended that the Catholic Aristotelian-Platonic synthesis still ranked as the dominant tradition of Western philosophy. *See* C.E.M. Joad, *Decadence: A Philosophical Inquiry* (London, 1948), p. 33.

53. Hilaire Belloc, *The House of Commons and Monarchy* (London, 1920), p. 69.

54. *Ibid.*, pp. 101-102.

55. *Ibid.*, p. 110.

56. *Ibid.*, p. 95.

57. *Ibid.*, p. 184. Belloc's monarchical ideas were very close to those of Maurras, though unlike the *Action Française*, he was impatient with constitutional purism and never wholly a royalist. Belloc cared little about who the monarch might be, nor was he concerned about how he might acquire his authority. What mattered was the fact that he could be a personal leader ruling with defined areas of responsibility. Moreover, Belloc had no special affection for the ruling house of England, which he regarded as a German import, having essentially German tastes and nothing in common with monarchy as the Middle Ages or the Renaissance understood it.

CHAPTER V

1. Maurice Reckitt, *As It Happened* (London, 1941), p. 108.

2. Shaw and a person unknown to him (Lewis Wallace, a merchant banker) put down five hundred pounds apiece to found *The New Age*. (Letter to *The New English Weekly*, VI [15 Nov., 1934], p. 99. As cited in Wallace Martin, *The New Age Under Orage*, [N.Y., 1967], p. 1).

Notes

221

3. Circulation figures were generally kept secret. Wallace Martin estimates *The New Age*'s circulation to have been under 3,000 a year. (Martin, *New Age*, p. 10).

4. *The New Age*, IV (28 Jan. 1909), p. 280.

5. "Notes of the Week," *The New Age*, January 2, 1913.

6. For Belloc's contribution to Guild Socialism *see* C. Bechofer and Maurice Reckitt, *The Meaning of the National Guilds* (London, 1918), pp. 407-409.

7. Dame Margaret Cole, *The Life of G.D.H. Cole* (London, 1971), p. 50.

8. Niles Carpenter, *Guild Socialism* (New York, 1922), pp. 82-83.

9. Stanley James, "Arthur Penty; Architect and Sociologist," *The American Review*, April 1937, p. 83.

10. Arthur J. Penty, *Old Worlds For New* (London, 1917), pp. 11-12.

11. Arthur J. Penty, *Towards a Christian Sociology* (London, 1923), p. 45.

12. Arthur J. Penty, "Am I a Distributist?" *G.K.'s Weekly*, April 22, 1926.

13. The "Arts and Crafts" movement was inspired by Morris and Ruskin. It represented a reaction against the dehumanization of the worker by industrialism and the misuse of machinery in industrial production. The "arts and crafts" people believed that architecture, painting, sculpture, and the crafts should be reintegrated into one discipline, much as it was in the Middle Ages.

14. For more details *see* A.R. Orage (ed.), *The National Guilds* (London, 1919), and *The New Age* articles on Guild Socialism commencing in April 1912.

15. Penty, *Post-Industrialism* (London, 1922), pp. 98-99.

16. *The New Age* accepted Belloc's definition as an accurate description of its position.

17. Hilaire Belloc, "An Examination of the National Guild System," VIII, *The New Age*, December 4, 1913.

18. *See* Belloc's "An Examination of the Guild System," which ran in *The New Age* from the autumn through December 1913.

19. Maurice Reckitt, *G.K. Chesterton: A Christian Prophet for England Today* (London, 1950), p. 9.

20. Chesterton felt the same way: "I called myself a Socialist because the only alternative to being a Socialist was not being a Socialist." G.K. Chesterton, *The Autobiography of G.K. Chesterton* (New York, 1936), p. 107.

21. The Anglo-Catholic group was high church and identified as Catholic. In the 1920s and 1930s they made up about one-quarter of the entire Anglican Church. Out of approximately sixteen thousand priests in the Anglican fold, about four thousand considered themselves "Catholic." *See* Daniel Sargent, "The Catholic Church in Contemporary England," *The Catholic Historical Review*, April, 1932, p. 65.

22. R.J. Bocock, "Anglo-Catholic Socialism: A Study of a Protest Movement Within a Church," *Social Compass*, XX/I, 1973, pp. 31-48.

23. W.R. Titterton, *G.K. Chesterton: A Portrait* (London, 1936), p. 138.

24. As a writer for the *Penny Illustrated Paper*, for example, he was convicted of libel for publishing an article accusing the editorial staff of the *Daily Express* of being German-Jewish spies. *See The Times*, March 9 and 10, 1911.

25. Eric Gill, *Eric Gill: Autobiography* (New York, 1941), p. 108.

26. Letter to William Rothenstein (January 29, 1912), ed. Walter Shewring, *Letters of Eric Gill* (New York, 1948), p. 44.

27. Rayner Heppenstall, *Four Absentees* (London, 1960), p. 41.

28. Eric Gill, *Engravings by Eric Gill* (Bristol, England, 1929), p. 10.

29. For more details on life at Ditchling *see* Stephen Hobhouse, *Forty Years and an Epilogue* (London, 1951) (Hobhouse lived at Ditchling and was well known as an interpreter of Jacob Boehme); Brocard Sewell, *My Dear Times Waste* (London, 1966); Peter Anson, *A Roving Recluse: More Memoirs* (Cork, 1946); W.H.G. Armytage, *Heavens Below: Utopean Experiments in England, 1560-1960* (Toronto, 1961); Heppenstall, *Four Absentees*; *The Aylesford Review*, Spring, 1965, Special issue devoted to H.D.C. Pepler; Robert Speaight, *The Life of Eric Gill* (New York, 1966); and Barbara Wall, "Eric Gill, Hilary Pepler and The Ditchling Movement," *The Chesterton Review*, Spring/Summer, 1979.

30. Of all the Distributists, Gill seems to have been the only one to acknowledge its link with anarchism. Writing to Herbert Read about Read's pamphlet "The Philosophy of Anarchism," Gill said that he concurred with the author about the necessity of anarchism, the ultimate truth of it, and its immediate practicality as syndicalism. (Herbert Read, *A Coat of Many Colours* [London, 1945], p. 5.) Read, for his part, called Gill an "anarchist in thought if not yet in name" and recommended Gill's essay "Ownership and Industrialism" (in *Sacred and Secular*) as an excellent introduction to the principles of anarchism.

31. O'Connor translated Maritain's *Art et Scholastique* into English, this being one of the first books printed and published by the Ditchling Press. Gill was enormously impressed with Maritain's work, hailing him as "a Daniel come to judgment" (Gill, *Autobiography*, p. 217). Gill seems to have used *Art et Scholastique* as a textbook for guiding himself through all problems relating to religion, social affairs, the arts, and the whole of life. Renée Haynes wrote that Gill used this book as the major source for his own education. *See* Donald Attwater, *A Cell of Good Living: The Life and Works and Opinions of Eric Gill* (London, 1969), p. 82.

32. Gill, *Autobiography*, p. 219.

33. Eric Gill, *Money and Morals* (London, 1934), pp. 21-22.

34. Attwater, *Cell of Good Living*, pp. 145-146.

35. Eric Gill, "The Factory System and Christianity," (1918), Eric Gill, *It All Goes Together* (London, 1944), pp. 25-27.

36. There are a number of interpretations given for Gill's leaving Ditchling, one of which centers on a personal feud between Gill and his friend, Hilary Pepler. For a more detailed discussion of this, *see* Barbara Wall, "Eric Gill, Hilary Pepler and The Ditchling Movement," *The Chesterton Review* (Spring/Summer, 1979), pp. 179-181.

37. Ferdinand Valentine, O.P., *Father Vincent McNabb, O.P.* (Westminster, Maryland, 1955), p. 141.

38. Eric Gill, "Art in England Now . . . as It Seems to Me," (a broadcast talk given in Jerusalem, June 15, 1937; with additions), Gill, *It All Goes Together*, p. 91.

39. *See* David Kindersley, *Mr. Eric Gill: Recollections of David Kindersley* (New York, 1967), p. 15.
40. Walter Shewring, *Blackfriars*, April, 1938.
41. In later years, Carey tried to convince Gill to move to America where there were plans to set up a Distributist commune in Vermont. The outbreak of World War II made this impossible. Carey did much to make Gill's work and ideas known in the U.S. After his death, Carey kept Gill's name in the public eye through the Catholic Art Association and its quarterly review, *Good Work*, which he edited.
42. Tom O'Brien, M.P. and former Secretary of the Trades Union Congress, wrote that McNabb's views on industrial society and his ability to reach the common people by insisting on the principles contained in *De Rerum Novarum* had a considerable impact on English trade unionism. (Ferdinand Valentine, *McNabb*, p. 172.)
43. McNabb used to describe himself as "a bit of old England walking about." (Brocard Sewell, "Father Vincent McNabb," *Aylesford Review*, Summer, 1968, p. 9.) Since he preferred to don the Dominican white habit and black cappa in public, he tended to look like a character out of a Zoé Oldenbourg novel.
44. Ferdinand Valentine, *McNabb*, p. 142.
45. *Ibid.*, p. 172.
46. From a letter written on a turnleaf from a discarded exercise book, Attwater, *Cell of Good Living*, p. 59.
47. *See* Brocard Sewell, *My Dear Time's Waste* (London, 1966), pp. 74-76.
48. Sir Henry Slesser, *Judgement Reserved* (London, 1941), p. 21.
49. *Ibid.*, p. 21.
50. It should be pointed out that although Slesser became a Roman Catholic later in life, he was not at this time a member of the Roman Church. He believed in an essentially Catholic dogma indistinguishable from that of the Roman Catholics, but he arrived at this on his own consideration and not by reason of Papal authority. In short, he considered himself a Thomist, but not a Roman Catholic. *See* Slesser, *Judgement Reserved*, p. 269.

CHAPTER VI

1. Dudley Barker, *G.K. Chesterton* (London, 1973), p. 261.
2. Chesterton, in particular, wrote numerous, rather vitriolic editorials defending the Church against the assaults of Dean Inge and Bishop Gore.
3. Mother Mary M. Loughran, "Catholics in England Between 1918 and 1945" (unpublished Ph.D. thesis, Department of History, University of Pennsylvania, 1954), pp. 74-75.
4. It appears that the Catholic clergy had generally ignored or misunderstood the social teachings of the papal encyclicals before 1930. The publication of *De Rerum Novarum*, for example, was greeted by a variety of conflicting interpretations. One Catholic writer argued that it indicated the Pope's rejection of

social democracy, while another saw it as justifying Fabian collectivism. (K.S. Inglis, *Churches and the Working Class in Victorian England* [London, 1963], p. 317.) But generally, English Catholics paid little attention to the encyclical; indeed it was not even mentioned in the Catholic Truth Society's official short history of the Catholic Church (1895), nor was there any reference to it in Purcell's biography of Manning (1895) or in Snead-Cox's life of Vaughn (1910). Since Catholics knew little of the content of the encyclicals, they tended to oppose trade unionism as much as they did socialism and communism. This greatly annoyed Gill, who explained that when it came to discussing matters of human work and the responsibility of workingmen, ordinary parish priests and laymen were either not interested (probably owing to their ignorance of the encyclicals) or frankly antagonistic to any reform whatsoever.

5. Anthony Everett Herbold, "Chesterton and *G.K.'s Weekly*" (unpublished Ph.D. thesis, Department of English, University of Michigan, 1963), p. 37.
6. Barker, *Chesterton*, p. 266.
7. W.R. Titterton, *G.K. Chesterton: A Portrait* (London, 1936), pp. 166-167.
8. *Ibid.*, p. 172.
9. As Went quoted Francis Bacon in a letter to the editor of the *Mid-Sussex Times*. As cited in *G.K.'s Weekly*, September 18, 1926.
10. G.K. Chesterton, "The League in Action," *G.K.'s Weekly*, November 20, 1926.
11. Maisie Ward, *Return to Chesterton* (New York, 1952), p. 273.
12. George Heseltine recollects that the paper showed a profit of 11 pounds, nobody being paid but the printers.
13. "A Note to the Reader," *G.K.'s Weekly*, December 3, 1927.
14. E.H. Haywood, "The Private Buses," *Weekly Review*, January 9, 1947.
15. G.K. Chesterton, "Straws in the Wind: The Mystery of Mussolini," *G.K.'s Weekly*, April 24, 1926.
16. G.K. Chesterton, "Straws in the Wind: The Distributist Schoolmaster," *G.K.'s Weekly*, August 16, 1930.
17. "The Education Bill," *G.K.'s Weekly*, June 7, 1930.
18. G.K. Chesterton, "Straws in the Wind: Representative Government," *G.K.'s Weekly*, April 17, 1926.
19. G.K. Chesterton, "Straws in the Wind: Wages and Profits," *G.K.'s Weekly*, April 24, 1926.
20. G.K. Chesterton, "Straws in the Wind: On Our Critics; the Individual and the Mine," *G.K.'s Weekly*, February 13, 1926.
21. Cardinal Bourne, head of the Roman Church in England, pointedly rebuked the miners in his Sunday sermon, arguing that there was no moral justification for their action. The general strike was considered a direct challenge to law and order, a sin against the obedience citizens owed to God. Bourne's position received further support in *The Tablet*, Britain's most influential Catholic monthly. Its editors argued that the strike was a ploy to "intimidate and even starve the electorate into wringing subsidies or sectional privileges from the people's Government as the price of ransom." Echoing the feelings of the Catholic hierarchy, *The Tablet* asserted that the trade unionists were becoming

too powerful, believed that the general work stoppage was a revolutionary act and against the teachings of the Church, and was relieved to see the strike defeated. ("The Challenge to Authority," *The Tablet*, May 15, 1926, pp. 638-639.)

22. "The Pride of England," *G.K.'s Weekly*, May 22, 1926. For a different view of *G.K.'s Weekly* and the general strike, *see* Gregory Macdonald, "And Now the Pink Legend; A Response to Jay P. Corrin," *The Chesterton Review*, Fall /Winter, 1976-1977. Macdonald strongly objects to my argument that *G.K.'s Weekly* had a radical public image. Concerning the paper and the general strike, he points out that Chesterton was away at the time, leaving the editorship in the hands of Titterton, who was unduly influenced by Mrs. Cecil Chesterton, "an admirer of Soviet Russia." Macdonald insists that after Chesterton returned to England, he softened the paper's position, and implies that, in the long run, it was not all that different from the stand taken by the official Church hierarchy. However, the record clearly indicates that Chesterton supported Titterton's line. Reckitt writes that when G.K. returned, he endorsed his assistant editor's slogan: "Keep calm, and stand up for the strikers." (Reckitt, *World and the Faith*: *Essays of a Christian Sociologist* [London, 1954], p. 58.) Also, Chesterton's editorial, "The Pride of England," May 22, 1926, reveals that he agreed with Titterton's position entirely. It seems to me that throughout the crisis, Chesterton was consciously following through on revolutionary principles laid down by the *Eye* and *New Witness* and *The New Age* during the prewar strikes. Politically speaking, these positions were far more radical than those of either the Anglican or Roman Church; indeed, as subsequent events reveal, Chesterton's stands were irreconcilable with those of the Roman Church.

23. "Distributism and the Mines," Parts I and II, *G.K.'s Weekly*, April 7 and April 14, 1928.

24. "The Respectable Radicals," *G.K.'s Weekly*, February 22, 1930. It is interesting to note that the communist leader, R. Palm Dutt, denounced the Mond-Turner talks on essentially the same grounds as the Distributists. Dutt wrote in the *Labour Monthly* that if the T.U.C. accepted the Mond-Turner proposals it would have begun the process of converting the Labor movement from an organ of class struggle into a tool of the industrial capitalists. *See* "Notes of the Week," *The Commonwealth*, September 1928.

25. "The Distributist League," *G.K.'s Weekly*, August 9, 1930.

26. Maurice Reckitt, "The Cockpit," *G.K.'s Weekly*, August 23, 1930.

27. "The Distributist League," *G.K.'s Weekly*, October 4, 1930.

28. "The Trades Union Bill," *G.K.'s Weekly*, February 27, 1931. For an opposite view of the League's position *see* Gregory Macdonald, "And Now the Pink Legend," *Chesterton Review*, Fall/Winter, 1976-1977.

29. "Among the Branches," *G.K.'s Weekly*, June 4, 1927.

30. H.S.D. Went, "Democracy," *G.K.'s Weekly*, August 17, 1929.

31. Hilaire Belloc, "The Breakup," *G.K.'s Weekly*, October 31, 1931.

32. Hilaire Belloc, "Were We Wrong?" II, *G.K.'s Weekly*, November 5, 1932.

33. G.K. Chesterton, "The First Reply to Fascism," *G.K.'s Weekly*, August 29, 1935.

CHAPTER VII

1. "The Distributist League," *G.K.'s Weekly*, December 13, 1930.
2. G.C. Heseltine, "Distributism," *Catholic World*, January, 1932, p. 388.
3. Harold Robbins, "Foundations with a Celler," *G.K.'s Weekly*, January 9, 1926.
4. Most agricultural-minded Distributists emphasized the need to revive farming for the purpose of a better-balanced economic structure. Only a small minority of these men believed that Britain should completely give up industrialism for agriculture. McNabb was this latter group's most eloquent representative.
5. G.C. Heseltine, *The Change: Essays on the Land* (London, 1937), p. 107.
6. Vincent McNabb, *The Church and Land* (London, 1926), p. 189.
7. *Ibid.*, p. 191.
8. H.E. Humphries, *Liberty and Property: An Introduction to Distributism* (London, 1928), pp. 12-13.
9. This discussion of Gill's attitudes toward work and the ownership of property are taken from a number of articles that were written for *G.K.'s Weekly*. They were published in 1937 under the title *Work and Property* (London, 1937).
10. Maurice Reckitt, "Machinery and the Distributive State," *G.K.'s Weekly*, June 6, 1925 and "The Mechanical Navvy," *G.K.'s Weekly*, May 9, 1925.
11. A.J. Penty, "Machinery and Employment," *G.K.'s Weekly*, June 27, 1925.
12. A.J. Penty, "Fundamentalists and Empiricists," *G.K.'s Weekly*, January 2, 1926.
13. This was the result of what Douglas called "the intricacies of cost accounting," which created price increases that rose faster than purchasing power. (Wallace Martin, *The New Age Under Orage* [New York, 1967], p. 27.)
14. Maurice Reckitt, "Two Views of Distributism," *G.K.'s Weekly*, March 31, 1928.
15. Maurice Reckitt, "Social Credit and the Worker," *The Commonwealth*, August, 1922.
16. Indeed, even seasoned literary critics had difficulty understanding the themes of his novels. For example, *see* the unsigned reviews in *The Glasgow Citizen*, March 3, 1910; *Punch*, March 9, 1910; *The Saturday Review*, July 30, 1910; and Henry Murray in *The Bookman*, August, 1910.
17. A study of Chesterton's fiction also reveals significant data on his political views. For an examination of G.K.'s political attitudes as demonstrated in his novels, *see* Ian Boyd, *The Novels of G.K. Chesterton* (London, 1975).
18. Several people involved in the Distributist movement have written about the League's anti-machine faction and have commented on the poor image this group created for Distributism as a whole. It must be made clear, however, that such attitudes were shared by only a very small minority of Distributists. This so-called "extremist" position was never the official League policy and its leading officials continuously denounced those men who promoted this view.

L.J. Clipper in his study of Chesterton (*G.K. Chesterton* [New York, 1974]) gives the reader the impression that Distributism aimed to return everyone to the soil (*see* pp. 77-78). As I shall explain in more detail, the essential aim of Distributism was economic balance, not the reconstruction of Arcadia.

19. A.J. Penty, "Am I a Distributist," Parts I and II, *G.K.'s Weekly*, May 22 and May 29, 1926.
20. G.K. Chesterton, "Straws in the Wind: The Aggression of Plutocracy," *G.K.'s Weekly*, June 12, 1926.
21. G.C. Heseltine, "Peasant Proprietorship," *G.K.'s Weekly*, July 17, 1926.
22. For a fuller explanation of this *see* Humphries, *Liberty and Property*, pp. 16-17.
23. G.K. Chesterton, "Straws in the Wind: What All Distributists Say," *G.K.'s Weekly*, July 23, 1927.
24. G.K. Chesterton, "Straws in the Wind: A Real Danger," *G.K.'s Weekly*, March 16, 1933.
25. G.K. Chesterton, "How Are You Going To Do It?" *G.K.'s Weekly*, October 1, 1927.
26. G.K. Chesterton, *The Outline of Sanity* (New York, 1927), p. 247.
27. Hilaire Belloc, *An Essay on the Restoration of Property* (London, 1936), p. 11.
28. *Ibid.*, p. 48.
29. Hilaire Belloc, *The Crisis of Our Civilization* (New York, 1937), p. 214.
30. *Ibid.*, p. 235.
31. Letter to Mrs. Reginald Balfour (June 28, 1922), ed. Robert Speaight, *Letters from Hilaire Belloc* (London, 1958), p. 122.
32. A Guide Section entitled "Small Workshops" appeared each week in the small advertisement section of *G.K.'s Weekly*.
33. K.L. Kenrick, "Practical Distributism," Part III, *G.K.'s Weekly*, May 12, 1928.
34. Michael Derrick, "Distributism and Primitivism," *Blackfriars*, April, 1934.

CHAPTER VIII

1. The studies of Chesterton by Lawrence Clipper (*G.K. Chesterton*, New York, 1974); Dudley Barker (*G.K. Chesterton*, London, 1973); and Christopher Hollis (*The Mind of Chesterton*, Coral Gables, Florida, 1970) devote little space to Distributism. John McCarthy's book, *Hilaire Belloc: Edwardian Radical*, (Indianapolis, 1978), deals primarily with the early radical-liberal phase of Belloc's career but does not have much to say about Distributism. Rodney Barker (*Political Ideas in Modern Britain*, London, 1978) provides a good but brief review of Distributism. Two recent studies that have dealt more extensively with Chesterton's political views are Ian Boyd's, *The Novels of G.K. Chesterton* (New York, 1975) and Margaret Canovan's, *G.K. Chesterton, Radical Populist* (New York, 1977). The major surveys of modern British history (R.C.K. Ensor, *England: 1870-1914*, Oxford, 1936; C.L. Mowat, *Britain Between the Wars, 1918-1940*, Boston, 1971; and A.J.P. Taylor, *English History, 1914-1945*, Oxford, 1965) make no reference whatever to Distributism.

2. William Vincent Baker, *The New Maryland* (London, 1935), pp. 8-9.
3. The six Catholic land associations were: 1) Scottish, the Rev. John McQuillan, D.D., Chairman; J.P. Magennis, Secretary; 2) South of England, the Rev. Herbert Vaughan, D.D., Chairman; Brian Keating, Secretary; 3) Midlands, Rt.Rev. Msgr.J. Dey, D.S.O., Chairman; Harold Robbins, Secretary; 4) North of England, Rev. T. Fish, D.D., Chairman; D.J. Jones, Secretary; 5) Nottingham, Rt.Rev. Msgr.J. Bigland, Chairman; H.G. Weston, Secretary; and 6) Liverpool, Dom Gregory Buisseret, O.S.B., Chairman; J. Gavin, Secretary.
4. Msgr. Dey, "The Back to the Land Movement," *Dublin Review*, April, 1935, p. 262; *see* also "Why We Do It," *The Cross and the Plough*, Easter, 1935.
5. G.C. Heseltine, "Marydown," *G.K.'s Weekly*, October 26, 1933.
6. Baker, *New Maryland*, p. 44.
7. T.W.C. Curd, "Marydown, A Catholic Land Colony," *The Month*, July, 1933, p. 29.
8. Elsmere Harris, "The Cockpit," *G.K.'s Weekly*, January 3, 1935.
9. John L. Finlay, *Social Credit: The English Origins* (London, 1972), p. 49.
10. *See* "The Revival of What?" *The Cross and the Plough*, Michaelmas, 1936.
11. *See* "Unemployed on the Land," *The Times*, March 6, 1934 and J.W. Scott, "A Paradox of Progress," *The Times*, August 7, 1934.
12. *See* Victor Bonham-Carter, *Dartington Hall: The History of an Experiment* (Ithaca, 1958).
13. For additional information on these land experiments *see* W.H.G. Armytage, *Heavens Below: Utopean Experiments in England, 1560-1960* (Toronto, 1961); John Hoyland, *Digging for a New England* (London, 1936); and Hilda Jennings, *The New Community* (London, 1934), and *Brynmawr* (London, 1934).
14. "Second Thoughts on 'Back to the Land,' " *The Tablet*, December 28, 1935.
15. "Strangers Within Their Gates," *Blackfriars*, November, 1941.
16. Maisie Ward, *Return to Chesterton* (New York, 1952), pp. 274-275.
17. Harold Robbins, *The Sun of Justice; an Essay on the Social Teachings of the Catholic Church* (London, 1938), pp. 148-149.
18. This was a specious book—"The Greatest Forgery of the Century" (Edward A. Flannery, *The Anguish of the Jews* [New York, 1965], p. 191)—outlining a plan by the princes of the 12 tribes of Israel to take over the world. The *Protocols* was exposed as a forgery of Russian anti-Semites by a London *Times* correspondent in 1921.
19. H.E.G. Rope, "Looking Before and After," *Flee to the Fields*, John McQuillan *et al.*, pp. 208-209.
20. *See* letter from W.P. Witcutt in support of Harold Robbins, *Blackfriars*, December, 1938, p. 933.
21. In addition to this, various studies appeared by the middle of the 1930s arguing against the efficacy of the Catholic Land Association's programs. C.S. Orwin and W.F. Darke's book, *Back to the Land* (1935) and *The Agricultural Dilemma*, a report of an inquiry organized by Viscount Astor and B. Seebohm Rowntree, both concluded that a return to the land would have no significant

impact on unemployment. The researchers believed that city dwellers would have great difficulty adjusting to farm life and that the small, self-sufficient farm was not economically viable.

22. G.M. Turnell, "Our Debt to Chesterton," *Arena*, July, 1937, p. 74.
23. Michael Derrick, "Distributism and Primitivism," *Blackfriars*, April, 1934, p. 169
24. "The Distributist League," *G.K.'s Weekly*, April 12, 1930.
25. N.E. Egerton Swann, *Is There a Catholic Sociology* (London, 1922), pp. 15-32.
26. *See* D.G. Peck, "Collectivism and the Catholic Tradition Regarding Property," II, *Christendom*, September, 1941.
27. John L. Finlay, in his extensive examination of the social credit movement, discovered that Major Douglas borrowed heavily from Distributist philosophy to form the basis of his own system. *See* Finlay, *Social Credit*, pp. 45-46, 121.
28. *The American Review*, April, 1933, pp. 122-126.
29. "Editorial Notes," *The American Review*, April, 1934, p. 119.
30. *Ibid.*, p. 198.
31. Arnold Lunn, *Now I See* (London, 1956), p. 56.
32. Christopher Hollis, *Along the Road to Frome* (London, 1958), p. 79.
33. Douglas Jerrold, *Georgian Adventure* (London, 1937), pp. 81-82.
34. Stanley B. James, "The Happy Warriors," *The Month*, September, 1932, p. 108.
35. Hollis, *Road to Frome*, pp. 80-81.
36. Douglas Jerrold, "The Future of the English Political Parties," *The English Review*, October, 1933, pp. 338-339.
37. Douglas Jerrold, "Hilaire Belloc and the Counter-Revolution," *For Hilaire Belloc*, ed. Douglas Woodruff (London, 1946), p. 5.
38. Douglas Jerrold, "Current Comments," *The English Review*, June, 1933, pp. 600-601.
39. Douglas Jerrold, "English Political Thought and the Post-War Crisis," *The American Review*, May, 1933, p. 178.
40. Mosley, a former minister in the Labour government, was the leader of the British Union of Fascists. Many of Chesterbelloc's followers have refused to acknowledge the rightist image of Distributism (*see* Gregory Macdonald, "And Now the Pink Legend: a Response to Jay P. Corrin," and Lewis Filewood, " 'Fascism' and the *Weekly Review*: A Response to Gregory Macdonald and Jay P. Corrin," *The Chesterton Review*, Fall/Winter, 1976-1977). Yet amongst historians and students of modern British history there has been a general tendency to classify the Chesterbelloc and Distributism as right wing (*see* J.R. Jones in *The European Right: A Historical Profile*, eds. Hans Rogger and Eugen Weber, Berkeley, 1966). Perhaps this is an oversimplification, for Distributism defies any neat classification, though, as this study attempts to demonstrate, there have been sufficient reasons for historians to pass such judgement.
41. J.M. Cleary, *Catholic Social Action in Britain, 1910-1959* (Oxford, 1961), p. 119.
42. *See* Mary Vivian Brand, *The Social Catholic Movement in England, 1920-1955*

(New York, 1963). Chesterton's latest biographer, Dudley Barker, makes similar derisive remarks about Distributism and the League. *See* his *G.K. Chesterton* (London, 1973), pp. 258-259; 266-267.

43. In Somerville's opinion, it was a "bad," "ignorant," or "rebellious" Catholic who disputed Cardinal Bourne's pronouncement on the evil of the general strike. (Henry Somerville, "The Question of Strikes," *Christian Democrat*, June, 1926.)

44. "More Comments on Some Distributists," *Christian Democrat*, September, 1927.

45. This seems to be the position taken by Brand, *Social Catholic Movement*.

46. Cleary, *Catholic Social Action*, p. 119.

47. *Ibid.*, p. 171.

48. Wilfred Sheed, *The Morning After* (New York, 1972), p. 271.

CHAPTER IX

1. G.K. Chesterton, "Straws in the Wind: Are We Inconsistent?" *G.K.'s Weekly*, June 26, 1926.

2. Hilaire Belloc, "The Two Foreign Policies," *G.K.'s Weekly*, February 14, 1931.

3. G.K. Chesterton, "The Core of It," *The Cross and the Plough*, Christmas, 1935.

4. G.K. Chesterton, "Straws in the Wind: Are We Inconsistent?" *G.K.'s Weekly*, June 26, 1926.

5. "The Modern Hypocrisy," *G.K.'s Weekly*, October 31, 1925.

6. Belloc seems to have neglected that Trieste was turned over to Italy at the peace settlement in 1918.

7. Hilaire Belloc, "The Truce," *G.K.'s Weekly*, November 9, 1929.

8. Gregory Macdonald, "Looking On," *G.K.'s Weekly*, May 7, 1936.

9. G.K. Chesterton, "Straws in the Wind: Is It Peace?" *G.K.'s Weekly*, July 18, 1931.

10. Hilaire Belloc, "The Truce," *G.K.'s Weekly*, November 9, 1929.

11. "The Crisis in France," *G.K.'s Weekly*, February 15, 1934.

12. Hilaire Belloc, "Current Affairs," *G.K.'s Weekly*, April 27, 1929.

13. G.K. Chesterton, "Straws in the Wind: Exodus from Europe," *G.K.'s Weekly*, December 28, 1929.

14. Hilaire Belloc, *The Cruise of the Nona* (London, 1925), p. 154.

15. G.K. Chesterton, *The Resurrection of Rome* (London, 1930), p. 225.

16. *Ibid.*, p. 263.

17. *Ibid.*, p. 256.

18. G.K. Chesterton, "Straws in the Wind: The Mystery of Mussolini (IV)," *G.K.'s Weekly*, August 14, 1926.

19. Chesterton, *Resurrection of Rome*, p. 289.

20. J. Desmond Gleeson, "The March on Rome," *G.K.'s Weekly*, November 12, 1932.

21. John A. Toomey, "An Interview with Hilaire Belloc," *America*, March 23, 1935, pp. 563-565.
22. Although Belloc rejected representative government because it could be corrupted too easily ("oligarchy in the hands of an intriguing caucus," as he called it), he did believe that there was an irrefutable moral argument for "majority government." There were certain conditions when majority rule was just and necessary: 1) when the question arises from a homogeneous community; 2) when there is an active popular demand for its settlement; 3) when the matter under discussion is reasonably familiar to all; 4) when it concerns all, or nearly all, directly, and in much the same degree; 5) when the majority is substantial. (Hilaire Belloc, *Cruise of the Nona*, p. 156.)
23. Douglas Jerrold, *The Necessity of Freedom* (London, 1938), p. 242.
24. A.J. Penty, "Communism and Fascism," Part II, *American Review*, October, 1936, p. 495.
25. Mussolini used the term to define Fascism in the *Enciclopedia italiana*, though this essay was actually written by Giovanni Gentile.
26. Not all the better-known Distributists supported Italian Fascism. Slesser, Gill, McNabb, and Reckitt always disapproved of Mussolini. Some of the members of the League's London branch also seemed to develop a lingering dislike of Italian Fascism. In June 1930, after Dr. Alexander Magri gave an unflattering account of Fascism as he had witnessed it in Italy, the secretary of the Central branch concluded that Mussolini might have been a decent fellow but that Distributists could not approve many of his policies. ("Distributist League," *G.K.'s Weekly*, June 14, 1930.)
27. Harold Robbins, *The Sun of Justice; An Essay on the Social Teachings of the Catholic Church* (London, 1938), p. 69.
28. "Notes of the Week," *G.K.'s Weekly*, October 17, 1931.
29. In her biography of Chesterton, Maisie Ward reproduces a letter from Rabbi Stephen Wise, a well-known American Jewish leader, who praised G.K. for "being one of the first to speak out with all the directness and frankness of a great and unabashed spirit" against Hitlerism. *See* Maisie Ward, *Gilbert Keith Chesterton* (New York, 1943), p. 265.
30. G.K. Chesterton, "Straws in the Wind: The Tool," *G.K.'s Weekly*, September 6, 1934.
31. G.K. Chesterton, "Straws in the Wind: The Gangster," *G.K.'s Weekly*, August 30, 1934.
32. G.K. Chesterton, *The End of the Armistace* (New York, 1940), p. 113.
33. Donald Attwater, "English Catholic Fascists?" *Commonweal*, January 10, 1941, pp. 296-302. Attwater described a "latinophile" attitude, produced largely by Hilaire Belloc, which created the impression that Italy and France could do no wrong because they were rooted in Catholic culture. Attwater was commenting on a group of writers who had fallen under the sway of such attitudes, and who had thereby created a fascist image for English Catholics in the American press. Attwater went on to describe some of the ideas put forth by this group of

Catholic writers, whom he intentionally did not name, because they did not form a homogeneous body and were not necessarily in complete agreement on all things. Generally, the Latinophiles pushed for closer political cooperation between Britain and Mussolini, and excused Italy's imperialism on the grounds that she was anti-communist and forced into Abyssinia by the "folly of sanctions." The group also had a preoccupation with communist conspiracies (they blamed the fall of France on the "Reds," i.e., the Popular Front, and saw Franco defending Christianity against communism), and believed that Europe was dominated by a combination of bankers, secret societies (Freemasons), and Jews.

34. Jerrold, *The Necessity of Freedom*, pp. 249-250. This was also Mosley's position. *See* Colin Cross, *The Fascists in Britain* (London, 1961).
35. Marshall McLuhan, "The Cockpit," *G.K.'s Weekly*, October 3, 1935.
36. *See* C.F. Hammond, "Financial Armageddon, Second Phase," *G.K.'s Weekly*, October 24, 1935, and Gregory Macdonald, "Looking On," *G.K.'s Weekly*, October 17, 1935.
37. "The Black Peril," *G.K.'s Weekly*, December 12, 1925.
38. Pound congratulated *G.K.'s Weekly* for its considerate defense of Mussolini. The paper was seen to have made the best possible contact with Fascism. (Ezra Pound, "The Cockpit," *G.K.'s Weekly*, October 3, 1935.)
39. Letter to Reckitt (September 19, 1935), Maisie Ward, *G.K. Chesterton* (New York, 1943), p. 548.
40. A.J. Penty, "Communism and Fascism," Part II, *The American Review*, October, 1936, p. 501.
41. G.K. Chesterton, "Straws in the Wind: The First Reply to Fascism," *G.K.'s Weekly*, August 29, 1935.
42. G.K. Chesterton, "Straws in the Wind: Which is the Herring?" *G.K.'s Weekly*, September 19, 1935.
43. Chesterton had consistently denounced Japan's China policy.
44. Conrad Bonacina, "The Cockpit," *G.K.'s Weekly*, September 26, 1935.
45. Gerald Flanagan, "The Cockpit," *G.K.'s Weekly*, May 21, 1936.
46. Mrs. Cecil Chesterton, *The Chestertons* (London, 1941), p. 298. *See also* Frank A. Lea, *The White Knight of Battersea: G.K. Chesterton* (London, 1946), p. 74.
47. Hilaire Belloc, "Moscow," *G.K.'s Weekly*, August 13, 1936.
48. "What a Russian Alliance Means," *Weekly Review*, June 1, 1939.
49. Stephen Spender, *World Within World* (Los Angeles, 1966), p. 187.
50. A.J. Brock, "Correspondence," *Weekly Review*, February 23, 1939.
51. Douglas Jerrold, *Georgian Adventure* (London, 1937), p. 384.
52. Franco brought the radical right, Catholic traditionalists, and monarchists together into the Falange Española Tradicionalista y de las Juntas de Ofensiva Nacional Sindicalista (F.E.T. y J.O.N.S.), which served as the official political party of the Nationalist forces.
53. Arnold Lunn, *Spanish Rehearsal* (New York, 1937), p. 176.
54. Gregory Macdonald, "Looking On," *G.K.'s Weekly*, August 20, 1936.
55. *See* Hilaire Belloc's "Another Five Facts," *G.K.'s Weekly*, September 27, 1936;

"The Breach," *G.K.'s Weekly*, September 23, 1937; and "The Two Monarchies," *Weekly Review*, August 25, 1938.

56. "Hispanis Victrix," *Weekly Review*, April 6, 1939.

57. In August 1937, Belloc claimed that he no longer had the time to edit the journal, whereupon R.D. Jebb took over the job.

58. Benvenisti's book received a highly favorable review by A. Raven Thomson in *The British Union Quarterly*, April-July, 1937. Thomson considered Benvenisti's doctrine of Distributism to be very attractive. In another book published in the same year, *The Iniquitous Contract*, Benvenisti applauded both Mosley and Hitler, the latter of whom he saw to be carrying out the policy of Pope Pius V.

59. Vincent Wright, "Conscription," *Weekly Review*, June 1, 1939.

60. A.K. Chesterton, "The Alternative," *Weekly Review*, May 25, 1944. The *Weekly Review*'s advocacy of a self-contained empire was remarkably similar to the B.U.F.'s imperialist line. Mosley proposed a Britain for the British and an empire based on the simple principle that the British people shall consume what they produce.

61. Belloc's commentaries on Italy and Spain were outrageous at times. In June 1939, for example, he claimed that Mussolini's fascist dictatorship not only saved Italy from communism but European civilization as well. *See* "Mussolini and the Guild," *Weekly Review*, June 15, 1939.

62. Letter to Lady Phipps (June 27, 1939), Robert Speaight, *The Life of Hilaire Belloc* (New York, 1957), p. 483.

63. Maurice Reckitt, *As It Happened* (London, 1941), p. 185.

CHAPTER X

1. *See* J.A. Hall, "Chesterton's Contribution to English Sociology," *Chesterton Review*, Spring/Summer, 1977.

2. Herbert Marshall McLuhan, *The Mechanical Bride: Folklore of Industrial Man* (Boston, 1967), p. vi.

3. Donald Attwater, "The Decline of Distributism," *Commonweal*, February 2, 1951.

4. Len Murray, "Slings and Arrows," *Manchester Guardian Weekly*, February 9, 1974, p. 20.

5. G.K. Chesterton, "Straws in the Wind: The Place of Nonsense in Sense," *G.K.'s Weekly*, January 19, 1926. As cited in A. Herbold, "Chesterton and *G.K.'s Weekly*" (unpublished Ph.D. thesis, Department of English, University of Michigan, 1963), p. 41.

6. Douglas Jerrold, *The Tablet*, June 27, 1936.

7. However, one finds similar sentiments in nineteenth-century romantic writers. In particular, *see* Novalis' (Friedrich von Hardenberg) *Die Christenheit oder Europa* (1799) and the works of the French writers, Chateaubriand, Bonald, and de Maistre.

8. For additional insight into Chesterton's political philosophy, especially his

populist tendencies, *see* Margaret Canovan, *G.K. Chesterton, Radical Populist* (New York, 1977).

9. A term used by John Harrison in *The Reactionaries* (London, 1966).
10. For example, compare Chesterton's "Is Humanism a Religion?" *The Criterion*, April, 1929, with Eliot's views on the subject. *See also* Eliot's obituary piece on Chesterton in *The Tablet*.
11. Geoffrey Wagner, *Wyndham Lewis: A Portrait of the Artist as the Enemy* (London, 1957), p. 36.
12. This is the view of John Harrison. *See* his *The Reactionaries*, p. 200.

Name Glossary: Distributists And Their Adversaries

Herbert Agar. American proponent of Distributism. A Pulitzer prizewinning writer, Agar served as editor of *Free America* and was associated with the Southern Agrarians.

Donald Attwater. Journalist friend of Eric Gill. Attwater was involved with the back-to-the-land movements but was a critic of certain aspects of Distributism and Belloc's political writings. Author of an excellent book on Eric Gill.

Maurice Baring. Man of letters, close personal friend of Chesterton and Belloc.

J.L. Benvenisti. Regular writer for the *Weekly Review*. Benvenisti came to believe that Distributism could be achieved through fascist means.

A.K. Chesterton. Britain's leading fascist intellectual and long-time Mosley supporter. Became a frequent contributor to the *Weekly Review* after 1938.

Cecil Chesterton. Brother of G.K.C. and editor of the *Eye* and *New Witness*. Collaborated with Belloc in writing the *Party System* (1911).

Seward Collins. Radical American Distributist, editor of *The American Review*.

T.W.C. Curd. Editor of *Towards* and founder of the Marydown Farming Association.

Major C.H. Douglas. Founder of the economic theory called "social credit."

Montague Fordham. Leader of the Rural Reconstruction Association. Fordham hoped to combine guild ideas, Distributism, and social credit as a basis for the reconstruction of British agriculture.

Eric Gill. Radical sculptor-craftsman and neo-Thomist philosopher. Established the Ditchling craft-guild, a Distributist commune designed to promote the principles of economic self-sufficiency.

J.Desmond Glesson. Active Distributist Leaguer, who has provided a colorful account of League meetings and various back-to-the-land experiments.

E.H. Haywood. Major Distributist leader (League's Central branch) who also claimed to be a socialist. A regular contributor to *G.K.'s Weekly* and the *Weekly Review*.

G.C. Heseltine. A leading Distributist (Birmingham branch), Director of *G.K.'s Weekly* and author of several back-to-the-land tracts.

S.G. Hobson. Along with G.D.H. Cole and A.R. Orage, a major advocate of the so-called "national guilds," which, as opposed to Penty's guild theories, would provide labor with greater economic and political power but preserve the modern factory system.

Christopher Hollis. Militant Catholic journalist and influential proponent of Distributism.

H.E. Humphries. Author of the League's first textbook, *Liberty and Property* (1927).

Reginald Jebb. Son-in-law of Hilaire Belloc, one-time editor of the *Weekly Review*.

Douglas Jerrold. Right-wing journalist and supporter of Mussolini and Franco. Jerrold served as editor of *The English Review* from 1931 to 1936.

Ada Jones. Wife of Cecil Chesterton. Jones was a well-known journalist (G.K. called her the "Queen of Fleet Street"), writing under the pen name of J.K. Prothero.

K.L. Kenrick. Secretary of the League's Birmingham branch. Along with Harold Robbins, Kenrick drew up the so-called "Birmingham Plan," a proposal to ameliorate unemployment by training workers for agriculture.

Arnold Lunn. Influential Roman Catholic convert and religious propagandist. Lunn was best known as a writer for conservative causes.

Edward J. Macdonald. The brother of Gregory Macdonald. Played a significant role as assistant editor of *G.K.'s Weekly*.

Gregory Macdonald. Foreign Affairs journalist. Active as a writer for *G.K.'s Weekly* and the *Catholic Times*. Later served as Director of the B.B.C.'s Central European Service.

C.F.G. Masterman. One-time friend of Hilaire Belloc's who became a target of Distributist criticism for his conduct as a Liberal M.P.

Father Vincent McNabb. A well-known Dominican friar, McNabb was a major figure in the Distributist League, the back-to-the-land movements, and the Catholic Social Movement. Close personal friend of Hilaire Belloc.

E.D. Morel. Radical social reformer and founder of the Congo Reform Association. Frequently attacked by Chesterton and Belloc as a financial manipulator and traitor to Britain.

Father John O'Connor. The spiritual adviser to G.K.C. and Eric Gill. Thought to be the man upon whom G.K. based the Father Brown mystery stories.

F. Hugh O'Donnell. Regular political commentator for the *New Witness*. Follower of Charles Maurras.

Lucean Oldershaw. G.K. Chesterton's friend and brother-in-law. A Radical member of the *"Speaker"* group.

A.R. Orage. Editor of *The New Age*, one of the leading intellectual journals of the early 1900s.

A.J. Penty. Responsible for introducing the guild idea into modern thinking. Advocated the abandonment of the factory system and a restoration of medieval guilds as instruments of social, economic, and political control.

H.D.C. Pepler. Close friend of Eric Gill who left a career with the London County Council to work at Ditchling Common. Became a highly regarded printer and in his later years assumed the editorship of the *Weekly Review*.

Maurice Reckitt. Leader of the Christian Socialist Movement.

Reckitt was an important link between the C.S.M. and Distributism. He was on the board of directors of *G.K.'s Weekly*, editor of *Christendom* and unofficial chairman of the Chandos group.

Harold Robbins. Editor of *The Cross and the Plough*, and one of the leaders of the Birmingham branch of the Distributist League.

H.E.G. Rope. A member of the "radical" wing of the Distributist movement. Father Rope was an unqualified machine-hater and frequently wrote for *The Cross and the Plough*.

Peter Scott. Established a cooperative commune along Distributist lines at Bryn Mawr in 1929. Scott's programs had considerable influence in launching similar experiments in England and Wales.

J.W. Scott. Founder of the National Homecrofts Association, which worked to establish self-sufficient farming communities in Wales.

Brocard Sewell. An early worker for the Distributist movement and *G.K.'s Weekly*. Biographer of Cecil Chesterton.

Herbert Shove. One of the leading figures in the Distributist League, for a time the organization's Honorary Secretary.

Sir Henry Slesser. Appointed Solicitor-General in 1924 in the first Labour government and later served as Lord Justice of Appeal from 1929 through 1940. While a Labour M.P., he attempted to convert that party to Distributism.

Perceval Smith. Hard-hitting financial correspondent for Cecil Chesterton's *New Witness*. Smith's specialty was the exposition of suspected corruption involving well-known financiers and industrialists.

Henry Somerville. Leader of the Catholic Social Guild; founder and editor of the C.S.G.'s journal, *The Christian Democrat*.

W.R. Titterton. Well-known Fleet Street journalist and long-time associate of G.K.C. Served as assistant editor of the *New Witness* and *G.K.'s Weekly*.

H.S.D. Went. Developed the organizational plans for the Distributist League.

P.E.T. Widdrington. One of the leading figures in the League of the Kingdom of God, a movement which utilized Distributist principles in its development of Anglo-Catholic social philosophy.

Douglas Woodruff. Conservative journalist. As editor of the Catholic lay-monthly, *The Tablet*, Woodruff made that journal one of the most influential Catholic publications in Britain.

Select Bibliography

I. Journals and Periodicals Extensively Consulted

The Age of Plenty
The American Review
The Aylesford Review
Blackfriars
Blackshirt
The British Union Quarterly
The Chesterton Review
Christendom
The Christian Democrat
Clergy Review
The Commonwealth
The Cross and the Plough
Daily Herald
The Distributist

The English Review
The Eye-Witness
The Fascist Quarterly
Fascist Week
G.K.'s Weekly
The Listener
The Month
The New Age
The New Witness
The Paternoster
The Speaker
The Tablet
The Times (London)
The Weekly Review

II. Works by G.K. Chesterton

Alarms and Discursions. London, 1910.
All I Survey. New York, 1933.
All Is Grist. London, 1931.
All Things Considered. New York, 1909.
As I Was Saying. New York, 1936.
The Autobiography of G.K.C. New York, 1936.
The Ball and the Cross. London, 1910.
The Catholic Church and Conversion. New York, 1936.
Come to Think of It. New York, 1931.
The Common Man. New York, 1950.
The Crimes of England. London, 1915.
The Defendant. London, 1901.
Do We Agree? A Debate Between Chesterton and Shaw, With Hilaire Belloc in the Chair. New York, 1964.
The End of the Armistice. New York, 1940.
The End of the Roman; A Pageant of Wayfarers. London, 1924.

240

The Everlasting Man. New York, 1925.
Francies Versus Fads. New York, 1927.
Four Faultless Felons. London, 1930.
Generally Speaking. London, 1928.
George Bernard Shaw. New York, 1950.
A Handful of Authors. London, 1953.
Heretics. New York, 1905.
I Say a Democracy Means . . . . New York, privately printed [n.d.]
Irish Impressions. New York, 1919.
Lunacy and Letters. New York, 1958.
Manalive. London, 1912.
The Man Who Was Thursday. London, 1907.
Miscellany of Men. London, 1912.
The Napoleon of Notting Hill. London, 1904.
The New Jerusalem. New York, 1921.
Orthodoxy. London, 1908.
The Outline of Sanity. New York, 1927.
The Resurrection of Rome. London, 1930.
The Return of Don Quixote. New York, 1927.
A Short History of England. London, 1917.
The Spice of Life. Philadelphia, 1964.
Twelve Types. London, 1902.
Utopia of Usurers. New York, 1917.
The Victorian Age in Literature. London, 1913.
The Well and the Shallows. London, 1935.
What I Saw in America. New York, 1922.
What's Wrong with the World. New York, 1910.
Tales of the Long Bow. London, 1925.
William Cobbett. London, 1925.

III. Works by Cecil Chesterton

Chesterton, Cecil. *G.K. Chesterton—A Criticism.* London, 1908.
———. and Belloc, Hilaire. *The Party System.* London, 1911.
———. "Huxley and the Catholic Faith," *The British Review,* January 1913
———. "Israel a Nation," *The British Review,* May 1913.
———. *The Perils of Peace.* London, 1916.
———. *The Prussian Hath Said in His Heart.* London, 1914.

IV. Works by Hilaire Belloc

Belloc, Hilaire. *The Alternative.* London, 1947.
———. *Catholics and the War.* London, 1940.

———. *A Change in the Cabinet.* London, 1909.

———. *The Church and Socialism.* From a paper read at the Catholic Conference at Manchester, September 1, 1909.

———. *Mr. Clutterbuck's Election.* London, 1908.

———. *A Companion to Mr. Wells' Outline of History.* San Francisco, 1927.

———. *Conversation with a Cat.* London, 1931.

———. *The Crisis of Our Civilization.* New York, 1937.

———. *The Cruise of the Nona.* London, 1925.

———. *Danton.* New York, 1928.

———. *Economics for Helen.* London, 1924.

———. *Emmanuel Burden.* London, 1904.

———, and Hammond, J.L. (eds.). *Essays in Liberalism.* London, 1897.

———. *Essays of a Catholic.* London, 1931.

———. *An Essay on the Nature of Contemporary England.* New York, 1937.

———. *An Essay on the Restoration of Property.* London, 1936.

———. *Europe and the Faith.* New York, 1920.

———. *The Eye-Witness.* London, 1916.

———. *The Free Press.* London, 1918.

———. *The House of Commons and Monarchy.* London, 1920.

———. *How the Reformation Happened.* New York, 1928.

———. *The Jews.* Boston, 1922.

———. Lectures at Fordham University, *The Ram,* January 22, 1937.

———. *Mr. Belloc Still Objects to Mr. Wells' Outline of History.* London, 1926.

———. *Mrs. Markham's New History of England.* London, 1926.

———. *Napoleon.* London, 1932.

———. *On.* London, 1923.

———. *On Anything.* Freeport, N.Y., 1969.

———. *On the Place of Gilbert Chesterton in English Letters.* New York, 1940.

———, and Chesterton, Cecil. *The Party System.* London, 1911.

———. *The Path to Rome.* London, 1902.

———. *The Place of a Peasantry in Modern Civilization.* Manchester, 1910.

———. *Pongo and the Bull.* London, 1910.

———. *The Servile State.* New York, 1946.

———, and MacDonald, J.R. *Socialism and the Servile State.* London, 1911.

De Chantigny, J.A. (ed.). *Hilaire Belloc's Prefaces.* Chicago, 1971.

Speaight, Robert (ed.). *Letters From Hilaire Belloc.* London, 1958.

Thal, Herbert Van (ed.). *Belloc: A Biographical Anthology.* New York, 1970.

V. Works by Distributists

Baker, William Vincent. *New Maryland.* Ditchling, 1935.

Benvenisti, J.L. *Absent-Minded Revolution.* London, 1937.

———. *The Iniquitous Contract.* London, 1937.

Fordham, Montague. *The Rebuilding of Rural England.* London, 1924.

Gill, Eric. *Art-Nonsense and Other Essays*. London, 1934.

————. *Engravings by Eric Gill*. Bristol, 1929.

————. *Eric Gill; Autobiography*. New York, 1971.

————. *Essays: Last Essays and In a Strange Land*. London, 1942.

————. *It All Goes Together*. London, 1944.

————. *Money and Morals*. London, 1934.

————. *The Necessity of Belief*. London, 1936.

————. *Sacred and Secular*. London, 1940.

————. *Unemployment*. London, 1933.

————. *Unholy Trinity*. London, 1938.

————. *Work and Property*. London, 1937.

Gillett, Gabriel. *Politics and Religion*. London, 1912.

Heseltine, G.C. *The Change: Essays on the Land*. London, 1937.

————. *Town and Country*. London, 1933.

Hoffman, Ross J.F. *The Will to Freedom*. New York, 1936.

Hollis, Christopher. *Along the Road to Frome*. London, 1958.

————. *Oxford in the Twenties*. London, 1976.

————. *The Breakdown of Money*. New York, 1934.

————. *The Two Nations*. London, 1935.

Humphries, H.E. *Liberty and Property: An Introduction to Distributism*. London, 1928.

Jerrold, Douglas. *Georgian Adventure*. London, 1937.

————. *The Necessity of Freedom*. London, 1938.

Lunn, Arnold. *And Yet So New*. New York, 1959.

————. *Come What May*. London, 1940.

————. *The Good Gorilla*. London, 1944.

————. *Memory to Memory*. London, 1956.

————. *Now I See*. London, 1956.

————. *Revolutionary Socialism*. London, 1938.

————. *Spanish Rehearsal*. New York, 1937.

McNabb, Vincent. *The Church and the Land*. London, 1926.

————. *Communism or Distributism; A Debate Between Vincent McNabb and John Strachey*. London, 1937.

————. *Father McNabb Reader: Selections From the Writings of Vincent McNabb*. New York, 1954.

————. *From a Friar's Cell*. Oxford, 1923.

————. *Nazareth or Social Chaos*. London, 1933.

————. *Old Principles and the New Order*. New York, 1942.

McQuillan, John, *et al. Flee to the Fields*. London, 1934.

Penty, Arthur J. *Distributism: A Manifesto*. London, 1937.

————. *A Guildsman's Interpretation of History*. London, 1920.

————. *Post-Industrialism*. London, 1922.

————. *Old Worlds For New*. London, 1917.

————. *Towards a Christian Sociology*. London, 1923.

————. *Tradition and Modernism in Politics*. New York, 1937.

Pepler, Douglas, and Gill, Eric. *The Devil's Devices.* London, 1915.
———. *The Hand Press.* Ditchling, 1934.
———. *A Letter from Sussex by H.D.C. Pepler About His Friend Eric Gill.* Chicago, 1950.
Reckitt, Maurice. *As It Happened.* London, 1941.
———, and Hudson, G.E. *The Church and the World.* London, 1938.
———. *G.K. Chesterton: A Christian Prophet for England Today.* London, 1950.
———. *Maurice to Temple.* London, 1947.
——— (ed.). *Prospects for Christendom: Essays in Catholic Social Reconstruction.* London, 1945.
———, et al. *The Return of Christendom.* London, 1922.
———. *The World and the Faith.* London, 1954.
Robbins, Harold. *The Sun of Justice: An Essay on the Social Teachings of the Catholic Church.* London, 1938.
Ryan, John Augustine. *Distributive Justice.* New York, 1916.
Shewring, Walter. *Letters of Eric Gill.* New York, 1948.
Shove, Commander Herbert. *The Fairy Ring of Commerce.* Birmingham, 1930.
———. "Fascism and Religion," *The Catholic Mind,* March 22, 1934.
Slesser, Sir Henry. *Judgement Reserved.* London, 1941.
———. *Machinery: Its Masters and Its Servants.* London, 1909.
———. *Religio Laici.* London, 1927.
Titterton, W.R. *A Candle to the Stars.* London, 1932.
———. *G.K. Chesterton; A Portrait.* London, 1936.
Witcutt, W.P. *Dying Lands.* London, 1937.

VI. Works Dealing with Chesterbelloc and Distribution

Anson, Peter. *A Roving Recluse.* Cork, 1946.
Armytage, W.G.H. *Heavens Below: Utopian Experiments in England, 1560-1960.* London, 1961.
Attwater, Donald. *A Cell of Good Living: The Life and Works and Opinions of Eric Gill.* London, 1969.
———. *Modern Christian Revolutionaries.* New York, 1947.
Auden, W.H. (ed.). *G.K.C.—Selections From His Non-Fictional Prose.* New York, 1970.
Baring, Maurice. *The Puppet Show of Memory.* London, 1922.
Barker, Dudley. *G.K. Chesterton.* London, 1973.
Barker, Rodney. *Political Ideas in Modern Britain.* London, 1978.
Bechhofer, C., and Reckitt, Maurice. *The Meaning of National Guilds.* London, 1918.
Beecham, Thomas. *A Mingled Chime.* New York, 1943.
Bentley, E.C. *Those Days.* London, 1940.
Boyd, Ian. *The Novels of G.K. Chesterton.* London, 1975.
Braybrooke, Patrick. *Gilbert K. Chesterton.* London, 1922.

_____. *I Remember G.K. Chesterton*. Epsom, England, 1938.

_____. *Some Thoughts on Hilaire Belloc*. London, 1923.

Cammaerts, Emile. *The Laughing Prophet: The Seven Virtues of G.K. Chesterton*. London, 1937.

Canovan, Margaret. *G.K. Chesterton: Radical Populist*. New York, 1977.

Carol, Sister, A.C. *G.K. Chesterton: The Dynamic Classicist*. Delhi, 1971.

Chesterton, Mrs. Cecil. *The Chestertons*. London, 1941.

Clements, C. *G.K. Chesterton As Seen By His Contemporaries*. New York, 1939.

Clipper, Lawrence J. *G.K. Chesterton*. New York, 1974.

Conlon, D.J. (ed.). *G.K. Chesterton: The Critical Judgements, Part I: 1900-1937*. Antwerp, Belgium, 1976.

Ervine, St. John. *Some Impressions of My Elders*. New York, 1922.

Evans, Maurice. *G.K. Chesterton*. Cambridge, 1939.

Furlong, William B. *GBS/GKC: Shaw and Chesterton, The Metaphysical Jesters*. University Park, Penn., 1970.

Gill, Cecil; Warde, Beatrice; and Kindersley, David. *The Life and Works of Eric Gill*. Papers read at a Clark Library Symposium, 22 April 1967, Los Angeles, 1968.

Hamilton, Robert. *Hilaire Belloc*. London, 1945.

Haynes, Renée. *Hilaire Belloc*. London, 1953.

Heppenstall, Rayner. *Four Absentees*. London, 1960.

Hobhouse, Stephen. *Forty Years and an Epilogue*. London, 1951.

Hobson, S.G., and Orage, A.R. (eds.). *National Guilds*. London, 1919.

Hollis, Christopher. *G.K. Chesterton*. London, 1950.

_____. *The Mind of Chesterton*. London, 1970.

Irvine, William. *The Universe of G.B.S.* New York, 1949.

Jebb, Eleanor (Belloc). *Testimony to Hilaire Belloc*. London, 1956.

Kenner, Hugh. *Paradox in Chesterton*. New York, 1947.

Kiernan, Edward J. *Arthur J. Penty: His Contribution to Social Thought*. Washington, D.C., 1941.

Kindersley, David. *Mr. Eric Gill: Recollections of David Kindersley*. New York, 1967.

Knox, Ronald A. *Captive Flames*. London, 1940.

las Vergnas, Raymond. *Chesterton, Belloc, Baring*. New York, 1938.

Lea, Frank A. *The Wild Knight of Battersea: G.K. Chesterton*. London, 1946.

Lowndes, Marie Belloc. *Where Love and Friendship Dwelt*. New York, 1943.

Lynd, Robert. *Old and New Masters*. New York, 1919.

Mandell, C.Creighton, and Shanks, Edward. *Hilaire Belloc: The Man and His Work*. London, 1916.

Mann, J.E.F. (ed.). *The Real Democracy*. London, 1913.

Maycock, A.L. *The Man Who Was Orthodox*. London, 1963.

McCarthy, John P. *Hilaire Belloc: Edwardian Radical*. Indianapolis, 1978.

Morton, J.B. *Hilaire Belloc: A Memoir*. London, 1955.

O'Connor, John. *Father Brown on Chesterton*. London, 1937.

Pfleger, Karl. *Wrestlers With Christ*. New York, 1938.

Siderman, E.A. *With Father Vincent at the Marble Arch.* Oxford, 1947.
Speaight, Robert. *The Life of Eric Gill.* New York, 1966.
————. *The Life of Hilaire Belloc.* New York, 1957.
Sewell, Brocard. *Cecil Chesterton.* Whitefriars, Faversham, Kent, 1975.
————. *My Dear Times Waste.* London, 1966.
Slosson, Edwin Emery. *Six Major Prophets.* Boston, 1917.
Sokolow, A.D. *The Political Theory of Arthur J. Penty.* New Haven, 1940.
Sullivan, John. *G.K. Chesterton: A Bibliography.* London, 1958.
———— (ed.). *G.K. Chesterton: A Centenary Appraisal.* London, 1974.
Swann, N.E. Egerton. *Is There A Catholic Sociology?* London, 1922.
Thorp, Joseph. *A Study of Eric Gill's Achievements and Ideas.* London, 1929.
Valentine, Ferdinand. *Father Vincent McNabb, O.P.* Westminster, Maryland, 1955.
Ward, Maisie. *G.K. Chesterton.* New York, 1943.
————. *Return to Chesterton.* New York, 1952.
West, Julius. *G.K. Chesterton: A Critical Study.* New York, 1916.
Wilhelmsen, Fredrick. *Hilaire Belloc: No Alienated Man, A Study in Christian Integration.* New York, 1953.
Wills, Garry. *Chesterton, Man and Mask.* New York, 1961.
Woodruff, Douglas. *For Hilaire Belloc; Essays in Honor of His 71st Birthday.* New York, 1942.

VII. General Works

Beck, George Andrew (ed.). *The English Catholics, 1850-1950.* London, 1950.
Benewick, Robert. *Political Violence and Public Order: A Study of British Fascism.* London, 1969.
Bonham-Carter, Victor. *Dartington Hall, The History of an Experiment.* Ithaca, N.Y., 1958.
Brand, Mary Vivian. *The Social Catholic Movement in England, 1920-1955.* New York, 1963.
Bridson, D.G. *The Filibuster: A Study of the Political Ideas of Wyndham Lewis.* London, 1972.
Brown, E.H. Phelps. *The Growth of British Industrial Relations.* London, 1952.
Bull, Paul. *The Economics of the Kingdom of God.* New York, 1927.
Cantuar, William (ed.). *Towards a Christian Order.* London, 1942.
Carpenter, L.P. *G.D.H. Cole: An Intellectual Biography.* Cambridge, 1973.
Carpenter, Niles. *Guild Socialism.* New York, 1922.
Carter, April. *The Political Theory of Anarchism.* London, 1971.
Carthy, Mary Peter. *Catholicism in English-Speaking Lands.* New York, 1964.
Catholicism and Property. Report of the Third Annual Anglo-Catholic Summer School of Sociology, 1927.
Cleary, J.M. *Catholic Social Action in Britain, 1909-1959.* Oxford, 1961.
Cole, Dame Margaret. *The Life of G.D.H. Cole.* London, 1971.
Cole, G.D.H. *Guild Socialism Restated.* London, 1919.

_____. *A History of the Labour Party From 1914.* London, 1948.

_____. *A History of Socialist Thought.* New York, 1953.

_____. *The World of Labour.* London, 1913.

Crawford, Virginia M. *Catholic Social Doctrine, 1891-1931.* Oxford, 1933.

Cross, Colin. *The Fascists in Britain.* London, 1961.

Derrick, Paul. *Lost Property.* London, 1948.

Donaldson, Frances. *The Marconi Scandal.* London, 1962.

Egbert, Donald D. *Social Radicalism and the Arts.* New York, 1970.

Emy, H.V. *Liberals, Radicals and Social Politics, 1892-1914.* Cambridge, 1973.

Finlay, J.L. *Social Credit: The English Origins.* London, 1972.

Glass, S.T. *The Responsible Society.* London, 1966.

Goodman, Paul. *New Reformation: Notes of a Neolithic Conservative.* New York, 1970.

_____. *People or Personnel: Decentralizing and the Mixed System.* New York, 1965.

Gooch, G.P. *History and Historians in the Nineteenth Century.* Boston, 1913.

Greenslade, S.L. *The Church and Social Order.* London, 1948.

Griffiths, Richard. *The Reactionary Revolution: The Catholic Revival in French Literature, 1870-1914.* New York, 1965.

Gwynn, Denis Rolleston. *A Hundred Years of Catholic Emancipation (1829-1929).* London, 1929.

Halévy, Elie. *The Rule of Democracy, 1905-1914.* London, 1932.

Harrison, John. *The Reactionaries.* London, 1966.

Hobson, S.G. *Guild Principles in War and Peace.* London, 1918.

Hyde, H. Montgomery. *Lord Reading: The Life of Rufus Isaacs, First Marquess of Reading.* New York, 1967.

Inglis, K.S. *Churches and the Working Classes in Victorian England.* London, 1963.

Jackson, Holbrook. *The Eighteen Nineties: A Review of Art and Ideas at the Close of the Nineteenth Century.* London, 1922.

Jennings, Hilda. *Brynmawr.* London, 1934.

_____. *The New Community.* London, 1934.

Jones, A.R. *The Life and Opinions of Thomas Ernest Hulme.* Boston, 1968.

Jones, Peter d'A. *The Christian Socialist Revival, 1877-1914.* Princeton, 1968.

Kenyon, Ruth. *The Catholic Faith and the Industrial Order.* London, 1931.

_____. *An Introduction to Christian Social Doctrine: Essays.* London, 1941.

Kingsmill, Hugh, and Pearson, Hesketh. *Talking of Dick Whittington.* London, 1947.

Lester, John A. Jr. *Journey Through Despair, 1880-1914.* Princeton, 1968.

Ludovici, A.M. *The Sanctity of Private Property.* London, 1932.

Mairet, Philip. *A.R. Orage: A Memoir.* London, 1936.

Martin, Wallace. *The New Age Under Orage.* New York, 1967.

Masterman, Lucy. *C.F.G. Masterman: A Biography.* London, 1939.

Mathew, David. *Catholicism in England, 1535-1935.* London, 1936.

Maurois, André. *Prophets and Poets.* New York, 1935.

McEntee, Georgiana Putnam. *The Social Catholic Movement in Great Britain.* New York, 1927.
Mosley, Oswald. *The Greater Britain.* London, 1934.
Mullally, Frederic. *Fascism Inside England.* London, 1946.
O'Connor, John Joseph. *The Catholic Revival in England.* New York, 1942.
Oliver, John. *The Church and the Social Order.* London, 1968.
Orage, A.R. *Political and Economic Writings of A.R. Orage.* London, 1936.
Palmer, Herbert. *Post-Victorian Poetry.* London, 1938.
Pelling, Henry. *A History of British Trade Unionism.* Baltimore, 1963.
Pope Leo XIII. *Five Great Encyclicals.* New York, 1939.
Read, Herbert. *A Coat of Many Colours.* London, 1947.
Roberts, Michael. *T.E. Hulme.* New York, 1971.
Rogger, Hans, and Weber, Eugen (eds.). *The European Right: A Historical Profile.* Berkeley, 1966.
Scott, J.W. *Syndicalism and Philosophical Realism.* London, 1919.
Selver, Paul. *Orage and the New Age Circle.* London, 1959.
Semmel, Bernard. *Imperialism and Social Reform.* London, 1960.
Sheed, F.J. *Sidelights on the Catholic Revival.* London, n.d.
Sheed, Wilfred. *The Morning After.* New York, 1972.
Smith, R.A.L. *The Catholic Church and the Social Order.* London, 1933.
Somerville, H. *The Catholic Social Movement.* London, 1933.
Stebbing, George. *The Position and Prospects of the Catholic Church in English-Speaking Lands.* London, 1930.
Steed, H. Wickham. *The Press.* London, 1939.
Swinnerton, Frank Arthur. *The Georgian Literary Scene.* London, 1935.
Wagner, Geoffrey. *Wyndham Lewis: A Portrait of the Artist as the Enemy.* London, 1957.
Ward, Wilfred. *Men and Matters.* New York, 1914.
Watkin, Edward Ingram. *Roman Catholicism in England From the Reformation to 1950.* Oxford, 1957.
Watt, Lewis. *Capitalism and Morality.* London, 1929.
Weber, Eugen. *Action Française.* Stanford, 1962.
Wilson, R. MacNair. *Monarchy or Money Power.* London, 1933.
Woodcock, George. *Anarchism.* London, 1971.
Woodlock, Francis. *Modernism and the Christian Church.* London, 1925.
Wright, A.W. *G.D.H. Cole and Socialist Democracy.* Oxford, 1979.

VIII. Articles

Agar, Herbert. "A Great Democrat," *The Southern Review,* Summer, 1937.
Amis, Kingsley. "The Poet and the Lunatics," *New Statesman,* February 26, 1971.
Attwater, Donald. "The Decline of Distributism," *Commonweal,* February 2, 1951.
———. "English Catholic Fascists?" *Commonweal,* January 10, 1941.
Benvenisti, J.L. "Is Britain Going Red?" *Commonweal,* December 26, 1941.

Bergonzi, Bernard. "Chesterton and/or Belloc," *Critical Quarterly*, I, 1959.

Bocock, R.J. "Anglo-Catholic Socialism: A Study of a Protest Movement Within a Church," *Social Compass*, XX/I, 1932.

The Canisius Monthly. November, 1930. Special issue on G.K.C.

"Chesterton as Essayist," *Times Literary Supplement*, June 16, 1950.

Collins, Edward J. "Distributism," *The Irish Monthly*, January, 1944.

Cowley, Malcolm. "Chesterton's Later Years," *New Republic*, December 20, 1943.

Cuffe, Edwin D. "G.K.C.: No Common Man," *America*, October 19, 1974.

Curd, T.W.C. "Marydown, a Catholic Land Colony," *The Month*, July, 1933.

Day, A.E. "The Story of *G.K.'s Weekly*," *Library Review*, Spring, 1974.

Derrick, Christopher. "G.K. Chesterton: An Intellectual Passion For Ultimates," *Times of London*, August 28, 1971.

Dey, Msgr. "The Back to the Land Movement," *Dublin Review*, April, 1935.

Dickens Studies Newsletter. June, 1974. Special issue on G.K.C.

Diggens, John P. "American Catholics and Italian Fascism," *Journal of Contemporary History*, Vol. II, no. 4, 1967.

"Ditchling's Twentieth Century Guild Colony," *The Catholic World*, August, 1932.

Eaker, J. Gordon. "G.K. Chesterton Among the Moderns," *The Georgia Review*, Spring, 1959.

Ferkise, V. "Populist Influences on American Fascism," *Western Political Quarterly*, 1957.

"Fleet Street Line," *Times Literary Supplement*, May 17, 1974.

Foot, Dingle. "G.K. Chesterton: Poet with an Historian's Eye," *Times of London*, May 29, 1974.

"G.K. Chesterton: Crusader for the Common Man," *Times Literary Supplement*, April 15, 1944.

Gwynn, Denis. "Catholic England Under King George V," *The Catholic World*, April, 1936.

Hart, Jeffrey. "In Praise of Chesterton," *Yale Review*, October, 1963.

Heseltine, G.C. "Distributism," *Catholic World*, January, 1932.

_____. "Fresh Fields," *English Review*, November, 1933.

Kelly, Hugh. "G.K. Chesterton: His Philosophy of Life," *Studies*, March, 1942.

Lunn, Arnold. "The Catholics of Great Britain," *Atlantic Monthly*, October, 1944.

"Man With Gusto," *Times Literary Supplement*, August 7, 1970.

The Mark Twain Quarterly. Spring, 1937. Special issue on G.K.C.

Maynard, Theodore. "A Literary Freelance in London," *The Catholic World*, June, 1931.

Muggeridge, Malcolm. "G.K.C.," *The New Statesman*, August 23, 1963.

Pearson, Hesketh, "G.B.S. Versus G.K.C.," *Living Age*, Vol. CCXIX, 1923.

Quinn, Edward. "Catholics in Contemporary England," *Catholic World*, September, 1937.

Reynard, H. "The Guild Socialists," *Economic Journal*, September, 1920.

Sheed, Wilfred. "Chesterbelloc and the Jews," *New York Review of Books*, September 25, 1971.

Speaight, Robert. "The European Mind: Hilaire Belloc's Thought and Writings," *Times Literary Supplement*, May 21, 1954.

———. "Personal Column." For *The Tablet*. Copy sent to Mr. T.F. Burns, October 20, 1969. Special Collections, Mugar Library, Boston University.

Spode House Review. August, 1972. Special issue on Hilaire Belloc.

———. December 1974 and January 1975. Special issue on G.K.C.

Toomey, John A. "An Interview with Hilaire Belloc," *America*, March 23, 1935.

Turnell, G.M. "Our Debt to Chesterton," *Arena*, July, 1937.

Waugh, Evelyn. "Chesterton," *The National Review*, April 22, 1961.

IX. Unpublished Material

Belloc Correspondence. Berg Collection, New York Public Library.

Herbold, Anthony E. "Chesterton and *G.K.'s Weekly*." Unpublished Ph.D. Thesis, University of Michigan, 1963.

Higgins, Michael W. "Ruskin and Chesterton: A Common Spirit." Paper delivered at the National Conference of the Chesterton Society, Strong College, York University, Toronto, Ontario, June 28, 1977.

Loughran, Mother Mary Malachy. "Catholics in England Between 1918 and 1945." Unpublished Ph.D. Thesis, University of Pennsylvania, 1954.

Mason, Gertrude. "The Social Philosophy of G.K. Chesterton." Unpublished Ph.D. Thesis, University of Chicago, 1950.

McCarthy, John P. "Hilaire Belloc: Critic of the New Liberalism." Unpublished Ph.D. Thesis, Columbia University, 1969.

Phillips, Paul David. "The Drama of Distributism." Unpublished Honors B.A. Thesis, Harvard University, 1973.

Ryan, James Marcus. "G.K. Chesterton as Literary Critic." Unpublished Ph.D. Thesis, Boston University, 1950.

INDEX